Sams Teach Yourself Comm[...] [...]ference
FrontPage 2000 Toolb[...]

G000144655

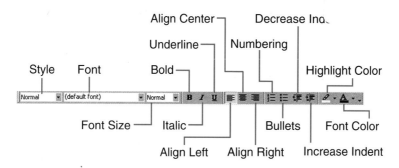

The Standard Toolbar

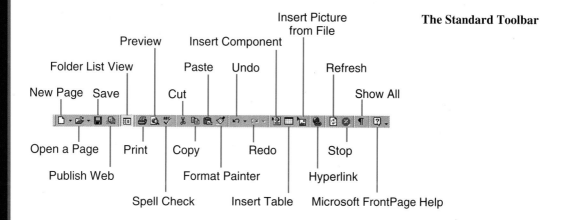

The Tables Toolbar

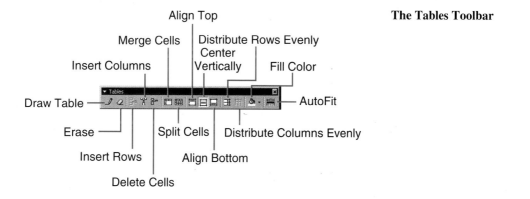

FrontPage 2000 Keyboard Shortcuts

Keyboard shortcuts for FrontPage 2000's top-level menus are accessed by pressing Alt+ except where indicated.

Ctrl+PgDn cycles between FrontPage Views (Normal, Source, and Preview)

FILE MENU

New	Ctrl+N
Open	Ctrl+O
Close	Ctrl+F4
Save	Ctrl+S
Save As	
Preview in Browser	
Print	Ctrl+P
Exit	

EDIT MENU

Undo	Ctrl+Z
Redo Last Action	Ctrl+Y
Cut	Ctrl+X
Copy	Ctrl+C
Paste	Ctrl+P
Delete	Del
Select All	Ctrl+A
Find	Ctrl+F
Replace	Ctrl+H

VIEW MENU

Reveal Tags	Ctrl+/
Refresh	F5

INSERT MENU

Break	
Horizontal Line	
Date and Time	
Symbol	
Comment	
Navigation Bar	
Page Banner	
Component	
Database	
Form	
Advanced	
Picture	
File	
Bookmark	
Hyperlink	Ctrl+K

FORMAT MENU

Font	
Paragraph	
Bullets and Numbering	
Position	
Dynamic HTML Effects	
Style	
Style Sheet Links	
Theme	
Shared Borders	
Page Transition	
Background	
Remove Formatting	Ctrl+Shift+Z
Properties	Alt+Enter

TOOLS MENU

Spelling	F7
Thesaurus	Shift+F7

Rogers Cadenhead

SAMS
Teach Yourself

Microsoft®
FrontPage® 2000

in 24 Hours

SAMS

A Division of Macmillan Computer Publishing
201 West 103rd St., Indianapolis, Indiana, 46290 USA

Sams Teach Yourself Microsoft® FrontPage® 2000 in 24 Hours

Copyright © 1999 by SAMS Publishing

International Standard Book Number: 0-672-31500-9

Library of Congress Catalog Card Number: 98-87801

Printed in the United States of America

First Printing: May 1999

02   01   00   4   3

Trademarks

Warning and Disclaimer

EXECUTIVE EDITOR
Mark Taber

ACQUISITIONS EDITOR
Randi Roger

DEVELOPMENT EDITOR
Scott D. Meyers

MANAGING EDITOR
Lisa Wilson

PROJECT EDITOR
George E. Nedeff

COPY EDITOR
Sean Medlock

INDEXER
Aamir Burki

PROOFREADER
Kim Cofer

TECHNICAL EDITOR
Paul Colligan

INTERIOR DESIGN
Gary Adair

COVER DESIGN
Aren Howell

LAYOUT TECHNICIANS
Brian Borders
Susan Geiselman
Mark Walchle

Overview

Introduction

Contents

About the Author

ROGERS CADENHEAD is a writer and Web developer who has written seven books on Internet-related topics, including *Sams Teach Yourself Java 2 in 21 Days* and *Sams Teach Yourself to Create a Home Page in 24 Hours*, but not *Teach Yourself Microsoft Bob in a Holiday Weekend*. Cadenhead is also the author of a trivia column for the *Fort Worth Star-Telegram* and Knight-Ridder News Service, and the publisher of the Web sites Cruel Site of the Day (`www.cruel.com`) and the Drudge Retort (`www.drudge.com`). Actively involved in computers since childhood, Cadenhead invented the BBS door game in 1982 and left the field without realizing that more than 500,000 of these games would be sold to BBS operators during the next 15 years.

Dedication

To my wife, Mary Christine Moewe, for the first 12 years of forever. We'll always have Arlington, Denton, Fort Worth, Denver, Peoria, Dallas, and Jacksonville. You made my whole century.—Rogers Cadenhead

Acknowledgments

I'd like to thank the team at Macmillan Computer Publishing, including Mark Taber, Scott Meyers, Randi Roger, Sean Medlock, Paul Colligan, Tina Perry, and Howard A. Jones. With a group like this working to make the book good, I'm proud to have my name on the cover so I can claim a disproportionate share of the credit.

I'd also like to thank David and Sherri Rogelberg at my agency, Studio B. When I made some unfortunate decisions in regard to small-cap Internet stocks this past spring, you helped me hit up some of the people in the preceding paragraph for money. That's always appreciated.

I also must thank my wife Mary and son Max. You've given patience, support, humor, and love to someone who spent enough time at a computer this past year to qualify as a plug-and-play device. I love you at least 200 percent above the recommended daily allowance.

Finally, I'd like to thank Microsoft Bob.

Tell Us What You Think!

As the reader of this book, *you* are our most important critic and commentator. We value your opinion and want to know what we're doing right, what we could do better, what areas you'd like to see us publish in, and any other words of wisdom you're willing to pass our way.

You can fax, email, or write me directly to let me know what you did or didn't like about this book—as well as what we can do to make our books stronger.

Please note that I cannot help you with technical problems related to the topic of this book, and that due to the high volume of mail I receive, I might not be able to reply to every message.

When you write, please be sure to include this book's title and author as well as your name and phone or fax number. I will carefully review your comments and share them with the author and editors who worked on the book.

Fax: 317-581-4770

Email: office_sams@mcp.com

Mail: Mark Taber
           Associate Publisher
           Sams Publishing
           201 West 103rd Street
           Indianapolis, IN 46290 USA

Introduction

With the release of FrontPage 2000, Microsoft's Web publishing software has climbed a rung on the social ladder. There are two kinds of software products at Microsoft—those that stand on their own, and those that are part of a larger product.

The standalone programs can be huge successes—you may have heard of Microsoft Windows 95. They also can end up as what-were-we-thinking failures—another 1995 product, Microsoft Bob, sold around 13 copies worldwide (including two to the author of this book).

FrontPage has always done well on its own, offering an easy way to publish your own World Wide Web pages without needing to learn the complexities of HTML and JavaScript. Now FrontPage has become part of Microsoft Office, the most popular productivity suite in the world.

You may be familiar with FrontPage 98 or one of the older versions of the software. FrontPage has always been one of the most popular Web editing tools because it makes creating a Web page as easy as writing a letter in Microsoft Word.

FrontPage 2000's inclusion in the Office suite shows how important the World Wide Web has become. Today, putting yourself and your company on the Web is an everyday part of life. People are using this medium to shop, learn, communicate, play, and teach. A network that once was occupied by a few thousand scholars, students, and military officials is now as ubiquitous as television. Millions of dollars are spent on Super Bowl commercials for the sole purpose of launching a Web site. People who don't even own computers are familiar with Internet companies like Amazon.com and Yahoo. Thousands of new Web sites are launched each day by a variety of publishers—corporations, small businesses, organizations, and individuals.

For these reasons and more, Microsoft has put a lot of emphasis on FrontPage 2000. The software is enormously improved from the previous edition, offering enhanced editing, publishing, and site maintenance capabilities.

FrontPage 2000 makes it simple to master the complex tasks required of a Web publisher, but you must first master the software itself. The fastest way to do this is with *Sams Teach Yourself Microsoft FrontPage 2000 in 24 Hours*.

During the 24 one-hour lessons in this book, you'll develop hands-on skills with each feature of FrontPage 2000:

- Creating new Web sites quickly with templates, themes, and wizards.
- Bringing existing sites into FrontPage 2000 without losing any of their HTML coding.
- Editing Web pages exactly as they will appear in a browser.
- Switching effortlessly between normal editing and HTML coding.
- Turning features of FrontPage 2000 on and off depending on the Web browsers used by your audience.
- Using FrontPage Server Extensions to add interactive capabilities like surveys, discussion forums, and feedback pages.
- Connecting your Web site to a Microsoft Access database or Microsoft Excel spreadsheet.
- Integrating your Web seamlessly with the other programs in the Office 2000 suite.
- Editing, cropping, and adding transparencies to images within FrontPage instead of using an image-editing program.
- Telling FrontPage 2000 what you want and letting the software figure out how to implement it through sophisticated Web technology like Cascading Style Sheets, JavaScript, and Active Server Pages.

Creating a FrontPage Web site has never been easier, even though the software's features have literally doubled from its previous version.

As you work with FrontPage 2000, you'll also build skills in Office 2000, which shares a common interface and some features with its new suitemate.

Whether you're using FrontPage 2000 at your office, home, or home office, *Sams Teach Yourself Microsoft FrontPage 2000 in 24 Hours* provides the skills you need to publish your own Web sites. By the time you've completed the lessons in this book, you'll be taking part in the same publishing revolution that spawned Yahoo, Amazon.com, The Fray, and thousands of other sites.

You'll also become well-acquainted with one of the first Web sites created with FrontPage 2000: this book's official site at `http://www.fp2k.com/24`. You'll find the following features there:

- Updates to the material covered in the book.
- Solutions to the exercises at the end of each hour.
- Answers to questions commonly asked by other readers.
- A way to contact author Rogers Cadenhead with your own questions, comments, and corrections.

As one of the first people to publish and maintain a Web site with FrontPage 2000, I've been surprised by how quickly I came to rely on its features. Web publishers tend to be "Amish" in their approach to new technology, favoring traditional techniques over the changes in software like FrontPage. Over the past five years, for example, most of my sites have been created with the HTML equivalent of the horse and buggy: Windows Notepad.

Sams Teach Yourself Microsoft FrontPage 2000 in 24 Hours is a guide to 21st century Web site design. Soon, thousands of people will be publishing on the World Wide Web without slowing down to learn HTML, CSS, and other alphabet-soup jargon, and they'll be using software such as FrontPage 2000 to do it.

By the time you finish this book, you'll be equally surprised by how much FrontPage 2000 can do for you. It can make Web sites much easier to create and manage. You'll be able to finish tasks in minutes that took hours for us old-fashioned types to do "way back when." (Whether you share this good news with your employer is up to you, of course. That's one of the fringe benefits of adopting Microsoft FrontPage 2000 as quickly as I adopted Microsoft Bob.)

PART I
Starting Strong with FrontPage 2000

Hour

Hour 1

Set Up and Run FrontPage 2000

Today, somewhere in the neighborhood of one million books have been released about the subject of World Wide Web publishing. Wait—I just heard a report on the radio—there are now one million and five.

These books normally start with an introduction to the World Wide Web, a mass medium that was born in the early 1990s and has blossomed into an amazing way to receive and send information.

At this time, you probably have heard about the Web. Otherwise, there isn't much reason for you to be interested in FrontPage 2000, Microsoft's Web site creation software. (This kind of keen analytical insight is why I'm writing computer books today and have completely abandoned my previous career in salads, fries, and milkshakes.)

Although the Web may be old news to you, there's a lot of new news to report about FrontPage 2000. With the release of this software, Microsoft has made Web publishing a core part of its Microsoft Office productivity suite. Many features of past FrontPage versions have been improved or expanded. Many others are completely new.

All 24 chapters of this book are used to cover FrontPage 2000, arguably the most sophisticated Web publishing software on the market today. You'll learn how to use each important feature of the software in easy-to-handle one-hour lessons.

Each chapter focuses on tasks you can accomplish rather than procedures you must memorize. By the time a day's worth of these hours has been completed, you'll be an expert user of FrontPage 2000, publishing your own Web sites, attracting visitors, receiving feedback, updating your sites, and attracting more visitors.

The best place to start is with a copy of FrontPage 2000 somewhere in the vicinity of your computer.

Acquaint Yourself with FrontPage 2000

Microsoft FrontPage 2000, like all elements of the Office 2000 productivity suite, was named after a year. Once you begin to use the software, you may start to think that FrontPage was named for the number of different things you have to learn to use it.

FrontPage 2000 comprises all the tools you need to create, publish, and manage a World Wide Web site. Each of these tools is integrated into a single program, which is one of those good news, bad news kind of things.

The bad news is that there are a large number of things to learn about this all-in-one software package. Creating, publishing, and managing a Web site are all substantive tasks that have traditionally been handled by several different types of software: page editors, file transfer programs, hyperlink verifiers, and more.

The good news: You don't have to learn the quirks of several different programs or to keep track of which program handles which task. In previous versions of FrontPage, the software's page editor and site explorer were separate programs. This could easily cause users to zig by running one program when they should have zagged by running the other.

Learning to use FrontPage is like learning to use Microsoft Word, the popular word-processing software that's also part of Office 2000.

Although Word has hundreds of different features, the basic mechanics of creating and editing a document are fairly simple. You type text into a window, click a few buttons or menu options to format the text, and save your work. You can start using Word long before you have mastered its more sophisticated features.

More good news: For the most part, you can learn to use FrontPage 2000 the same way.

Have you ever used a word processor like Microsoft Word to create a nice-looking business letter, produce an effective resume, or butter up an older relative to get into her will? If so, you have most of the skills you need to master FrontPage 2000 and create your own Webs.

> Although most people call a collection of related Web pages a Web site, Microsoft FrontPage refers to them as *Webs*. This term is used throughout the book, because you'll be encountering it often when using the software and its built-in help system.

Discover FrontPage 2000's New Features

Before the release of FrontPage 2000, thousands of people were using earlier versions of the software to publish their Web sites. To get an idea of its popularity, FrontPage is referred to on more than 120,000 Web pages, according to the World Wide Web search engine AltaVista at `http://www.altavista.com`.

FrontPage 2000 is the fourth major release of the Windows version of the software (another product, FrontPage 1.0, is currently available for Apple Macintosh users).

Like most major software releases from Microsoft, FrontPage 2000 introduces dozens of new features. People who are upgrading to FrontPage 2000 from a previous version will find the following improvements:

- *Custom themes*—Select one of the 60 existing themes and personalize it by selecting new colors, logos, images, and other page elements.
- *Color tools*—Color selection is enabled throughout the software with a color picker, color wheel, and a dropper that can grab a color from a graphic.
- *Roundtrip HTML*—For the first time, FrontPage can read in an existing Web page and save it without changing any of the existing HTML code or its formatting.
- *Visible HTML tags*—While still viewing a page normally in the editing window, you can make the HTML tags that comprise the page visible.

- *Easy access to Microsoft Access*—Incorporate Access database files into Web pages for viewing and editing. Users can even create Access databases from within a Web page.
- *Web components*—Add sophisticated interactive features to a Web page with FrontPage and Office components such as an Excel Spreadsheet component and a Search component.
- *Automatic page linking*—By using the new AutoLink component, adding a new page to a Web can automatically cause related hyperlinks to appear on other pages.
- *Browser targeting*—If you decide which browsers and features you're creating a Web for, FrontPage 2000 will restrict its features to those supported by that target audience.

This list represents a selection of the changes introduced with this upgrade to the software. Many others are related to FrontPage 2000's new membership in the Office 2000 productivity suite. FrontPage shares common user interface elements like toolbars, shortcuts, and menus with other Office applications.

FrontPage 2000 also shares a common file format with the other applications such as Excel and Word: HTML. Each Office program can save its documents as Web pages. These pages can be loaded by FrontPage for editing without losing any of their information. A Word document can go from Word to FrontPage and back to Word, never losing its font selections or paragraph formatting.

If you're already familiar with FrontPage 98, the most significant thing you'll be adapting to is the software's strong connection to the rest of the Office suite.

Install the Software

Microsoft FrontPage 2000 uses an Installation Wizard to set up the software. Wizards, as you may know from experience with other Microsoft software, are dialog boxes that make complicated tasks easier by breaking them down into a series of simple steps.

Whether you're installing FrontPage 2000 alone or as part of Office 2000, the setup process is mostly self-explanatory.

The easiest way to start the Installation Wizard is to open your CD-ROM drive door, insert Disc 1 of the program's CDs, and close the CD door. The wizard should start automatically, as shown in Figure 1.1.

If the wizard doesn't start, you can begin the installation yourself. Click
Start, Run, open the CD's root folder, and select the program file Setup.exe.

FIGURE 1.1

*Using the Installation
Wizard.*

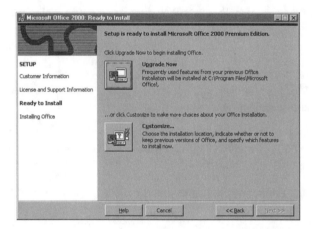

There are two ways to install the software: Install Now and Custom Install. Install Now
will delete any previous versions of the software that it finds before adding the current
version to your system. One of the things that it adds is the most up-to-date edition of
Internet Explorer, Microsoft's Web browser.

If you need to save old versions of your software or an older Internet Explorer, select the
Custom Install option. You'll be able to control where the software is installed and which
older versions of the software to keep.

Another reason to use Custom Install is that it provides more control over how some
FrontPage 2000 features are set up.

When FrontPage 2000 is installed, the default behavior of the wizard is to save most of
its files to your system's hard drive. If your system cannot make use of some files, they
will not be saved at all.

The main reason some files may not be usable is related to differences
between Windows 95/98 and Windows NT. For example, the FrontPage
Server Extensions resource kit only runs under NT, so the wizard prevents
you from installing it on any other operating system.

You can save disk space by running some files from the FrontPage CD—the built-in help files, FrontPage Web examples, and a tutorial. These files load more slowly from CD-ROM than they would from your hard drive.

You also can install additional FrontPage 2000 themes during a custom installation. Themes are an easy way to give a Web page or an entire Web a well-coordinated graphic appearance. FrontPage 2000 comes with two sets of themes: a group of two dozen that are automatically included with the software and an extra group of optional themes.

By default, the optional themes are only installed when you try to use them for the first time while using FrontPage 2000. One of the options during a custom installation is to go ahead and add them right away.

Figure 1.2 shows an Installation Wizard dialog box that's being used to customize how FrontPage 2000 is installed. The icon next to each element of FrontPage 2000 in Figure 1.2 shows how it will be installed:

- The hard drive icon indicates that the file should be saved rather than run from CD.
- The red X indicates the file cannot be installed at all.
- The hard drive number 1 icon indicates the file will be installed upon its first use.

FIGURE 1.2

*Customizing an instal-
lation of the software.*

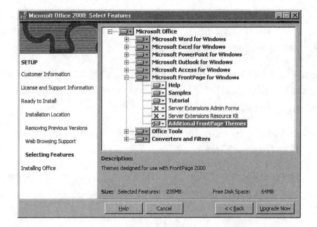

Once you've told the wizard how to install FrontPage 2000, the process takes around 5–15 minutes, depending on your system's capabilities. The last step requires a system reboot, so you should close any other programs and files that were left open during installation.

After the system has rebooted, the installation wizard will make changes to your system's registry and Start menu. This also may take 5–15 minutes.

> Looking for a good book to read while you're waiting for the software to be installed? The author of this book is trying to convince Sams to publish *Teach Yourself Not To Be in Such a Hurry About Everything in 24 Hours.* If my editors weren't taking so long to evaluate my proposal, you could be reading the book now.

1

Run the Software for the First Time

After the installation has been completed, you'll be able to run FrontPage 2000 from your Start menu.

FrontPage 2000 is the first version of the software that combines all of its features into a single interface. You will be able to create, edit, and publish a Web without leaving FrontPage. You can keep hyperlinks up-to-date, manage files, and even create a task schedule to organize your Web publishing projects.

The FrontPage 2000 graphical user interface is shown in Figure 1.3.

FIGURE 1.3

Running FrontPage 2000.

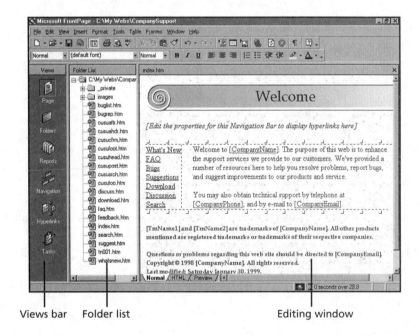

Views bar   Folder list   Editing window

In Figure 1.3, FrontPage 2000 is being used to edit a page that's part of a customer support Web. The three main sections of the interface consist of a Views bar, Folder list, and Editing window.

The FrontPage user interface takes on six different appearances depending on the view you've selected. *Views* are different ways that you can explore a Web as you work on it in FrontPage.

Views are chosen by using a set of icons inside the Views Bar identified in Figure 1.3. The view you select determines the kind of work you can do to the Web, and the following icons can be selected:

- *Page*—Edit a Web page
- *Folders*—Explore a Web's file folders and files
- *Reports*—View reports related to a Web
- *Navigation*—Navigate a Web's organizational structure
- *Hyperlinks*—View the way a Web's pages have been hyperlinked
- *Tasks*—Plan the upcoming tasks in a Web's development

All work that you do within FrontPage revolves around the Views bar.

The Folder list shown in Figure 1.3 lists all files and folders associated with the current Web. Clicking one of the listed Web pages opens that page in the Editing window.

> The Views bar and Folder list can be closed to make room for other windows on the FrontPage 2000 interface. Use the View, Views Bar and View, Folder List menu options to close these windows. You can use the same options to open these windows if they have been closed.

The Editing window functions like a word processor's editing window. You can add, edit, and delete Web page elements such as text and images.

There are two toolbars running along the top of the FrontPage 2000 interface, as shown in Figure 1.4.

FIGURE 1.4

The Standard and
Formatting toolbars.

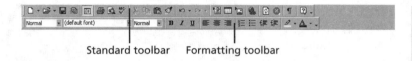

Standard toolbar   Formatting toolbar

The Standard toolbar and Formatting toolbar are used primarily when you're editing a Web page in the Page view. These toolbars are dockable, which means that you can move them around the FrontPage 2000 interface if you don't like where they have been placed.

To dock a toolbar, grab it with your mouse and drag it to the left, right, top, or bottom edges of the FrontPage 2000 interface. If you place the toolbar on the left or right edge, it will be displayed vertically instead of horizontally. You also can drag a toolbar off the FrontPage interface entirely, which puts it into a new window on your system desktop.

If you can't find a way to grab a dockable toolbar in a Windows program, look for a line that separates two buttons on the toolbar—the Standard toolbar in FrontPage 2000 has several of them. Click your mouse on top of one of these lines and hold down your mouse button to drag the toolbar around.

Take Different Views of a Web

Most of the work you do in FrontPage 2000 will be accomplished in the Page view. Each of the other fives views is more specialized.

The Folders view opens a Windows Explorer-style list of the files and folders that make up a Web. You can use it to do any of the things that Windows Explorer is used for: Opening, moving, renaming, and deleting files. You also can see the title, size, and modification date of each page in a Web.

The Tasks view is used to create and manage a to-do list of the tasks associated with your Web. If you're working on a Web alone and want to keep track of your progress, or collaborating with others who need to see what you've been doing, the Tasks view provides a built-in project manager. Task management is covered during Hour 14, "Manage Your Web."

View Reports about a Web

The Reports view, shown in Figure 1.5, opens a list of reports that tell you more about your Web.

FIGURE 1.5

The Reports view.

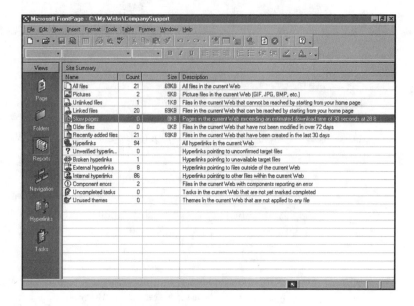

Each report in this view has a description that explains its purpose. Eight of the reports list files included in the Web based on a specific criteria.

The report that lists unlinked files is useful to determine when one or more Web pages are not connected to the rest of your Web. These pages can't be reached by a person who goes to the main page of your Web and uses hyperlinks to visit every page in your site. Unless there's a reason not to make these pages a part of the Web, you can use this report when either deleting the files to save space or adding links on those pages.

Another useful report lists the pages in a Web that would take 30 seconds or more to download using a 28,800-baud Internet connection (also called a 28.8).

One of the things you must keep in mind as a Web developer is the way your audience connects to the Internet. Most people are using a 28.8 modem to dial up an Internet service provider, load their Web browser, and start viewing pages, although this will change as ISDN and cable modems become more commonplace.

The 30-second report considers all parts of a Web page: text, images, interactive programs like Java applets, and anything else that is downloaded when the page is viewed in a browser.

Is 30 seconds a long time to wait for a page to load when you're surfing the Web? It depends on whether you're the kind of person whose loved ones would give you *Teach Yourself Not to Be in Such a Hurry in 24 Hours* as a present. The half-minute wait is a reasonably good benchmark for when you should start worrying if a page contains too much text, graphics, and other elements.

The 28.8 connection and 30 seconds can both be customized. You can set a different speed and different time by selecting the Tools, Options menu item and opening the Reports View tabbed dialog box. Figure 1.6 shows this dialog box and the speeds that can be used: 14.4, 28.8, 56.6, ISDN, T1, and T3.

FIGURE 1.6

Customizing several Web reports.

The Reports View dialog box also can be used to change the number of days that constitutes a recently added or older file in a Web—two other reports you can run.

Five reports that you can see in the Reports view concern the hyperlinks used in a Web. These reports enable you to find links that will cause a "file not found" error if they are used. You can report on bad links that are a part of your Web and bad links to other addresses on the World Wide Web.

In order to see a fully up-to-date hyperlinks report, you must click Tools, Recalculate Links before selecting the report. FrontPage will check all links, including external ones to other Web addresses if you're currently connected to the Internet. This can take five minutes or longer, depending on how many other Web addresses are contained in hyperlinks on your Web.

When you find a bad link, you can update it directly from within the Reports view by clicking the line in the report that displays this link. This can be a huge timesaver if your Web contains a large number of hyperlinks, because it's faster than loading each page into the Editing Window and finding the erroneous link.

View the Structure of a Web

The last two views of FrontPage 2000 are the Navigation and Hyperlinks views, which provide two different ways to look at your Webs in a visual manner.

The Hyperlinks view displays the relationship between a page and all Web addresses that it hyperlinks to, whether they're part of the same Web or available somewhere else on the World Wide Web. This view is shown in Figure 1.7.

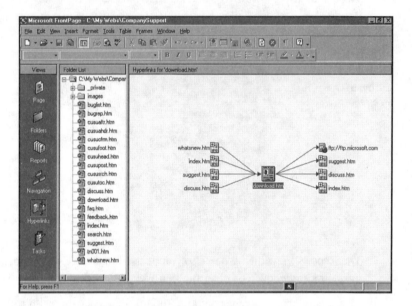

By clicking the + icon on any page in the Hyperlinks view, you can see all of its hyperlinks. You also can move a page to the center of the Hyperlinks view by right-clicking the page's icon and selecting the Move to Center pop-up menu item.

Pages can be opened for editing, deleted, and opened in a Web browser for viewing from the Hyperlinks view.

The Navigation view is used to establish a Web's navigational structure. Figure 1.8 shows the Navigation view for a customer support Web.

Each icon in the Navigation view represents a page in the Web. You might think that this view is redundant, because hyperlinks already establish the way a Web is navigated.

FrontPage 2000 supports the use of navigation bars—a group of common hyperlinks that can be placed on all pages of a Web for easy navigation. These bars can be made up of graphics or text.

FIGURE **1.8**

The Navigation view.

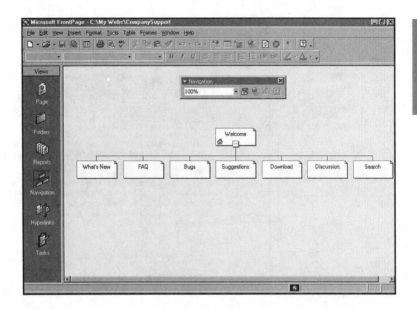

Almost all large Webs have a common navigational structure. A sports site could have a navigation bar that enables visitors to go to specific hockey-, baseball-, football-, and basketball-related pages. A political news site could have a navigation bar with links to elections, allegations, resignations, condemnations, and legislation.

As shown in Figure 1.8, the customer support Web has several pages that can be immediately loaded using its navigation bar: What's New, FAQ, Bugs, Suggestions, Download, Discussion, and Search.

Putting this bar on each page of the Web makes it easier for people to go directly to the information they want from your Web. Navigation bars also can include a link to the Web's home page and establish an order in which pages should be viewed.

Figure 1.9 shows a page of the customer support Web with two navigation bars:

- A vertical bar with home, back, and next graphics
- A horizontal bar with text links for What's New, Bugs, Suggestions, Download, Discussion, and Search (there's no FAQ link because it's the current page)

Links added to a page through a navigation bar do not show up in the Hyperlinks view. You'll have a chance to work with navigation bars during Hour 6, "Manage a Web."

Graphic
navigation—
bar

Text
navigation—
bar

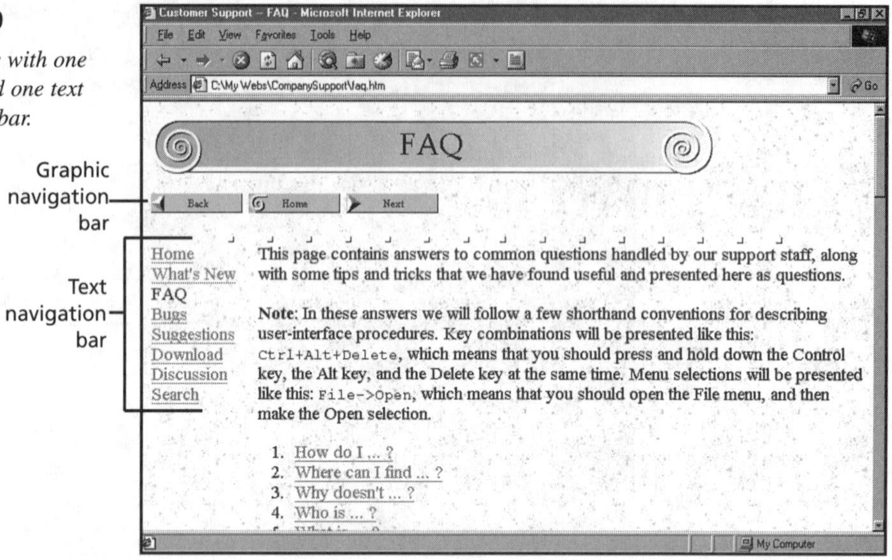

Workshop: Explore the FrontPage 2000 User Interface

This hour's workshop is to familiarize yourself with the FrontPage 2000 interface.

Before you can do that, you need a Web to work on. The fastest way to create one is to use one of the default Webs that FrontPage 2000 knows how to build by itself.

One of these is almost identical to the customer support Web shown throughout this hour.

To begin creating a default Web, select File, New Web. A dialog box opens, listing each of the Webs FrontPage 2000 can build (see Figure 1.10).

Double-click the Customer Support Web icon to create this Web and all of its folders and pages on your hard drive. FrontPage 2000 creates this Web using a template, a blueprint for a Web and all the files it contains. The customer support template is designed for Webs that support a company's products.

FIGURE 1.10

The New Web dialog box.

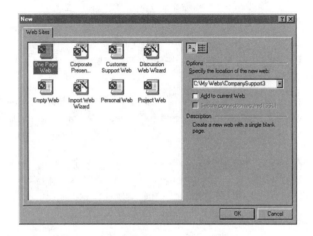

To see what this Web looks like, select the menu item File, Preview in Browser. (There's also a Preview in Browser button on the Standard toolbar.)

Use this new Web to answer each of the following questions:

1. What's the title of the discuss.htm Web page?

2. How many files of the Web are pictures?

3. How many hyperlinks does the page faq.htm contain?

4. How many hyperlinks does the entire Web contain?

5. What happened to the site on Wednesday, July 26?

Solution: Viewing a Web

There are several ways to come up with some of the answers to this workshop. The following solutions are either the fastest to accomplish or the most definitive:

1. Title of discuss.htm: In the Folders view, you can see that the title of this page is "Customer Support — Discussion." This title is displayed in the title bar of a Web browser when the page is loaded.

2. Number of pictures in Web: According to the Reports view, two of the 21 files in the Web are pictures.

3. Number of hyperlinks in faq.htm: If you open the Hyperlinks view and make faq.htm the center page, you'll see that it links to six pages. This is a different total than you'd get by loading the page into the Editing Window and counting the links by hand, because the Hyperlinks view does not include navigation bars.

4. Number of hyperlinks in Web: There are 87, according to one of the items of the Report view.

5. What happened on July 26: The customer support Web was placed online, according to whatsnew.htm.

The last solution is more labor-intensive than the others. Using what you learned during this hour, you could either look at each page in the Web in the Page view or preview the Web in a browser and visit each of its pages until you came across a reference to July 26.

A faster method is to use the Edit, Find menu option available in many of the programs of Microsoft Office. One of the most significant upgrades to FrontPage 2000 is to make it part of Office 2000, sharing many of the same features of programs such as Word and Excel.

Those programs have Edit, Find menu options that can search through entire documents to find specific text. FrontPage 2000 has one that can search an entire Web, making it impossible for "July 26" to hide.

Summary

If you've accomplished all of the tasks from the first hour, you now have a copy of FrontPage 2000 somewhere inside your computer. This copy has been used it to create a Web and explore the FrontPage interface.

All work you do in FrontPage 2000 begins by selecting a view—the six different ways to look at a Web. The Views Bar contains icons for each of these options: Page, Folders, Reports, Hyperlinks, Navigation, and Tasks.

Moving from view to view, you can do everything that's needed to create a Web, keep its content up-to-date, and easily fix things such as broken hyperlinks.

This hour presented a bird's-eye view of the views in FrontPage 2000. You'll be swooping down for a much closer look at this interface in each of the 23 hours to follow.

In case you're counting along at home, the number of books published about the World Wide Web is now one million two hundred and twelve.

Q&A

Q **What modem speed should my Webs be designed for?**

A The answer depends largely on the kind of Web you're producing. Most Web publishers who are going after the widest possible audience take care of the person on a 28,800-baud connection. Alienating them with a lot of slow-loading pages narrows the audience considerably.

Some publishers organize a Web into pages for slower connections like 28.8 and pages for faster ones like cable modems and T1 lines. It's more time-consuming, but you can experiment with more graphics and interactive page elements without worrying as much about the time-to-load report.

Exercises

Challenge your knowledge of the FrontPage 2000 graphical user interface with the following exercises:

- Create another new Web using a different template such as Personal Web or Project Web. Explore each of the views with this Web, especially Navigation and Hyperlinks, to see how different it appears from the Web you created during this hour.

- Using the customer support Web that FrontPage created, give your company a name. Make sure each page of the Web contains this name and preview the whole site in Internet Explorer.

HOUR 2

Use Templates to Quickly Create a Web

Historians believe that one of the most remarkable achievements of mankind is the completion of the Great Wall of China, the 1,500-mile fortification built by some 300,000 laborers in the third century B.C.

Personally, I've always had more respect for the guys who started the thing. Looking out on miles and miles of unspoiled mountains, a group of workers had to put down the first stone, knowing that millions more must be stacked before their job was over and employee benefits were fully vested. As someone who faces paralyzing indecision in a buffet line, I can't imagine what it was like to place the Great Wall's first brick.

As you get ready to create your first Web in FrontPage 2000, the program may look as imposing as a line of Chinese mountains in need of a wall. Knowing where to start, and what to do, can be a daunting task when you've never used the software.

FrontPage 2000 makes the task less daunting through the use of templates, built-in Webs that the software knows how to create by itself.

Templates enable you to develop a complete Web in a few minutes, then spend your efforts customizing that Web rather than creating it from scratch.

Although they won't work with all Webs, templates are a huge timesaver when they are suitable for your projects. During this hour, you'll create your first Web in a matter of minutes, an accomplishment made possible through the use of a template.

Discover FrontPage 2000 Templates

Templates are standard Webs or Web pages that FrontPage 2000 can build upon request. The software includes 48 different templates, and they match some of the most common ways that publishers use the World Wide Web.

The built-in templates include a personal Web, a corporate Web, customer feedback Web pages, and site search pages.

During the previous hour, you used a template to quickly create a Web you could experiment with. The 19-page customer support Web included numerous hyperlinks, a navigation bar, and other features common to FrontPage Webs.

To create a new Web with a template, use the File, New, Web menu command. To create a new page, use File, New, Page instead. In either case, a dialog box will open listing the templates that are available, along with a list of wizards.

Wizards, like the Installation Wizard used during the previous hour, simplify a task by breaking it down into discrete steps. In FrontPage 2000, wizards can create a Web or Web page based on the answers you provide in a series of dialog boxes.

Figure 2.1 shows a dialog box listing the templates and wizards that you can use to create a new Web.

All Webs and Web pages start from templates, even if you don't want FrontPage 2000 to do any work for you. If you're creating a Web that should not contain any built-in pages, choose the Empty Web template. If you're creating an empty page, the Normal Page template should be selected.

Wizard   Template

FIGURE 2.1

*Selecting a template
for a new Web.*

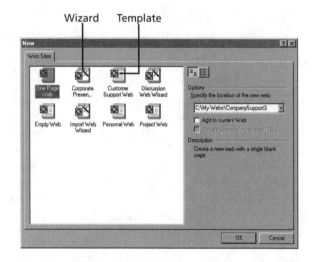

2

Select a Web Template

Before you can create a page in FrontPage 2000, you must create a Web that will contain that page. Because all Webs start from a template, you must choose one to start a project.

The following templates can be used to start a Web:

- *Empty Web*—A Web containing no pages.
- *One Page Web*—A Web with a single blank page.
- *Personal Web*—A Web for personal information.
- *Customer Support Web*—A 19-page Web that enables a company to offer customer support for one or more of its products.
- *Project Web*—A 23-page Web devoted to a collaborative project, with pages for member information, project status, a schedule, group discussions, and an archive.

When choosing a template, you must also choose the location where the Web will be saved. Webs can be saved to disk or to a World Wide Web server.

If you save a Web to disk, you must save it again on a World Wide Web server to make it publicly available. This is also called publishing a Web, because it's analogous to publishing things such as books. A Web must be made available on a Web server before the outside world can visit it.

Before you can save a Web to a Web server, you must have a username and password for that server. You'll learn more about this process during Hour 13, "Publish Your Web."

To save a Web to disk, specify a folder where the Web should be stored. This folder should only be used to store files related to your Web. If it doesn't already exist, FrontPage 2000 will create it.

Although it adds an extra step, you should save all Webs to disk and publish them on the Web separately. This prevents you from losing any files in the event that the Web server crashes or the server's administrator deletes your site.

After a template and location have been selected for a new Web, FrontPage 2000 creates all pages contained in the Web, and any subfolders that are needed. Each of the built-in templates includes private and images subfolders.

The images subfolder holds any graphics files that are part of the Web. The private sub-folder, which initially contains no files, can be used as a place for files that should be hidden from visitors to your Web. If you create a Web that collects information such as a visitor's name and mailing address, the private subfolder is a good place to keep it away from prying eyes.

Despite its name, the _private folder is actually as public as everything else when your Web is created. You must use FrontPage security features to hide the folder's contents, which is possible only on Web hosts that are equipped with FrontPage Server Extensions.

If the template contains any pages, the main page of the Web will be named index.htm.

The filename index.htm is one of several names that are commonly used for a Web's main page—also called its *home page*. Others are index.html, default.htm, and default.html.

Customize a Template

After a new Web has been created from a template, you can begin making changes to customize the Web.

If you're creating a home page for yourself or someone you're exceptionally familiar with, the Personal Web template is a good starting point.

This five-page template includes the following elements:

- A main page with space for an introduction
- A page to display photos
- A page to describe several hobbies and interests
- A page to list your favorite Web sites

A navigation bar provides links to each of these pages, as shown in Figure 2.2.

FIGURE 2.2

The hyperlinks page from the Personal Web.

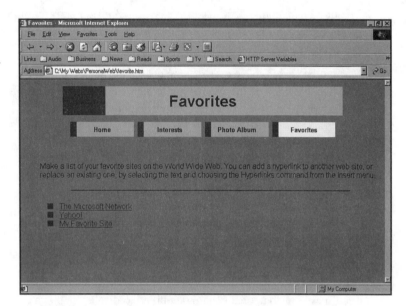

By loading each of these pages in the Page view, you can edit several different things: text, hyperlinks, navigation bars, timestamps, and page banners.

Edit text by placing your cursor anywhere within the text and using your keyboard. You also can employ features common to most word processors: text highlighting, cut-and-paste, and the Formatting toolbar.

Some things on a page look like text but are actually something else, such as hyperlinks or timestamps.

As you move the cursor over different parts of a page, the cursor changes depending on what it's placed on. FrontPage 2000 also may display a ToolTip—a short box of informative text—that describes how you can modify that part of the page.

Navigation bars, timestamps, and page banners are all components—special page elements that add functionality to a FrontPage 2000 Web.

The main page of this Web, index.htm, contains a timestamp component immediately after the text "This page last updated on" and before the period at the end of the sentence. The timestamp displays the date that the page was last edited, and changes automatically each time changes are made to the page.

The timestamp component makes it easy to tell visitors how current the information on a page is. You don't have to enter the date using text and change it manually during each page update.

Placing the cursor above a timestamp causes the cursor to change to a hand-and-page icon. Double-click the timestamp and a dialog box will open enabling you to edit how it is presented. This dialog box is shown in Figure 2.3.

FIGURE 2.3

Editing a timestamp component.

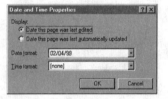

Each FrontPage 2000 component is edited using a dialog box like the one shown in Figure 2.3.

The timestamp component can be modified to display a date, a time, or both. You also can choose the format that the time and date are displayed in. After making the change, press the F5 function key, also called the Refresh button.

The Refresh button works like the one on a Web browser, which causes a Web page to be completely redrawn. The Refresh button on FrontPage 2000 should be pressed after any components on a page are changed.

Another component that you can modify is the page banner, a heading atop a page that can serve as its title.

Each page in the personal Web template has a banner at the top. By default, the banner is graphical—text appears over a simple graphic file.

To change a banner, double-click it to bring up the Page Banner Properties dialog box, as shown in Figure 2.4.

FIGURE 2.4

Editing a page banner component.

You can change the text of a banner and determine whether it should be displayed as a picture or text.

Any changes to a page's banner will be made to that page's icon in the Navigation view, changing the text of navigation bars that link to the page. A page banner serves as a title for that page.

The Personal Web also includes several different hyperlinks. Some of these are part of the navigation bar, a FrontPage component that uses the Navigation view to determine which links should be displayed.

Other hyperlinks can be edited directly. The `favorite.htm` page of the Personal template contains three of these hyperlinks. One leads to Yahoo!, another to the Microsoft Network, and a third to something called My Favorite Site.

Each hyperlink consists of two things:

- The Web address that the link leads to
- The part of a page that should be clicked to visit the link

Hyperlinks can be associated with any element of a Web page, including text, graphics, or a combination of both. The Web address is also called a *URL*, an acronym that stands for *Uniform Resource Locator*.

The URL can link to anything on the World Wide Web, such as pages, graphics, and other files. It also can link to something within the current Web.

Text that is being used as a hyperlink can be changed with the keyboard like any other text on a page.

Changing a hyperlink's URL is different than editing a component. Right-click the hyperlink and select the Hyperlink Properties pull-down menu command. The Edit Hyperlink dialog box will open, which is shown in Figure 2.5.

FIGURE 2.5

Editing a hyperlink's URL.

The Edit Hyperlink dialog box looks like the one that appears whenever you're opening a file in Windows. If you're linking to another page or file in the current Web, you can select it using this dialog box.

If the link is to an address on the World Wide Web such as `http://www.fp2k.com/24`, enter this in the dialog's URL field.

After changing the URL, you can test it in a Web browser by clicking Preview in Browser on the Standard toolbar. If the URL links to an address on the World Wide Web, you need to connect to the Internet before trying it out.

Workshop: Create Your Own Personal Web

You now should be able to create a personalized Personal Web, your first real Web in FrontPage 2000.

Use the Personal Web template to create a person's home page. The person in question can be you, someone you're familiar with, or someone you hope to become familiar with—once they see the Web that has been created in their honor.

This Web should have each of the following:

- An introduction on the main page that describes the person in a few sentences.
- An interests page that describes three of the person's interests.
- A hyperlinks page that links to three of the person's favorite Web sites.

If you have photos of the person, you should use some of them on the photo page that's part of a Personal Web.

Also, change the page banner of the interests page to Hobbies instead of Interests. This change will require some changes to the text of that page, and it also should appear on the navigation bar throughout the Web.

While you're working, you may accidentally delete a component or hyperlink you're working on. You can add a new one to replace it using one of the following menu commands:

- Insert, Date and Time for a timestamp
- Insert, Page Banner
- Insert, Hyperlink

The last thing you should do is to personalize the text on each of the pages, removing anything that doesn't make sense. Use interesting, energetic language to describe the subject of this Web, especially if you're developing it in someone's honor.

> If you're creating a personal Web to honor someone, please stay away from phrases like "Your No. 1 fan," "We were meant to be together," and "If I can't have you, no one else will." Also be sure to obey any mail that has the words "restraining order" in it.

After making all of these changes, preview the Web in a browser. Before previewing the pages, FrontPage 2000 will give you an opportunity to save anything that hasn't been saved yet.

Solution: Getting Personal

An example of a Web that was produced for this workshop can be found on this book's official Web:

`http://www.fp2k.com/24`

Each hour of the book has its own page on this Web, offering workshop solutions, corrections, clarifications, and answers to reader questions.

Figure 2.6 illustrates the main page of this workshop's solution: Misery Loves Company, the home page of Annie Wilkes.

FIGURE 2.6

The Personal Web of
Annie Wilkes.

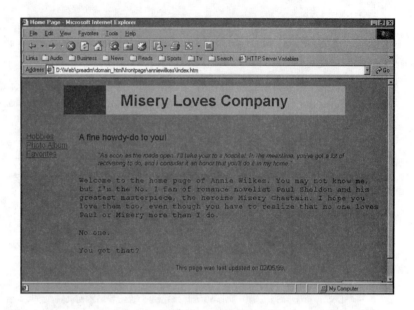

Using FrontPage 2000, Annie was able to quickly create a personal home page for herself. Templates free up time that can be spent on other pursuits, such as rescuing your favorite romance novelist after a car accident and holding him hostage until he brings your favorite character back from the dead.

Most of the changes required to customize the Personal Web template can be handled with text editing in the Page view.

Since there already are three hyperlinks on favorites.htm for Yahoo!, Microsoft Network, and a third site, these hyperlinks can be modified to suit the person you're creating the Web for.

As you're working on the hyperlinks, you may run across a page of the Web called myfav3.htm. This page is included in the Personal Web template simply to provide a destination page for the My Favorite Site hyperlink. You should delete myfav3.htm in the Folders view if the page isn't being used in your Web.

If you changed the page banner on interests.htm so that the text is Hobbies, you might have run into problems displaying this change in a Web browser.

To fix this, load the page in Page view and press F5—the Refresh button. This is a common oversight when you're changing components, and the first thing you should try when a page doesn't look right during a browser preview.

Summary

Templates are a great way to reduce the amount of time it takes to develop a Web. When they are applicable to a project you're working on, they're a great timesaver. Your efforts are spent customizing a template instead of starting from a bunch of empty Web pages.

There is always something to be said for doing everything by hand, of course.

If 1,500-mile Chinese wall templates were available when a certain project was started by Emperor Shihuangdi, it might be known today as the Good Wall of China. Centuries of international tourism would have been greatly reduced.

2

Q&A

Q How can you change the appearance of a Web template?

A The colors and graphics in a template such as Personal Web are controlled by its theme. Themes, as you will discover during the next hour, are a way to establish a consistent and pleasing visual appearance for a Web.

The theme of a built-in template can be changed easily within FrontPage. You can change everything about the way the Web looks, including its background color, background image, component graphics, text color, and hyperlink color.

Q Earlier, you said that the main page of a Web can have different names, such as `index.htm`, `default.htm`, and `index.html`. Which should be used?

A The one you choose depends on which one your Web hosting provider looks for when someone tries to pull up the Web without naming a page. For example, if someone visits `http://www.prefect.com`, the server will actually look for `http://www.prefect.com/index.html`. This occurs because the Web server is configured to add `index.html` to any address that doesn't include a page reference.

FrontPage 2000 calls any new page `index.htm`. You can easily rename this file in the Folders view to conform with your Web hosting provider.

Exercises

Challenge your knowledge of FrontPage 2000 templates with the following exercises:

- Expand the Personal Web that you created during this hour by adding short reviews of all three sites listed on the hyperlinks page. Put each of these reviews on its own page and move the URLs to these new pages.

- Using a portal such as Yahoo!, find a Web site that matches each of the things listed on your personal Web's hobbies page. Add hyperlinks on this page linking to these sites.

Hour 3

Apply a Theme to an Entire Web

This hour contains graphic descriptions. Reader discretion is advised.

Half the battle in any Web project is to create the information that will be displayed on the pages of your site. FrontPage 2000 makes this easier through the use of templates, which can generate pages—and even entire Webs—for you to customize.

The other half of that battle is to make that information look good.

There was a time when the World Wide Web was almost entirely text. The information contained on a Web was more important than the different ways that browsers displayed it.

That time ended a few minutes after a new Web page element was introduced—the image file. Images such as GIF and JPG files could be displayed on the Web as part of pages, creating a new expectation for what sites should look like.

Most Web users expect sites to be easy to use and visually interesting. FrontPage 2000 makes this part of Web design easier through the use of themes, packages of coordinated graphics that can be applied to your Webs.

During this hour, you'll learn how to apply themes to Webs and individual Web pages. You'll also be creating one of your own customized themes.

Sample the FrontPage 2000 Themes

As a Web publisher, one of your most important tasks is to establish the visual appearance of your site. This is determined by each of the following, among other things:

- The color of text and hyperlinks
- The color or image used as a background
- The fonts used
- The images and navigation bars

Another choice you must make is whether these things should vary from page to page or be consistent throughout an entire Web. Using the same visual elements makes it easier for a visitor to know they're still on your Web. It also can make a Web easier to navigate, if you've kept the layout consistent and used navigation bars.

FrontPage 2000 enables you to establish the visual identity of a Web by assigning a theme to it.

Themes establish the visual appearance of a Web or a Web page by defining its colors, fonts, text, and images.

Select a Web Theme

There are more than a dozen themes included with FrontPage 2000. Themes are selected by using the Format, Theme menu command. A Themes dialog box opens that enables you to preview each available theme before applying it to any part of your Web, as shown in Figure 3.1.

The themes in FrontPage 2000 are given short names that help describe their appearance. Blueprint is a technical-looking theme that resembles draftsman's markings. Citrus Punch features tropical flowers and bright colors. Blank, though not actually blank, is relatively plain.

Select each theme to see a preview of it in the dialog's Sample of Theme window. The Romanesque theme is shown in Figure 3.1.

FIGURE 3.1

Selecting a theme for a Web or a Web page.

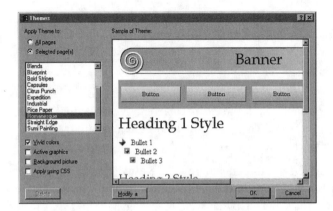

The first choice you must make is whether to apply your chosen theme to a page or your entire Web. If you choose a single-page theme, it will be applied to the page that's currently open in Page view.

> Themes are one of the easiest features to experiment with in FrontPage 2000. If you apply a theme to your Web and don't like it, you can easily wipe out the change by choosing a different theme. You also can remove all themes by choosing (No theme) in the Themes dialog box.

The next decision to make is whether to select any of the following options:

- Vivid colors
- Active graphics
- Background picture
- Apply using CSS

The Vivid colors option determines whether the theme will use a variety of bright colors or a white background and darker colors.

If a theme uses vivid colors, it will have a bright background color such as light green or yellow and other colors that work well on that background.

If a theme does not use vivid colors, the background will be white and all other colors will be darker, making them easier to read.

This color choice will not be as significant if you use the theme's background image. This causes a graphic to be tiled—repeated over and over like tiles on a kitchen floor—underneath the contents of a page. The difference between vivid and darker colors is less noticeable over a background image.

Choosing Active graphics adds some animation effects to the theme. One common feature of an animated theme is a navigation bar with buttons that change in response to mouse movement. These are called *hover buttons* in FrontPage 2000, because the buttons change when a mouse hovers over them.

FrontPage creates this effect through the use of one of the scripting languages that it supports: JavaScript or VBScript. All of the scripting is handled internally by FrontPage, so you don't have to be familiar with these languages to make use of them on your Webs.

Like all features offered through scripting, hover buttons are not supported by all browsers. Versions 3.0 and later of Microsoft Internet Explorer and Netscape Navigator support these buttons. On browsers that don't support them, a non-animated version of the graphics will appear.

The last option you can enable with a theme is to apply it using *CSS—Cascading Style Sheets*. Style sheets are a standard for Web browsers that has been recently implemented in Navigator and Internet Explorer. They enable the basic visual elements of a page—its text, colors, fonts, and formatting—to be defined separately from the information the page contains.

Since a theme is a representation of a Web's visual appearance, it makes sense to define it through the use of Cascading Style Sheets.

However, the most important thing to note about Cascading Style Sheets are the words "recently implemented." Although a standard for Cascading Style Sheets has existed since December 1996, at the time of this writing Microsoft and Netscape are offering different and occasionally incompatible implementations of style sheets in their browsers.

If you apply a FrontPage theme using Cascading Style Sheets, it should be fully supported by the current version of Internet Explorer. This is the first version of FrontPage that offers support for style sheets, and its implementation is most compatible with Microsoft's Web browser. You should test the Web in other browsers to make sure that their users are able to successfully view the site.

Removing Unused Themes

Every theme that you apply to a Web adds more than a dozen graphics files to it. These files are used behind-the-scenes by FrontPage 2000, and they include hover buttons, the background picture, and the graphic behind every page banner.

If you apply a theme to a specific page, the files used by this theme stay around even if that page is later deleted.

You can find and delete these files with the Unused Themes report on the Reports view. This report lists the number of themes that are no longer associated with any part of the current Web.

To remove these files, double-click the line of the Reports view that lists Unused Themes. FrontPage 2000 must recalculate the hyperlinks of the Web before it can finish this task, so you need to be connected to the Internet.

3

Assign a Theme to a Web

During the last hour, you created a Web using the Personal Web template. Although you might not have realized it at the time, you were using a theme. The Personal Web, like all built-in templates, has a default theme that it applies to all pages in the Web.

Depending on the person for whom you were creating that Web, the theme may not have been quite what you were looking for. A Jimmy Buffett home page is a lot more comfortable in Citrus Punch than Industrial. A Web devoted to the French mathematician and scholar Marin Mersenne probably is more suited to Blueprint than the Artsy theme.

> As you're selecting a theme, you might notice the (Install Additional Themes) option. Select this to install more than 45 additional themes from the FrontPage 2000 CD. These themes take up approximately 3M of disk space.

As the first project of this hour, load the personal Web that you created and apply a new theme to all of its pages.

Because it's so easy to experiment with themes, preview the Web in a browser in three different ways:

- With active graphics
- With non-active graphics and a background image
- With vivid colors and no background image

Figure 3.2 shows last hour's Annie Wilkes home page with a different theme and a background image.

FIGURE 3.2

Trying a new theme on a personal Web.

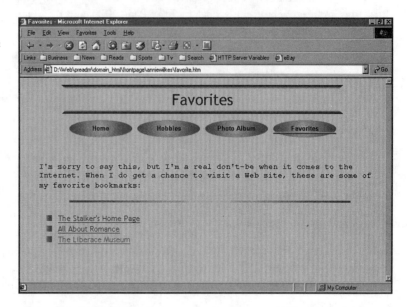

Create Your Own Theme

As you have seen, themes are a quick way to establish the appearance of a Web. Whether your Web contains 5 or 500 pages, the same minimal amount of work is required to apply a theme.

If none of the built-in themes suit the Web you're trying to create, you can develop your own.

To create a new theme, you can begin by modifying an existing one. Start by selecting the existing theme as if you're going to apply it to a Web, and click Modify in the Themes dialog. Three new buttons will appear: Colors, Graphics, and Text. Each of these enables you to change part of the selected theme.

Selecting a Color Scheme

The Colors button is used to pick the five colors that make up the theme's color scheme. These colors can be selected in three different ways:

- Selecting from a list of available schemes
- Using a color wheel
- Manually assigning a color to each Web element that can be placed on a page, including headings, text, and hyperlinks

Many of the listed colors correspond with existing themes, so you can borrow them for your new theme.

The color wheel is shown in Figure 3.3.

FIGURE 3.3

Selecting a theme's colors from a wheel.

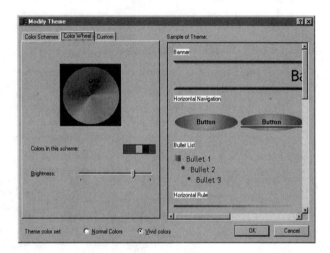

The color wheel is used to pick a set of five related colors. Picking a red area of the wheel creates a color scheme that is predominantly red, for instance.

The scheme changes as you move to different places on the wheel, making it easy to meander around until you find something you like.

Another thing you can do that greatly affects the scheme is to adjust the brightness level of the entire wheel. If you're looking for a gloomy range of colors, you will need to darken the entire color wheel first.

Every change you make while selecting colors is reflected in the Sample of Theme window, as shown in Figure 3.3.

One thing that isn't obvious about selecting a color scheme is what the five colors are used for. The color in the middle is the page's background color. The other colors are used in a variety of different ways, as you'll see in the Sample of Theme window.

The third way to select colors for a theme is to assign them manually. Instead of picking a five-color scheme, you assign specific colors to specific Web elements such as the page background, active hyperlinks, and body text. This is more time-consuming, but it provides total control over the colors employed in the theme.

After you have made changes to an existing theme, you can save them in the Themes dialog box by clicking Save As and giving the theme its own name. This is preferable to clicking Save because it doesn't wipe out the existing theme.

Selecting Text and Graphics

The Text button of the Themes dialog box is used to associate fonts with body text and the six different heading sizes that are used on Web pages. A dialog box opens, enabling you to select any font that's installed on your system, as shown in Figure 3.4.

FIGURE 3.4

Selecting fonts to use in a theme.

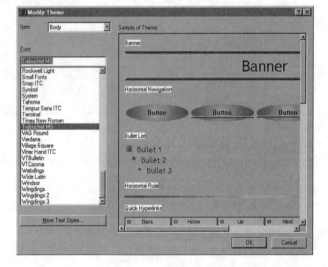

Fonts are a very system-specific element of Web page design. If you use a font on your Web that isn't present on a visitor's system, their browser will default to a standard font such as Arial, Helvetica, or Verdana.

If you're developing a Web that only will be seen on a company's intranet, you can use any font that you know will be present on the machines that have access to that Web.

If you're a corporate Webmaster, you can always order your colleagues to install a font. This might seem a little cheeky, but it's time someone showed why the word "master" is part of the job title. Harbormasters control traffic on a waterway. Jedi masters control potent Forces. Is it too much to ask that Webmasters have sovereign power over fonts?

3

Anything bound for the World Wide Web probably should stick to fonts that are the most widely supported. The built-in themes in FrontPage 2000 use the following fonts: Arial, Book Antiqua, Century Gothic, Helvetica, Times, Times New Roman, Trebuchet MS, and Verdana. The safest of these fonts to use are Arial, Helvetica, Times, and Verdana.

If you're concerned that a font won't be present, you can specify one or more alternate fonts when modifying a theme. Instead of picking a single font, enter a list of fonts separated by commas, such as "Verdana, Arial, sans serif" or "Times New Roman, Times, serif." Web browsers will look for each font in the list and use the first one that's present on the system running the browser.

The final way to create a new theme is to modify an existing theme's graphics.

Every theme has graphics files associated with 11 different page elements, including the background image, page banner, and both horizontal and vertical navigation bars. Some of these elements have several different graphics files associated with them—hover buttons have files for each image that appears on the button.

Changing graphics requires strong working knowledge of how the different page elements function.

To change the graphics associated with a theme, click Graphics from the Themes dialog box. A new dialog box opens, enabling you to select graphics and see how they look in a Sample of Theme window, as shown in Figure 3.5.

*Choosing new
graphics for a theme.*

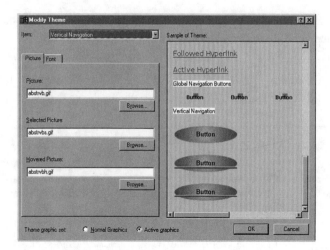

One of the simplest graphics to change is the background picture. This graphic is displayed beneath Web pages when the theme is applied with the Background Picture option selected.

Click Browse to choose a new graphic file. If this file is located anywhere on your system, you can find it using the standard Windows file open dialog box. If it is located on the World Wide Web, you can find it using the image's URL.

Regardless of where you find the file, FrontPage 2000 will make a copy of it for use with the theme. FrontPage will use a copy instead of the original whenever the theme is applied to a Web.

One thing FrontPage 2000 doesn't do for you is secure permission to use the graphics it can grab from the Web. Portals such as Yahoo! have dozens of links to sites that offer background images you can freely use on Webs. Search for text such as "Web page backgrounds" or "background archive."

Workshop: Develop Your Own Theme

The last project for this hour is to express your patriotism by developing a patriotic theme devoted to a country and the colors of its flag. If you're not feeling patriotic at the moment, your project is to express someone else's patriotism.

Take one of the existing themes and save a copy of it as Patriotic or a comparably inspiring name. Any of the themes can be used for this purpose, though some of the more generic themes such as Blank are probably the best choices.

Using this new theme, make each of the following changes:

- The predominant color of the theme should match the darkest color of the country's flag.
- The background color should match the lightest color of the flag.
- Hyperlinks should match a third color of the flag.

Some artistic license may be required if you're patriotic about a country with a one-color or two-color flag.

After setting the colors, select two new fonts that suit the theme—one for body text and the other for each heading. These fonts should be relatively common if you're going to employ the theme on your own Webs. Otherwise, you can take more liberties.

If you have graphics software such as Microsoft Image Composer, you can expand this project by creating a background picture and other graphics.

Figure 3.6 shows a version of the Patriotic theme created for the Republic of Palau, an island of 16,000 people in the Pacific.

FIGURE 3.6

A page featuring a new Patriotic theme.

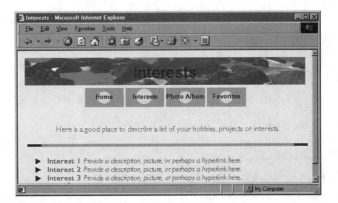

Summary

During this hour, you learned how to use FrontPage 2000's built-in themes to establish the graphic appearance of a Web. FrontPage has themes suited to a variety of purposes: corporate sites, personal home pages, hobbies, and more.

If the software's built-in themes did not fit a project, you learned how to create your own theme by customizing an existing one.

Themes define several different aspects of a Web, including its background picture, navigation bars, and the color of text, headings, and hyperlinks. They can make use of advanced Web design features like JavaScript to cause buttons to change in response to mouse movements on a page.

If you can develop your own graphics, plug them into new themes for an easy way to establish the appearance of a page or an entire Web.

If you're not graphically inclined, themes are a good way to hide this fact.

Q&A

Q I'm creating a new theme. I chose a background color as part of a color scheme, but it always shows up as white when I'm using the theme. What's causing this?

A The background color of a theme is affected by whether you've opted to use vivid colors when you apply it to a Web. If you have not chosen vivid colors, FrontPage 2000 will use a white background with a more muted version of your color scheme.

To put your missing background color to use, reapply the theme with the Vivid Colors option selected.

Exercises

Challenge your knowledge of FrontPage 2000 themes with the following exercises:

- Create a new theme inspired by your favorite holiday. In addition to picking colors and fonts that are suited to the occasion, search Yahoo! or another portal for free graphics you can incorporate into the theme.

- Create a new Web that you can use for some theme-related experimentation. Pick a theme for this Web that has animated graphics and is applied through Cascading Style Sheets. Try this out with each browser on your system to see whether it displays successfully.

Hour 4

Let Wizards Do the Hard Work

One of the things you learn quickly about FrontPage 2000 is how much work it can do without you. As you saw in past hours with templates and themes, FrontPage can create an entire Web and its graphic appearance with a few menu commands.

FrontPage automates even more complex tasks through the use of wizards.

Wizards, as you probably encountered using other Microsoft software, are programs that ask a series of questions about a project you're trying to complete. Your answers control how the program does its work.

You've already used a complex wizard with FrontPage 2000—the Installation Wizard that set the software up on your computer for the first time.

Wizards in Microsoft FrontPage 2000 can be thought of as templates with brains. They are used to create Webs and Web pages that are too variable to be handled with a template.

By breaking down a task into a series of simpler steps, wizards make it possible to create complex Webs—such as a 20-page professional site, a discussion forum, and an interactive form.

Employ a Web Wizard

There are two kinds of wizards in FrontPage 2000: Web wizards, which create entire sites, and single-page wizards.

As you learned when working with templates, wizards can be selected when you're creating a new Web or adding a new page to an existing Web. Click File, New, Web or File, New, Page and a dialog box will list the templates and wizards you can select.

Figure 4.1 shows the dialog box that appears when you're creating a new Web.

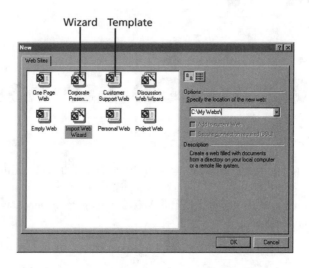

FIGURE **4.1**

Selecting a wizard or template for a new Web.

When you select one of the magic-wand wizard icons, a dialog box opens, describing the wizard and its purpose.

Create a Corporate Web

The Corporate Presence Wizard can be used to quickly establish a company's official Web.

If you're developing a site for your own company or for a client that isn't on the Web yet, this wizard guides you through the process of developing a professional Web. You'll be able to choose products or services that should be spotlighted, solicit feedback from customers, incorporate the corporate logo into each page, and other business-related tasks.

The Corporate wizard has numerous features that make it easier to establish a company's Web. One example: The wizard asks for some common information that should be available about any company: its mailing address, phone number, fax number, email address for customer inquiries, and the like. These things can be automatically placed on different pages, and when something changes, FrontPage 2000 will update every page where it appears.

For example, if your company has to relocate because no one ever taught your original architect about flood plains, you can change the address by selecting Tools, Web Settings and opening the Parameters tabbed dialog box, as shown in Figure 4.2.

FIGURE 4.2

Changing information used throughout a corporate Web.

Once this change is made, it will be updated on every page where the parameter appears. You don't have to edit each of the pages individually. The Corporate Presence Wizard offers several shortcuts that make creating and maintaining a company's Web easier.

When you select this wizard, you'll answer a series of questions on 13 different dialog boxes. To make the most effective use of the wizard, you should know each of the following things about the Web:

- The products or services that will be promoted on the Web
- Whether feedback will be solicited from visitors, and how it should be saved
- Whether the Web needs its own search engine

- The company's mission statement, if one should be displayed on the Web
- Other kinds of information, such as catalog requests, that will be collected
- All contact information about the company along with the email address to use for the company and for Web-related inquiries

If you don't know some of these, you can add them later, after the wizard has created the Web. As a general rule, though, you'll be much closer to completing the Web if you gather all the necessary information before calling the wizard.

Figure 4.3 shows the first dialog box that's used to tell the wizard what kind of corporate Web to create.

FIGURE 4.3

Selecting the main pages of a corporate Web.

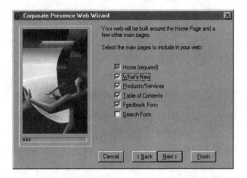

Like all FrontPage 2000 wizards, the corporate wizard includes a lot of explanatory text that describes what it is capable of creating. If you're still in the wizard and you change your mind about a previous answer, you can use the Back button to return to the dialog box and revise it.

One of the dialog boxes will ask exactly how many products and services you will be describing on the Web. A page will be created for each of these, along with a main page connecting all of them with hyperlinks.

If you're not sure whether to include a feature in your corporate Web, err on the side of excess. You can usually take things off a Web a bit easier than you can add them later. It's a gastronomic shame that life doesn't follow the same principle as FrontPage wizards.

For each product, you can determine whether to display an image or pricing information. Each service can be described along with the relevant capabilities and account information. You'll also be able to associate information request forms for each product and service, so prospective customers can use the Web to ask for more details about the company's offerings.

These aspects of the new Web are determined with the dialog box shown in Figure 4.4.

FIGURE 4.4

Customizing the products and services pages.

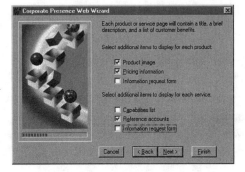

After you answer the questions on all 13 dialog boxes, the Corporate Presence Wizard is finally ready to create the actual Web itself.

The wizard creates each of the main pages that you requested—pages for products, services, and other features, and the start of a navigational structure for the Web.

Another thing it will do is add comments to each page offering tips on what you should add to that part of the Web.

These comments will show up in Page view, displayed in a lighter color than the body text of the page and preceded with the word "Comment." Comments are not displayed when the page is loaded by a Web browser, so you can leave them on the page while you're working on the Web.

To add your own comment to a page, click the menu command Insert, Comment. A dialog box will open, and the comment you enter into it will be added to the page at the current cursor location.

Import an Existing Web

One of the FrontPage 2000 wizards will bring an existing Web and all of its files into FrontPage. The Import Web wizard enables you to take advantage of FrontPage's features on a site that wasn't originally created with the software.

This wizard can import a site from two different places:

- A folder on a hard drive such as your own system or another system on a local network
- The World Wide Web

Local Webs are retrieved using the standard Windows file open dialog box. The Web and all of its pages are copied to a new folder, leaving the original intact.

When you retrieve a site over the World Wide Web, you specify its URL address. FrontPage 2000 will download the pages of the site, all of its images, and other files that are part of the same Web. It will even re-create the folder structure of the site—if the site stored all graphics files into an images subfolder, that will be maintained when the site is re-created on your system.

FrontPage 2000 will also retrieve any other pages that are part of the same Web. If there is a main home page and 20 other pages, each of these will be downloaded along with all of their images and other files.

 One thing this wizard won't grab are programs that run behind the scenes on a Web site: search engines, feedback forms, and the like. The output of these programs is saved, rather than a working copy you can run as part of your own Web.

As you might expect, this can be a time-consuming process. After you specify a site's URL, a dialog box will open that enables you to limit the amount of the Web you retrieve, as shown in Figure 4.5.

FIGURE 4.5

*Deciding how much of
a Web to retrieve.*

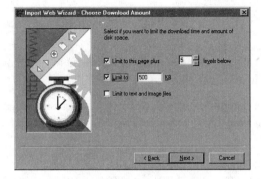

The download can be limited in three ways:

- Reducing the number of levels that are downloaded
- Limiting the Web to a maximum disk size
- Limiting the retrieval to text and image files only

Restricting the number of levels prevents FrontPage 2000 from digging any deeper when
it visits the pages of a Web. Each level represents a page—if FrontPage goes from the
main page to a "What's New?" page and then to a specific news item's page, it has tra-
versed three levels into the site.

Limiting the disk size and the type of files downloaded may cause FrontPage 2000 to
retrieve only a portion of the Web.

Once you retrieve a Web, you can begin working on it like any other FrontPage 2000 site
that you create.

Because FrontPage 2000 supports roundtrip HTML, the pages of the existing
Web should still display normally once they have been imported. As you
start making changes and using FrontPage features like navigation bars on
the Web, this may necessitate changes to existing features. You'll have to
test imported Webs thoroughly to make sure they function as intended.

As with other retrieval features of FrontPage 2000, the Import Web Wizard makes it easy
to incorporate existing Web content into your work. One thing it doesn't do is ask permission before making use of the content of other Web publishers, so you'll have to be
careful to secure permissions when using images, pages, and other material downloaded
directly from the World Wide Web.

Employ a Page Wizard

Most of the wizards you can use in FrontPage 2000 are used to create entire Webs. Because pages are generally simple, most can be added to a Web using a template that you customize within the Page view.

An exception to the rule is the Form Page Wizard, which simplifies the process of adding interactivity to your Web.

Add a Form to a Web

One of the new pages you can add to a Web uses a wizard instead of a template. The Form Page Wizard can create a form—a Web page with fields that collect information from a visitor to your site.

Forms can be created in FrontPage 2000 by adding the individual elements of a form directly to a page, such as text fields, drop-down menus, and buttons.

The Form Page Wizard can simplify this process for some of the common forms that appear on the World Wide Web:

- A page soliciting feedback from a visitor
- A page for ordering a product
- An entry for a Web guestbook

To use this wizard, you first choose a question or series of related questions that should be on the form. The wizard then will give you a chance to customize this further. Figure 4.6 shows how a set of ordering information questions can be customized.

FIGURE 4.6

Customizing a question on a form.

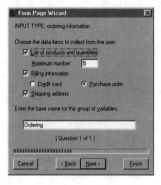

After you tell the wizard about all of the questions that should be on the form, you decide how the information should be saved. FrontPage 2000 can save the answers to a hidden data file on the Web, create a Web page that contains the answers, and mail a visitor's responses through email.

The wizard creates the form based on these specifications and adds it to the current Web. You'll be able to make changes to the form in the Page view after that point—working with a form the wizard built is no different than working with one you created by hand.

There's much more information on how to create forms in Hour 17, "Communicate on Your Web with Forms." You'll use the Form Page Wizard to create an extensive form and retrieve the data that was collected from a user.

Workshop: Create a Corporate Web

This hour's workshop is to create the official World Wide Web site for a fictitious company.

If you're not feeling particularly fictitious today, you can use the following work order as the basis for your Web:

```
MEMORANDUM

From:    I.M. Overpaid, V.P. of New Media and Interoffice Mail
Addr:    21st Century Cheese
    1 Milking Way
    Combined Locks, WI 54113
Phone:   (920) 555-JACK
Fax:     (920) 555-BRIE
To:      That person with the cubicle near the coffee machine who
surfs the Web all day on company time

Recently, it has come to my attention that our competition,
Dairy Godmother, has created their own World Wide Web site with
the intention of going public. They've received very favorable
coverage in both CheeseWeek and American Dairyperson, and are now
being described as "the big cheeses of the Fox River valley."

I would like you to create the official World Wide Web site for
21st Century Cheese. Our customers should be able to visit the
site to learn more about each of our brands:

Mo' Betta' Feta
Hit the Road Jack
```

4

```
Live Brie or Die
Gouda for You
Significant Udder
```

```
They also should be able to contact us with suggestions, and our
address and other contact information should be prominently
displayed.
```

```
I have been told that Web sites are highly complex projects that
take skilled professionals weeks, if not months, to create.
```

```
I expect to see the site online by two weeks ago last Wednesday.
```

```
Sincerely,
I.M.
```

Use a FrontPage wizard to create the Web presence for 21st Century Cheese or a fictitious company of your own creation. Be sure to include the kinds of information
requested by Vice President Overpaid even if you're working for an entirely different
company, and answer all of the questions about the business asked by the wizard. Some
of these you'll have to make up on your own, such as the email addresses for the company and the email inbox for information requests.

If you're working on I.M. Overpaid's assignment, under no circumstances are you to use
the expression "cut the cheese" on the company's Web. For a full explanation of the
company's reasoning, see Section 14-D of the 21st Century Cheese Employee's Manual,
"Why Hank Got Fired."

Solution: Using the Corporate Presence Wizard

Figure 4.7 shows the main page of a 21st Century Cheese Web.

In addition to the information found in Vice President Overpaid's work order, the following choices were made using the Corporate Web wizard:

- Three main pages: Home, Products/Services, and Feedback
- Two things on the home page: Introduction and contact information
- Number of products: 5
- Number of services: 0
- Product details: Pricing information and a request form

- Feedback requests: Full name, mailing address, email address
- Page contents: Page title, links to main pages, email address, and page modification date
- Theme: Arcs

The Web shown in this solution can be found on this book's official Web:

`http://www.fp2k.com/24`

Visit the Hour 4 section of the site to find a link to this version of 21st Century Cheese.

FIGURE 4.7

Customizing a question on a form.

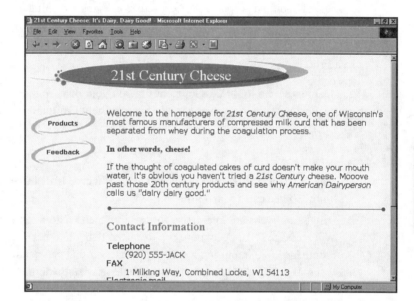

There also may be links to other fictitious companies created by readers of this book, provided that any of them take this very broad hint and contact the author after publishing their own workshop solutions on the World Wide Web.

Summary

During the first four hours of this book, you learned how to take advantage of three time-saving features of FrontPage 2000: templates, themes, and wizards.

Templates are default Webs and Web pages intended for use in your own projects. The template gets you part of the way on a task you're working on, and you finish it by customizing the template.

Themes are built-in graphic styles you can apply to either a Web page or an entire Web. They define the background, colors, image buttons, and fonts that are used, and you can quickly establish a consistent look-and-feel for a Web using themes.

Wizards are interactive programs that create templates based on your answers to a series of questions. You can create more complex Webs with wizards than are possible with templates, including a corporate Web, discussion Web, and an interactive form page.

By using these three features, you're able to solve one of the problems any Web designer faces: how to go from an empty file folder to an entire Web, complete with pages, images, hyperlinks, and a navigational structure.

These features save a lot of development time on your own Web projects. Whether you share this fact with your own version of Vice President Overpaid is entirely up to you.

Q&A

Q One of the wizards, the Discussion Web Wizard, isn't introduced during this hour. Where can I learn how to use it?

A Discussion Webs are interactive forums in which visitors can read and post their own messages. They are more sophisticated than the other Web wizards offered in FrontPage 2000, requiring a special Web server that can handle these kinds of Webs. You'll find out how to work with these wizards during Hour 22, "Enable Discussions on Your Web."

Exercises

Challenge your knowledge of FrontPage 2000 wizards with the following exercises:

- Using a portal such as Lycos or a search engine such as AltaVista, find a company's official Web site that doesn't appear to be more than 20 pages in size. Use the Import Web Wizard to bring this Web into FrontPage 2000 and use the Folders view to explore its structure.

- If you created the 21st Century Cheese Web, add a favorite cheese survey to the site on its own page by using the Form Page Wizard.

PART II

Designing Web Pages with FrontPage 2000

Hour

Hour 5

Create a Web Page

During this hour, you'll face something that has been avoided in the first part of this book:

The blank page.

Filling an empty page is a challenge that the World Wide Web inherited from its ancestors in the written family: books, magazines, and newspapers. Graven stone tablets also could be included in that list, but Moses produced them by dictation, so that's a different challenge altogether.

Absent of divine commandment, you'll be filling blank pages with the basic elements of the Web: text and hyperlinks. You'll work with text in several different ways, changing its font and colors, aligning and formatting paragraphs, and turning text into attention-grabbing headings.

You also will associate text with hyperlinks that connect a page to other documents on your own Web and the World Wide Web.

While you are working with pages, you'll also learn to title a page and choose its own background picture or color.

It all starts with a single blank page in the current FrontPage 2000 Web.

Create and Title a Page

To edit a page, you first must load it into the Page view of FrontPage 2000.

Every Web page in FrontPage 2000 begins as a template. If you want to start from scratch on a new page, the closest you can get is the Normal Page template.

To begin a new page, click File, New Page or the New Page button on the Standard toolbar, which is shown in Figure 5.1.

FIGURE 5.1

The New Page button is located on the Standard toolbar.

New Page button ────

When you select a new page template, the page will appear in the Page view for immediate editing.

If the current Web does not have a theme applied to it, the new page will be completely blank. Otherwise, the theme's background, fonts, colors, and other formatting details will be applied to the page.

The new page will initially be given a unique filename such as newpage1.htm or newpage2.htm. You can give it a different name by clicking File, Save As, or rename it later in the Folders view. Right-click the file and select Rename from the pop-up menu that appears.

> If the Folders list is visible while you're in the Page view, you also can use it to rename files. Select View, Folder List to make it either appear or disappear.

If you close the current Web without making any changes to the new page, FrontPage 2000 discards the page. Otherwise, the software will remind you to save it when you close the Web or preview it in a browser.

Add Shared Borders to a Page

Another thing added to a new page upon its creation is any border that it shares with the rest of the current Web.

FrontPage 2000 enables you to create border areas that are common to all pages on a Web. Click Format, Shared Borders to see what shared borders are being used. A dialog box will open, indicating which borders are currently shared, as shown in Figure 5.2.

FIGURE 5.2

Adding and removing a Web's shared borders.

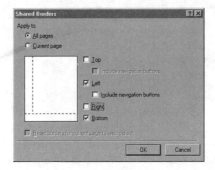

A FrontPage Web can share top, bottom, left, and right borders, though sharing all four doesn't leave a lot of real estate for the rest of each page. They are often used to provide room for things like navigation bars, site logos, and copyright notices.

Many of the built-in FrontPage themes use the left border for a navigation bar that appears on every page of a Web. A do-it-yourself fireworks site should probably consider a shared bottom border with a note disclaiming the publisher from any legal responsibility in the event of unexpected limb loss.

The Shared Borders dialog box can be used to add and remove these borders. Borders are marked in the Page view with dotted lines like those shown in Figure 5.2. Any change made to a border area on one page is instantly reflected on all pages that share the border.

Title a Page

Every Web page is entitled to a title. Although FrontPage 2000 will assign a default title, it's usually something along the lines of "New Page 5," which isn't terribly helpful to people navigating your Web.

A page's title appears in the title bar of most Web browsers—the topmost edge of the window containing the browser. (Non-visual and all-text browsers render it differently.)

To title a page, select File, Properties or right-click the page and select Page Properties from the pop-up menu that appears. A dialog box opens containing six tabbed dialog boxes that can be used to alter the page. Under the General tab, you can enter a new title. The General dialog box is shown in Figure 5.3.

5

FIGURE 5.3

Setting a new title for a page.

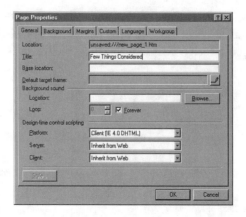

When you title a page, FrontPage 2000 uses this text for the page's banner and on navigation bars, if these are used. It also is suggested as a filename for the page when you first save it.

Although a title is initially copied to a page banner, these are separate elements in FrontPage 2000. Changing one does not automatically change the other, though you might expect that when you're first learning to use the software. You'll work with page banners more during Hour 9, "Display Graphics on a Page."

Choosing a succinct, descriptive title is important for two reasons—it helps people use your Web, and it helps others find it.

If you use the Table of Contents template to add that kind of page to your Web, each page's title is used in the resulting table of contents listing.

Also, the title of a page is the most prominent thing shown in a search engine when results are listed. For example, AltaVista lists the title of each page followed by a few lines of text pulled from its contents.

The title may also be used to determine how a Web is ranked during a search, so if you place "Totally Nude Furniture" in a page title, you'll get more visits from people searching for that topic than you might otherwise. (You'll also get more visitors who were expecting something other than unfinished rocking chairs, so keep that in mind when making any easily confused claims involving states of undress.)

Select a Background for Your Page

One of the ways you can dress up a Web is to give a page a background. The background can be either a solid color or a picture that's loaded from an image file.

Select Format, Background to open the Page Properties dialog box that's used to select a background (see Figure 5.4).

FIGURE 5.4

Selecting a page background.

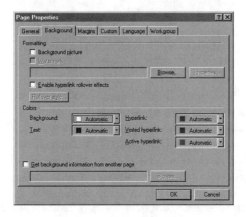

To use a background picture, click the Browse button and a file open dialog box enables you to choose any file on your system. A background picture must be in the GIF, JPG, or PNG format.

You can use a URL to specify the background picture, but this causes FrontPage 2000 to use a graphic that isn't part of your Web.

If the graphic is removed from that URL, it will stop appearing on your pages. For that reason, it's better to make a copy of the image on your system—if you have permission to do so—and work directly with that copy.

Background pictures are repeated under the contents of a page. This is called *tiling*, because each copy of the graphic is like an identical tile on a kitchen floor. If you would like the background to be displayed once, select the Watermark option. The background won't scroll along with the rest of the page.

To choose a background color instead of a picture, deselect the Background Picture check box and click the Background Colors pull-down menu. The standard FrontPage color selection dialog box appears with 16 basic colors to choose from. If none of these fit what you're looking for, click the More Colors button and a more advanced color dialog box will appear, as shown in Figure 5.5.

5

FIGURE 5.5

*Choosing a page's
background color.*

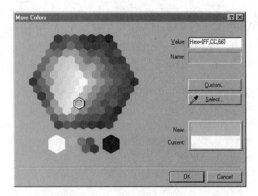

You can select one of the colors shown in the More Colors dialog box or enter a color's
hexadecimal value in the Value field. You also can click the Custom button to open a
third color selection dialog box with even more options.

> Knowledge of hexadecimal values is completely unnecessary to using FrontPage 2000
> because you can pick colors in other ways. For the curious: Hexadecimal values are num-
> bers on a base-16 system, which means there are 16 different single-digit numbers.
> They're often useful in computer programs because you can represent values up to 255 in
> only two digits. The first 20 hexadecimal numbers are 0, 1, 2, 3, 4, 5, 6, 7, 8, 9, A, B, C, D,
> E, F, 10, 11, 12, and 13. Microsoft could have impressed some people in the hexadecimal
> crowd by naming its software FrontPage 7D0.

The color you select is displayed underneath the contents of the page.

When a page has both a background color and a picture selected, the color will be
replaced by the picture when the page is fully loaded. To cause only the color to display,
deselect the Background Picture check box.

If you want to designate a background for an entire Web, it's much easier to create a new
theme with the desired background and apply that theme to the Web. The theme will also
be available for use in other projects, unlike a background that is selected manually.

Add Text to a Page

To add text to a Web page, open it in FrontPage 2000's Page view and begin typing. The
characters will appear at the currently selected cursor position, whether you are in a
shared border or the main part of the page itself.

Shared borders are indicated by dotted lines on the page. These lines won't show up when the page is viewed in a browser.

After you have entered some text on a page, you can highlight a selection of the text and use FrontPage's formatting options on it.

The Formatting toolbar contains the following buttons:

- *Bold*—Makes the text appear in boldface.
- *Italic*—Italicizes the text.
- *Underline*—Underlines the text.
- *Align Left*—Lines up all selected text and other page elements along the left margin of the page.
- *Center*—Centers the selected page elements.
- *Align Right*—Lines up the selected elements along the right margin.
- *Increase Indent*—Indents the selected elements more than they are currently indented.
- *Decrease Indent*—Reduces the indentation of the selected elements.

Most of these buttons are common to different software, especially the B, I, and U icons used for boldface, italics, and underlines.

> FrontPage 2000 can help you learn the purpose of each button on the Standard and Formatting toolbars. If you hover your cursor over a button for a few seconds, FrontPage displays a ToolTip naming that button.

5

When you are working with text on a Web page, you should let text wrap around the right margin at all times and only press the Enter key when you finish a paragraph. On most Web browsers, the text appears in block style, with each paragraph beginning at the left margin and a blank line separating paragraphs.

Pressing the Enter key causes a paragraph break to appear, even when you're arranging images and other page elements along with text.

The main reason you should not worry about the right-hand margin is that it varies depending on the browser and system being used to view a Web page. Someone on an 800-by-600 resolution monitor is going to see much more text per line than someone on a 640-by-480 monitor. A person who has enabled large text for easier reading will greatly reduce the number of characters that appear on a line. These are just two examples of the variability of Web presentation.

If you're using FrontPage 2000 to publish a Web page for the first time, you must become accustomed to the lack of control you sometimes have over a page's appearance.

Unlike a medium such as print, where a page looks exactly like the designer intended it to look, the Web is a fluid medium where pages can rearrange themselves to fit the space they have available to them.

To see this in action, connect to the Internet, load your favorite Web site, and resize your browser window so that it takes up a portion of your desktop instead of the whole thing. Figure 5.6 shows a page from one of my favorite sites, TeeVee, in two different browser windows.

FIGURE 5.6

How page presentation varies in different browsers.

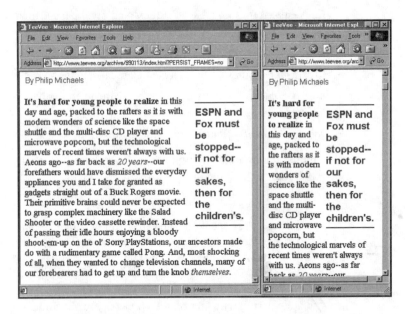

The text of the page wraps differently depending on the space that's available to it.

Every paragraph break on a Web page causes a blank line to appear in most browsers, including Netscape Navigator and Microsoft Internet Explorer. To begin text at the left margin without a paragraph break, you can insert a line break by selecting Insert, Break and choosing the Normal Line Break option from the subsequent dialog box.

There's a hidden shortcut for adding a line break without leaving the keyboard—hold down the Shift key while pressing Enter.

Line breaks can be used to ensure that text appears on different lines without a paragraph break separating them. They're also useful when you're aligning images and other page elements.

Turn Text into a Hyperlink

Documents on the World Wide Web are connected to each other through the use of hyperlinks. When you click on a link, your browser opens up the Web page or other type of file that has been associated with the link.

Hyperlinks can be associated with anything you place on a page: text, images, Java applets, QuickTime movies, WAV sound files—you name it. If my Uncle Kirby ever goes through with his plan to wire a TCP/IP port at an appropriate body juncture, you'll be able to create a hyperlink to him.

Text hyperlinks are displayed in a way that sets them apart from other text on a page. In most browsers, they are underlined.

> For this reason, underlining other text that isn't a hyperlink is frowned upon. Your users will click the underlined text and wonder why it isn't functioning as a hyperlink.

To create a hyperlink, highlight the part of the page that should be associated with the link and select either Insert, Hyperlink or the Hyperlink button on the Standard toolbar.

5

Hyperlinks can be associated with files on your system or any URL on the World Wide Web. If the file is another page in your Web, you can select it using a Windows file open dialog box.

A hyperlink to a URL should contain the full URL preceded by protocol information such as http:// or ftp://. Some examples are `http://www.mcp.com`, `http://www.fp2k.com/24` and `ftp://ftp.netscape.com`.

If you're linking to a file on your system, add it to your Web first by using the File, Import menu command. If you don't, the link will not be usable when the page is published to the World Wide Web.

After creating a hyperlink, you can edit it by right-clicking the link and selecting Hyperlink Properties.

Turn Text into a Heading

Text on a Web page can be set apart from other text by turning it into a heading. Headings range in size from 1 (largest) to 6 (smallest), and they can be used for the same purpose as a headline in a newspaper—succinctly describing the text that follows. They also can be used as subheads with a larger article, as enlarged quotations, and for other attention-grabbing purposes.

The easiest way to turn text into a heading is to use the Style pull-down menu on the Formatting toolbar, which is shown in Figure 5.7. This menu has several different options for formatting text, including choices for six heading sizes from 1 through 6.

FIGURE 5.7

The Style pull-down menu.

The actual size of a heading is browser-specific, but as a general rule you can rely on the 1-to-6 ranking system.

Headings can be associated with hyperlinks and used in most other ways as if they are text. One exception is that a heading must occupy its own paragraph.

To see this in action, highlight a single word in a paragraph and turn it into Heading 1 text. Everything else in that paragraph will be turned into that heading also, occupying a very large chunk of the page.

Change the Font and Color of Your Text

When you add text to a page that has a theme applied to it, the text will have the font and color assigned to body text in that theme. If no theme has been applied, the text will be displayed in the default font and color of the Web browser used to load the page—usually a Times Roman, Arial, or Helvetica font.

To override the font or color choice for text, highlight the text and click Format, Font to open the Font dialog box (see Figure 5.8). You can use this to select a new font and color for the selected text.

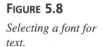

FIGURE 5.8

Selecting a font for text.

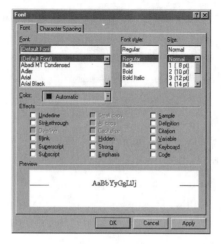

You can choose any font that's present on your system, but if it isn't present on the system of the person viewing your Web, a default font will be substituted for it.

As with font selection for themes, you should stick to common fonts such as Arial, Helvetica, Times, and Verdana because they are likely to be present on most systems. FrontPage 2000 also relies on Book Antiqua, Century Gothic, Times New Roman, and Trebuchet MS in many of its themes.

You also can specify a font and several alternatives in a list separated with commas, such as "Times Roman, Times, serif" or "Courier New, Courier, monospace".

The size of a font can be designated on a scale from 1 (smallest) to 7 (largest). The point size associated with each of these sizes is a rule of thumb rather than an exact measurement. Though the font will be displayed at that size within FrontPage 2000, it's another thing that differs according to the browsing software being used and how it is configured.

A font's color can be selected with the standard FrontPage 2000 color selection dialog boxes. You also can apply several different effects to the text:

- *Strikethrough*—Text will be marked with a line through it, ~~like this~~.
- *Blink*—Text will blink on and off.
- *Superscript and subscript*—Text will be shrunken and appear either above or below other text on the same line.
- *Hidden*—Text will be part of the page but not displayed.
- *Strong*—Text will be displayed with strong emphasis (in most browsers, this causes it to appear in boldface).
- *Emphasis*—Text will be displayed with emphasis (italics in most browsers).

5

Several of the other text effects are used to define the kind of information the text represents. They are presented differently in different browsers, and are not as commonly used today as effects that describe how text is presented.

The following are descriptive effects you can use:

- *Variable*—A variable name, describing a place used to store information in a computer program.
- *Keyboard*—Something that a user should enter with a keyboard.
- *Code*—Source code of a computer program.
- *Sample*—Sample output from a computer program.
- *Citation*—A citation crediting the source of information in an essay or similar paper.

Workshop: Write Your Autobiography

The project you'll be undertaking next is the authorship of your life story, background, and achievements. Since there isn't too much time left in the hour, I hope you're either succinct or extremely modest.

To get ready, create a new One-Page Web in FrontPage 2000 and give it a name such as "common." This Web will serve as a convenient holding place for pages that you can import into other Webs.

A page about you would be something you might want to reuse in several different Webs.

Create a new page with your name as the title and bio.htm as the filename. Use this page to answers each of the following questions:

- Where were you born?
- Where do you live today?
- What schools did you attend?
- What is your career and some of the jobs you have worked?
- What are your greatest professional achievements?
- What are your best personal accomplishments?
- Who's in your immediate family?

Answer each of these with enthusiasm—even if you have to fake some of it. My own career in academia had some low points I'd rather not discuss until the restraining order expires.

Use left-aligned headings to divide the body text into several different sections such as "Personal," "Professional" and "Educational." (If one of your sections is "Criminal," you might want to answer with a little less enthusiasm.)

Change the margins of each section of text so that there is some blank space between the text and the edges of the page.

As the last element of the assignment, add at least five hyperlinks: one back to index.htm and four to sites on the Web. If your schools or jobs have their own Webs, they would be good links. Your hometown and birthplace also should have Webs—if not, the portal Yahoo! has pages devoted to thousands of cities and countries.

Solution: Your Life and Times

After putting your life story into hypertext, you should have a better grasp on the basics of Web page creation. You also may have learned something about yourself, but that's entirely accidental.

Neither the author of this book, Macmillan Publishing, its employees or affiliates is responsible for any personal growth caused by this publication. Any incidental growth that may occur should not be interpreted as a reason to file this book in stores under "Self-Help" rather than "Web Publishing."

The trickiest part of the project was the requirement to set text apart from the margins of the page. That's achieved by using the Increase Indent button on the Formatting toolbar.

You can test your page out by clicking the Internet Explorer icon on the Standard toolbar. FrontPage 2000 will make sure you have a chance to save the page before it's loaded by a browser.

5

Summary

As a writer myself, I can attest to the power of the blank page. Regardless of the medium, there are few things on earth that can inspire more fear in writers [editor's note: other than editors].

After this hour, you should have some tools for keeping the blank page at bay.

Text, headings, and hyperlinks make up the largest part of the World Wide Web. By combining the three, you can create entire Webs that reach an audience of thousands.

Of course, that audience is going to wonder why you're not using any feature of the World Wide Web introduced after 1994.

You'll correct this perception in the next several hours as you work with lists, tables, and frames.

Q&A

Q I'm not a computer programmer. Why would I want to use text effects like variable, code, and keyboard?

A You probably wouldn't. Those effects date back to the first version of HTML, the language used to create Web pages, and they aren't used on many pages today—even when things like variables and source code are displayed on a page. Most browsers display these effects simply as boldface, italicized, or underlined text, so the Bold, Italic, and Underline buttons can be used instead.

FrontPage 2000 includes these effects primarily for the HTML users who are accustomed to them. You can probably avoid them entirely, especially if none of your own pages is on a technical subject.

Q During this hour, the serif and monospace fonts were mentioned. I've never encountered these when selecting a font. Are they new?

A Those fonts are generic, catch-all fonts that a Web browser matches to a real font that's present on the system. There are five of these: serif, sans-serif, cursive, monospace, and fantasy. The Web browser will choose the default font for each of these styles, which is most commonly a Times font for serif, Helvetica for sans-serif, Courier for monospace, and something like Zapf-Chancery for cursive and Western for fantasy. A good way to use these fonts is to put them last in a comma-separated list of fonts—such as "Verdana, Helvetica, sans-serif."

Exercises

Challenge your knowledge of FrontPage 2000 page creation with the following exercises:

- Load the corporate Web you created during Hour 4 and expand the pages that described its products and services. Add indented text and reformat the headings to a different size.
- Create a Halloween-oriented page with an orange background, black text, and headings in the scariest font installed on your system—choose a font that has "Gothic" in its name if all else fails.

Hour **6**

Manage a Web

If you have never used FrontPage before acquiring version 2000, you may be a little unclear about what the software means when it calls something a "Web."

On the World Wide Web, a Web is analogous to a Web site—the pages, images, programs, and other files that you view in a browser as you navigate through it.

In FrontPage 2000, a Web is a site that FrontPage knows how to edit, publish, and perform maintenance on. In all other respects, a FrontPage Web is like any other site that you have used, no matter what software created it.

All Webs must be FrontPage Webs in order for FrontPage 2000 to work on them.

This is not to say that you can't edit individual Web pages with FrontPage without it turning them into FrontPage Webs. You can. However, if you use any of the site management features, FrontPage will turn whatever you're are working on into a FrontPage Web.

During this hour, you'll learn about the life cycle of a FrontPage Web. You'll see how they are born, how they are killed, and how they can thrive in new locations.

Another thing you'll discover is how parent-child relationships can be fostered in the pages of a Web. You'll give children, parents, and siblings to a page and take them away again.

If you don't understand how this software can be so biological, keep reading. The first stop is the place where FrontPage Webs are born.

Create and Explore a Web

A FrontPage Web is created in two ways:

- Creating a new Web using a FrontPage template.
- Importing an existing Web using the Import Web wizard.

Once either of these tasks has been completed, you can work with these FrontPage Webs in the same manner.

Past versions of FrontPage loaded existing Webs and retranslated the HTML of the pages so that it was consistent with how FrontPage creates HTML. This resulted in some compatibility problems with tables and other page elements that change appearance depending on the way their HTML code was formatted. FrontPage 2000 has been developed to leave existing HTML unchanged, so you'll have much better success importing Webs.

A Web is begun with the File, New, Web command. A dialog box opens, listing the templates and wizards that can be used to create the new Web. The Import Web Wizard is one of these options.

Two of the Web templates are used to start a new Web from scratch: the Empty Web and One-Page Web. These Webs consist of the standard file folders, no themes, and no other extra features. The only difference between them is that one includes a blank Web page and the other doesn't.

Import Files to a Web

The World Wide Web is a conglomeration of different media. While pages consist of text documents, these pages can include a variety of different file types, including the following:

- GIF, JPG, and PNG graphics files
- WAV and MIDI sound files
- AVI, MOV, and MPG movies
- Java applets
- ActiveX components

To incorporate these media into your FrontPage 2000 Web, you should first make them a part of the Web using the File, Import command.

You can import files, entire folders, and World Wide Web sites. Requesting the latter causes the Import Wizard to be called so you can specify the site's URL and how it will be retrieved.

A convention of FrontPage is to create an images subfolder where a Web's images can all be stored. If you're working with other types of media, you might want to create folders for them as well—such as java for Java applets and sounds for any sound files you're using.

Once you have imported a file, it will become part of the Web. Whenever you copy the Web to a new folder or actually publish it to the World Wide Web, that file will be included.

Copy and Delete a Web

You can copy a Web to a new folder on your system by publishing it. In FrontPage 2000, the Publish feature will copy a Web to another location, whether it's on your computer's hard drive or a server that's connected to the World Wide Web.

You'll learn how to make your site available on the World Wide Web during Hour 13, "Publish Your Web."

6

It's easier to publish a Web to your own system because you don't require a username, password, or other special access.

To copy the current Web to a new folder, select File, Publish Web to open the Publish Web dialog box (see Figure 6.1).

FIGURE 6.1

Choosing how to publish a Web.

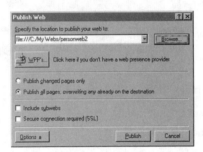

The Browse button on the Publish Web dialog box is used to select the location where the Web should be copied. It opens a Windows file open dialog box with some extra FrontPage-specific features on it.

If there's an empty folder on your system where the Web should be stored, you can use this dialog box to find the folder and open it.

You also can use the file open dialog box's New Folder button to create and name a new folder for the Web.

When you're copying a Web to a new folder, select the option to publish all of its pages so that nothing is omitted. After the Web has been published in full, you'll have two copies of it on your system.

You can delete a FrontPage 2000 Web in two different ways:

• Delete only the parts of the Web that control how it is edited in FrontPage.

• Delete the Web entirely.

To perform either deletion, open the Web and display its folder list (if this list isn't visible, use View, Folder List in the Page or Navigation views). Right-click the name of the Web—the top line in the folder list—and select the Delete command. A dialog box that enables you to delete FrontPage material or the entire Web opens.

Both of these actions are permanent, so you should handle them with due diligence—a phrase I picked up from stock traders that seems to mean "anything bad that happens as a consequence of my advice is entirely your fault."

Deleting an entire Web wipes out the folder containing the Web, all of its subfolders, and all of the pages, images, and other files that comprised the Web.

Deleting the FrontPage 2000 material of the Web only makes the site unrecognizable as a FrontPage Web. Everything else—pages, images, and other files—is not removed.

FrontPage 2000 places several files in a Web's folders that are used by the software to manage the Web. When you use the Import Web Wizard to bring an existing site into FrontPage 2000 for the first time, these behind-the-scenes files are created during the import process.

A Web with none of its FrontPage material can still be viewed normally with a Web browser, but you won't be able to open it for editing in FrontPage.

> If you ever change your mind after deleting this part of a Web, you can bring it back into FrontPage 2000 as a new Web by using the Import Web Wizard.

Add a Navigation Bar to a Web

It's easy to get lost when you're visiting the pages of a large site on the World Wide Web. One of the ways publishers make these Webs easier to use is through the use of navigation bars—common text or graphic links that are associated with the main pages of the site.

Most commercial news and sports sites have navigation bars that lead to the main topics they cover. A sports site such as ESPN.Com has links to its NFL, NBA, NHL, and Baseball pages on a navigation bar that's part of every page. If you dive down several links into ESPN's site while you're reading stories, you can get back to a starting point by using the navigation bar.

Navigation bars can be added to your own FrontPage 2000 Webs and placed in shared borders to make them appear on every page. There are four kinds of bars:

- Vertical lists of text links
- Horizontal lists of text links
- Vertical lists of graphic links
- Horizontal lists of graphic links

6

When you are working with a navigation bar, you don't create any of the hyperlinks that it contains. Instead, these links are determined by the navigational structure you have created for the Web in the Navigation view.

Figure 6.2 shows the Navigation view for a newly created site that used the Personal Web template.

FIGURE 6.2

Examining a Web's navigational structure.

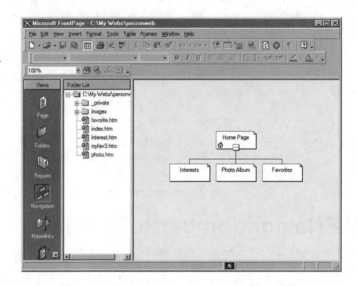

Four of the five pages in the Personal Web are represented in the Navigation view. The fifth, myfav3.htm, is not present because it is not yet part of the Web's navigational structure.

The Navigation view establishes a parent-child relationship between the pages of a Web. In Figure 6.2, the page labeled Home Page is the parent of the other three pages: Interests, Photo Albums, and Favorites.

Pages are added to the Navigation view by dragging them from the Folders list. You can try this out with a new Personal Web by dragging the icon next to myfav3.htm over the Navigation view.

When you drag a page onto the Navigational view, keep hold of it by holding your mouse button down. A dotted outline indicates the relationship that would be established if you dropped the page at that location. The outline changes depending on where you have dragged the page and which page it is closest to.

Figure 6.3 shows an outline around the cursor that shows a parent-child relationship between the Favorites page and a new page that hasn't been dropped. The cursor is closest to the Favorites page.

FIGURE 6.3

Dragging a new page into the Navigation view.

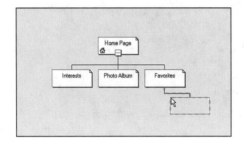

You can pick up pages in the Navigation view and drag them to new locations. The easiest way to get a feel for this view is to drag a new page around and drop it at several different places to see what relationship is established.

In general, a page dropped above another page becomes its parent. A page dropped below a page becomes its child. A page that's dropped beside a page is its sibling and shares the same parent.

An exception: Pages dropped above a Web's home page will be orphans—no lines will connect them to other pages. You can use this to start new parent-child groups that are completely unrelated to other pages of the Web.

In the Navigation view, a parent can have as many children as desired, but a child has only one parent.

> The one-parent rule is where the parent-child metaphor starts to get a little creepy. If you suspect something untoward is going on inside FrontPage 2000's Navigation view, think of these pages as paramecia. They also reproduce through a one-parent system that doesn't involve a stork.

Once you have established the Navigation view for a Web, it will be used to determine which links appear on the Web's navigation bars.

Navigation bars are added to a page with the Insert, Navigation Bar menu command. You also can edit an existing bar by double-clicking it in Page view. Both commands open the Navigation Bar Properties dialog box, shown in Figure 6.4.

6

FIGURE 6.4

*Working on a naviga-
tion bar.*

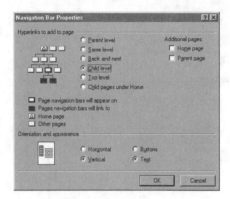

A navigation bar in FrontPage 2000 can display six different groups of hyperlinks:

- *Parent level*—Links to the parent of the current page and all of its siblings
- *Same level*—Links to all pages that are siblings of the current page
- *Back and next*—Links to the siblings immediately to the left (back) and right (next) of the current page
- *Child level*—Links to all pages that are children of the current page
- *Top level*—Links to all pages that have no parents
- *Child pages under Home*—Links to all pages that have the Web's home page as a parent

You also have the option of adding extra links for the Web's home page and the current page's parent, if these aren't already in the group.

The Navigation Bar Properties dialog box shown in Figure 6.4 contains a drawing of a Navigational view. As you choose the different hyperlink groups, this drawing will change to show the pages included in that group.

Two more things you can configure are a navigation bar's orientation (horizontal or verti-cal) and its appearance (buttons or text).

The selection that you make will be immediately reflected in the Web. You can easily experiment with the different styles until you find one that you like.

If your Web does not have a theme applied to it, you will not see buttons on your navigation bar even if you select that option instead of text. FrontPage 2000 relies on themes to provide the buttons that are used on graphic navigation bars.

The Navigation view is used to provide the text that's associated with each hyperlink on a navigation bar. To change this text, right-click a page's icon in the Navigation view and select the Rename menu option.

This text appears on all navigation bars that link to the page, so it should be reasonably short to provide room for other links. It also is used on the page's banner—a FrontPage 2000 component displayed in the top shared border of any Web that uses FrontPage's built-in themes.

Figure 6.5 shows the Favorites page from a Personal Web after myfav3.htm has been added to the Web's navigational structure. This page contains two navigational bars—a horizontal one along the top and a vertical one along the left side.

FIGURE 6.5

A page with two navigational bars.

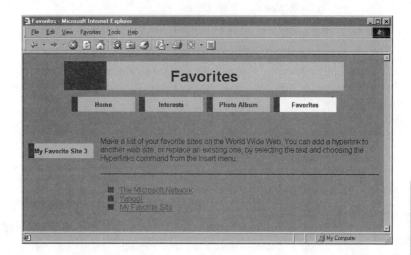

The horizontal bar along the top links to all pages on the same level and the Web's home page. (It also includes a button for the page itself, though FrontPage 2000 automatically removes this unnecessary link.)

The vertical bar only links to pages that are on a child level from the current page. Because myfav3.htm was established as a child to the Favorites page in the Web's Navigational view, it shows up on this bar.

6

Workshop: Create a FrontPage Family Tree

The parent-child relationships in the Navigational view can be thought of as a family tree.

If you're not familiar with the term, a family tree is a drawing that shows several generations of a family and how they are related to each other.

The Navigational view looks like one of these trees, though admittedly the family's a little odder than most. You can use the view to determine which pages have children, which children have grandchildren, and so on. The home page sits on top as the grandsire of many descendants.

This hour's workshop is to put three generations of your own family into the Navigational view.

Do the following:

- Create a new Web with no pages in it.
- Add a new page named after one of your grandparents.
- Add pages named after each child of that grandparent.
- Add pages named after you and each of your siblings.

Once this is done, you'll have several different pages with absolutely no connection to each other. Use the Navigational view to establish the correct parent, child, and sibling relationships between these pages.

When this is done, add a common navigation bar to the top of each page of the Web. This bar should contain only the children of the current page.

Add a second navigation bar to the right of every page that contains a link to all siblings and the parent.

Solution: Building a Web's Navigational Structure

Figure 6.6 shows a Navigation view family tree of the Bradfords from the 1970s TV drama *Eight is Enough*. If you're familiar with the show, the names of Tom Bradford and his eight kids are probably familiar to you. Sandra Sue may not be—she's the infant daughter of Susan and Merle the Pearl.

FIGURE 6.6

Three generations of pages in the Navigational view.

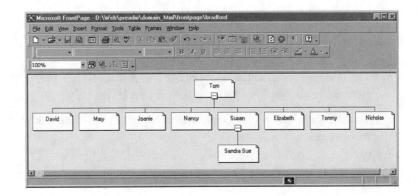

The quickest way to add empty pages to a Web and save them is to click the New Page and Save buttons on the Standard toolbar. FrontPage 2000 asks you to give the page a name before saving it.

Once all the pages have been created, you can drag them onto the Navigational view to establish the correct parent-child relationships. This view is also used to give each page a name, which you must do before the page's name will appear on navigation bars.

Shared borders are established through the Format, Shared Borders command. You can add top and right borders and apply the change to the entire Web.

Navigation bars are added through the Insert, Navigation Bar command. If you have applied a theme to the Web, you can use graphic buttons. Otherwise, all navigation bars will be displayed as text.

If you are creating Webs that have common groups of links on several different pages, the easiest way to handle this in FrontPage 2000 is through navigation bars.

Summary

Thus concludes the biological aspects of your FrontPage 2000 tutelage.

During the past hour, you've followed FrontPage Webs from their creation to their relocation to their final deletion. You should be comfortable giving life to new Webs and taking it away when you want to reclaim some disk space.

You also can bring Webs into FrontPage 2000 with the Import Web Wizard and take them back out again with the Delete command.

6

The real family ties in a FrontPage Web occur in the Navigational view, where you take a group of unrelated pages and turn them into a family, complete with parents, children, and siblings.

The navigational structure is one of the things that makes a FrontPage Web different from the other Webs you run across with your browser.

You'll encounter other differences in the coming hours that make the distinction even more clear.

Q&A

Q My Web isn't going to use any navigation bars. Is there any reason for me to use the Navigation view?

A Navigation bars are the main reason for but not the only benefit of a well-designed navigational structure for a Web. If your site is composed of 12 or more pages, the Navigation view can be a useful tool for finding your way around the Web while you're editing it.

The view also forces you to spend some time conceptualizing the structure of the Web. By looking at where pages are organized within the site, you may find ways to improve how users travel through its pages. You'll also have an easy place to title any page banners you're using on the Web.

Exercises

Challenge your knowledge of FrontPage 2000 Webs with the following exercises:

- Take a Web—preferably one you can afford to experiment with—through the following life cycle: creation, moving to a new folder, losing its FrontPage material, being imported back into FrontPage, and deletion.
- If you have created one of your own Webs prior to using FrontPage, import it into a new folder on your system and add a navigational structure to it.

Hour 7

Organize a Page with Lists and Tables

Anyone who has spent time decorating a house or an office knows the value of containers. An empty container is the best excuse for buying new things that need to be contained.

Today, entire stores are devoted to the subject of containment. You can spend hours figuring out ways to hold and store things you've never actually heard of, or things you're not actually using anymore.

I own more floppy disk containers today than floppy disks. If there's ever a run on the things, no one else will be more prepared.

With any luck, you'll feel the joy of containment—or should that be contentment—about the subject of this hour.

Lists and tables are two ways to contain something on a FrontPage 2000 Web page.

You'll learn how to package text and other information together into lists—groups of related items set apart from everything else with special symbols.

You'll also learn how to package anything on a Web page into tables—boxes that can hold text, images, Java applets, and even more tables.

Create Numbered and Unnumbered Lists

Text on a Web page is grouped into paragraphs that are normally displayed with no indentation and blank lines separating them.

Another way to organize text is to turn it into a list.

Lists, as the name implies, are groupings of related items. Each item is a paragraph of text or even a combination of text and other page elements.

Web pages can display two kinds of lists:

- Numbered lists, where each item is prefaced by a unique number.
- Unnumbered lists, where each item is prefaced by a character.

The text you just read is a two-item unnumbered list. The "•" character is similar to the ones commonly used on Web pages, which are also called *bullets*.

Text is formatted as a list by clicking the Unnumbered and Numbered List buttons on the Standard toolbar, as shown in Figure 7.1.

FIGURE 7.1

List buttons.

Numbered list

Unnumbered list

Numbered lists are in sequence, starting with the number 1 and counting upward. You can specify a different starting number in the List Properties dialog box, which is called up by right-clicking the list in the Page view.

Lists can be placed inside other lists, enabling you to present text in formats like the following:

```
1. Tables
     • Dining
     • Kitchen
     • Water
```

```
2. Chairs
     • High
     • Arm
     • Musical
```

An internal list is created by highlighting existing list items and clicking the Increase Indent button. You can create lists as many levels deep as needed, and the Decrease Indent button returns list items back to their enclosing list.

The bullets that are displayed next to items in an unnumbered list provide a visual clue about which list they belong to. If an unnumbered list is placed inside another, the two lists will have different styles of bullets.

If you put a list on a page that sports one of FrontPage 2000's built-in themes, graphic bullets that are coordinated with the overall theme will be used.

FrontPage Webs designed for current browsers can use collapsible outlines—bulleted and numbered lists that can change the number of displayed items. To make all or part of a list collapsible, select the list items, right-click the mouse, and choose List Properties. You can enable collapsible outlines, and you can display them initially in collapsed form.

Items in a collapsible list can be clicked to show or hide any of their sublists. If the preceding Chairs list was collapsible, you could click Chairs to make the High, Arm, and Musical items disappear. Clicking Chairs a second time makes them reappear.

The collapsible outlines feature can be selected in FrontPage 2000 only if your target audience is using version 4.0 or later of Netscape Navigator or Microsoft Internet Explorer. Choose Tools, Page Options, and click the Browser Compatibility tab to determine the audience for your Web. You'll learn more about this during Hour 16, "Make Your Web Compatible with Multiple Browsers."

Create a Table for Tabular Data

One of the things that befuddles Web page designers is the fluid state of a Web page. Text, images, and other page elements move around depending on the way they're presented. The same page can look remarkably different in two different browsers on different computer systems.

Web designers can achieve more control over the appearance of page elements by placing them into tables.

7

Tables are rectangular grids that are divided into individual cells that are themselves rectangular. Information can be placed into each of these cells to line it up vertically or horizontally with the information in other cells.

If you're having trouble conceptualizing a table as it relates to a Web page, think of a wall calendar:

```
SUN  MON  TUE  WED  THU  FRI  SAT
*    *    1    2    3    4    5
6    7    8    9    10   11   12
13   14   15   16   17   18   19
20   21   22   23   24   25   26
27   28   29   30   *    *    *
```

A calendar like this is a rectangular table containing a bunch of rectangular cells.

On a wall calendar, each day takes up its own cell in the table. The names of each weekday from SUN to SAT also occupy their own cells.

Tables are divided into vertical columns and horizontal rows. The wall calendar shown has seven columns and six rows.

The primary purpose of tables is to organize information that must line up into straight rows and columns. You can use it to display data like an expense report in easy-to-read columns.

They also are useful when structuring the content of a Web page. Anything that can be put on a Web page can be placed inside a table cell—even another table.

Most commercial World Wide Web sites use tables to lay out the contents of their pages.

As you work with tables, you'll see how this is useful.

Add a Table to a Page

Tables can be added to a page using the Insert Table button on the Standard toolbar. When you create a table, you immediately choose the number of rows and columns that it contains by dragging your mouse over a table-like grid.

The Insert Table button and this grid are shown in Figure 7.2.

FIGURE 7.2

Choosing a table's dimensions.

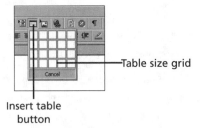

Table size grid

Insert table button

The number of rows and columns in a table determines the initial number of cells that it contains. If you add a 3-row by 3-column table, it will contain nine cells.

You will be able to easily add and subtract rows and columns from a table, so the initial choice isn't important. The Insert Table button only can be used to create tables that are a maximum of five rows long by five columns wide, but you can expand these dimensions easily after creation.

Tables can be limited to one row and one column, which creates a single-cell grid.

When you add a table to a page, it is placed at the spot of your cursor in the Page view. The table's borders and cell borders are visible, as shown in Figure 7.3.

FIGURE 7.3

Adding a new table to a page.

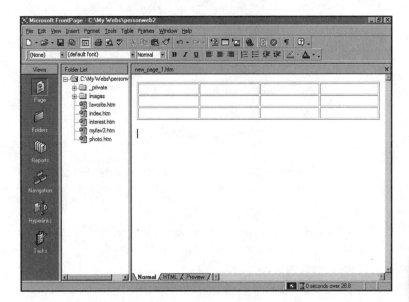

7

Add Data to a Table

Once you have a table on a page, click your cursor to place it inside a cell and you can begin adding text, images, and other things to that cell.

Tables begin with all cells and rows the same size, and FrontPage 2000 will attempt to keep them the same size while you're adding text. Words will wrap around the right edge of a cell as if it were the right margin of a page.

If you add an image or something else that's too large to fit into it, rows and columns will stretch to make room.

You also can make cells shrink to only take up the room they need by selecting Table, AutoFit.

Figure 7.4 shows a Web page that contains a table used to display the offensive statistics for several baseball players. The auto-fit feature has been selected for this table, so the leftmost row—which contains the last name of each player—takes up more space than the rows containing statistics.

FIGURE 7.4

A table for baseball statistics.

When you're adding things to cells you can use the Tab and Shift-Tab keys to jump from one cell to another. Tab advances to the next cell to the right or the next row. Shift-Tab moves left or to the previous row.

An unusual thing happens if you press Tab when you're in the cell that's on the bottom row and the far right-hand column: FrontPage 2000 creates a new row and moves the cursor into the first cell on this row.

This enables you to keep adding new data to a table like the player statistics table shown in Figure 7.4. If you don't know the number of rows you need, you can just start with a few and add them as you're entering data.

A new row or column can be added to an existing table by right-clicking a cell adjacent to where the row or column should be inserted. The resulting pop-up menu has Insert Row and Insert Column commands.

You can delete rows and columns by right-clicking in a cell that will be included in the deleted area. Click Delete Cells to remove the selected area from the table.

Resize a Table

By default, a table in FrontPage 2000 is sized in one of two ways:

- All cells take up the same size if they don't contain something that's too big for this to be possible.
- All cells are resized to be as small as they can be and still hold their contents.

You can resize a table so that its rows and columns have specific pixel widths.

To do this, place your cursor over any of the borders on the table. The cursor will switch to a double-sided arrow that points either up-down or left-right. This cursor indicates you can drag that border on the table to adjust the size of adjacent rows and columns.

Setting specific pixel dimensions for a table is something that can easily detract from the usability of a page, especially if you're making it larger than 640 pixels wide or 480 pixels tall. Those dimensions match the monitor resolution for a large number of Web users, so bigger tables will require scrolling to be seen in full.

You also can resize a table so that it takes up a percentage of the space that's available to it. This requires the Table Properties dialog box, which is called by right-clicking a table and choosing the Table Properties menu command.

This dialog box can be used to resize a table, align it on a Web page, and change the way cells are displayed in relation to each other. It's shown in Figure 7.5.

You can set the width and height of a table by pixels or by percentage. Choosing a width of 100 percent means that the table will take up all the space that's available to it—the entire width of the page, unless the table is inside another table that's restricted to a smaller size.

7

FIGURE 7.5

*The Table Properties
dialog box.*

Height isn't normally specified as a percentage, because Web pages are much more flexible in dimension from top to bottom than they are from side to side. Web users are accustomed to scrolling down a page to read it, while very few Webs require scrolling to the right.

When you set these dimensions for a table, you shouldn't use Table, AutoFit again or you'll wipe them out. Removing settings for height and width will cause tables to default to their normal sizing: all cells the same, or the minimum space needed for any cell.

The alignment options for a table are the same as they would be for anything else: left, centered, and right.

Three more things you can modify about a table are its cellpadding, cellspacing, and border values.

Cellpadding is the amount of empty space that surrounds the contents of every cell. If you increase it from the default value of 1, cells will grow bigger though their contents will stay the same size.

Cellspacing is the amount of space in the grid between each cell. This makes the height and width of the grid lines bigger, if they are visible. Increasing it from the default of 2 causes the table to grow while cells remain the same size.

The *border* determines the size of the border that surrounds the table. If it is set to 0, the table border and all of its grid lines will disappear. The cells of the table will still line up correctly, but it won't be as apparent to your visitors that a table is being used.

Many of the things you change about a table can also be done to individual cells. When you right-click a cell and choose the Cell Properties dialog box, it looks almost identical to the Table Properties dialog box shown in Figure 7.5.

You can change the height, width, and alignment of individual cells. You also can remove the height and width values to revert the cell back to the default sizing behavior.

Tables and even cells can have their own background. Like a page background, they can be a color or a graphics file that is tiled to fill the space.

Backgrounds are selected in the Table Properties and Cell Properties dialog boxes.

Use a Table to Layout a Page

Although tables were introduced to HTML as a means for displaying tabular data like the calendar and player statistics shown earlier during this hour, they were immediately appropriated for another purpose by Web designers: layout.

Tables are the way to rein in the fluidity of information on a Web page. By placing elements within tables and even nesting one table inside another, you can create page layouts that don't change substantively with every browser, monitor, and computer that's used to view them.

FrontPage 2000 uses tables for this purpose behind the scenes. Shared borders are implemented as cells in a table, and the page's content between all the borders also occupies a cell.

When tables are used to lay out a page, the border is usually set to 0 so the effect is transparent.

The main disadvantage of using a table for this purpose is that Web browsers can't display any part of the table until the entire table has been downloaded.

Ever wondered why so many professional World Wide Web sites have a banner ad that loads immediately while the rest of the page shows up sometime later that week? This happens because the banner is often outside the table that contains the rest of the page.

One feature of tables that's handy when you're laying out a page is the ability to combine cells. You can stretch a table cell so that it takes up the space normally occupied by several cells.

To do this, drag your cursor from the original cell and select an area that covers all of the cells you want to merge it with. The merged cell must be a rectangle, like any cell, but it can take up as many original cells as desired.

Right-click the selected area and choose Merge Cell to combine them into one new cell.

7

Figure 7.6 shows a new row atop the baseball statistics table. All four cells in the row have been selected, so the Merge Cell command will create a new cell that's four columns wide and one row tall.

FIGURE 7.6

Selecting cells to merge together.

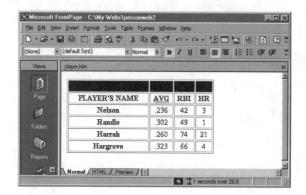

Workshop: Create a Monthly Calendar

This hour's workshop gives you a chance to revisit the topic of calendars by creating one of your own.

In a dummy Web or one of the ones you have already created, add a new page called calendar.htm. This page should contain the full calendar for the current month.

The calendar should include each of the following:

- Abbreviations for each day's name.
- A row across the top displaying the month and year.
- Each day's number lined up horizontally and vertically.
- Different colors to distinguish weekdays from weekends.
- A calendar color that's different than the page's background.

Solution: The Calendar Has Been Tabled

With the exception of the row across the top, the workshop's calendar can be created as a basic table with seven columns and enough rows to hold the weeks, the day abbreviations, and the month and year atop the calendar.

The top row of the calendar is a single cell—either the rightmost or leftmost cell on the first row had to be merged with all of the others.

Figure 7.7 shows a table calendar for June 1999.

FIGURE 7.7

A calendar for June 1999.

This calendar doesn't take up the entire width of the browser window, because the table is set to a width of 90 percent.

Unfortunately FrontPage 2000 does not allow background colors to be set for entire rows or columns. The colors for the weekends and the names of each day are set on a cell-by-cell basis.

Summary

Like a person coming home from a store with new containers, you now know two places to put stuff in your FrontPage 2000 Webs:

- *Lists*—Groups of related items set apart by bullets, symbols, or numbers
- *Tables*—Rectangular grids of cells that can hold anything Web pages can hold

Lists are primarily useful as a way to organize text within a larger document.

Tables are useful for presenting tabular data and organizing the layout of a Web page. FrontPage 2000 itself relies on the latter to implement features such as shared borders.

It is hoped that the presence of these containers will serve as an inspiration for you to find things that must be contained.

If not, contain yourself. In the next hour, you'll learn about something big enough to hold entire Web pages.

7

Q&A

Q **I've highlighted a group of cells to delete, but the Delete Cells command can't be selected when I right-click the area. What's wrong?**

A There are two ways to select a group of adjacent table cells in FrontPage 2000. One is to drag your mouse over the cells to highlight them in the same way that text is highlighted.

If this selection method doesn't allow the cells to be deleted, try the alternative. Hover your cursor at the outer border of a row or column you want to delete. The cursor will change to a thick arrow pointing at that row or column. Click once, the chosen area will be highlighted, and you can use the Delete Cells command on it.

Exercises

Challenge your knowledge of FrontPage 2000 lists and tables with the following exercises:

* Create a Web page that outlines a project you're planning to undertake, such as the first Web you are going to design after finishing this book. Use numbered lists for each major section of the outline and internal unnumbered lists breaking down those sections.

* Create a table that takes up an entire Web page and has around five rows and five columns. Give each cell a different background color, then add tables inside several of these cells. Give those different background colors, too. Repeat the process until your work qualifies as an homage to the artist Piet Mondrian.

HOUR 8

Divide a Page into Separate Frames

A few years after the creation of HTML and the World Wide Web, Netscape introduced a new feature for sites called *frames*. In keeping with their name, frames divide windows into smaller sections. They're used to subdivide the browser's window area into two or more areas, each of which holds its own Web page independently of all other frames. The experience is like having two browsers open at the same time. You can load separate pages into the frames and use them as if they were in separate browsers.

During this hour, you'll learn how to create frames and place pages into them. You'll discover how to resize a frame, take away features like its scrollbar, and convert existing Webs into frames.

Create a Frame

Frames divide a browser window into two or more separate windows. The size of each
frame is determined by the page designer, and each frame can have its own scrollbars.
You can also resize frames by dragging their borders to new locations. If you don't want
a frame to have scrollbars or be resizable, these features can be removed.

The simplest framed page contains two frames—either top and bottom or left and right.
Figure 8.1 displays a two-page framed Web page.

FIGURE 8.1

*A Web page with left
and right frames.*

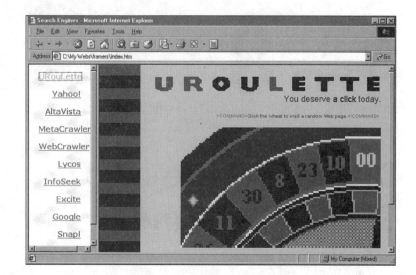

When you're working with frames, a hyperlink in one frame often causes something to
be loaded in the other. The frame in which the action happens is called the *target frame*.
In Figure 8.1, the frame on the left contains a list of hyperlinks to search engines and
other portal sites. When one of these is clicked, the site opens in the right frame.

URouLette, which is located at http://www.uroulette.com, is the namesake of one of the
World Wide Web's first random link generators. Clicking a link at URouLette opens a random page on the Web.

You also can cause a hyperlink to open a frame in the page that contains the link. The frame to be opened is determined by additional information in each hyperlink.

Add Framed Pages to a Web

In FrontPage 2000, the first step in creating framed pages is to choose one of the frame templates.

The Frames Pages tab, which you can open when selecting a new page template, contains 10 different combinations of framed pages (see Figure 8.2).

FIGURE 8.2

Selecting a frame template.

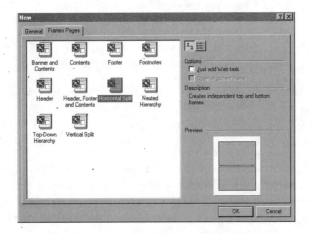

The tab's preview box displays the approximate size and alignment of the different frames. The following frame templates are available:

- *Banner and Contents*—A banner frame on the top, a contents frame on the left, and a main frame. Hyperlinks in the banner frame change the contents frame.

- *Contents*—A contents frame on the left and a main frame. Hyperlinks in the contents frame change the main frame.

- *Footer*—A footer frame on the bottom and a main frame. Hyperlinks in the footer change the main frame.

- *Footnotes*—A footnotes frame on the bottom and a main frame. Hyperlinks in the main frame change the footnotes frame.

- *Header*—A header frame on the top and a main frame underneath. Hyperlinks in the header frame change the main frame.

- *Header, Footer, and Contents*—A header frame on the top, a footer frame on the bottom, and a contents frame. Hyperlinks in the header and footer change the contents frame.

- *Horizontal Split*—Top and bottom frames that are independent of each other.

- *Nested Hierarchy*—A frame on the left that changes a frame on the right, leaving the main frame alone.

- *Top-down Hierarchy*—A frame at the top that changes a frame in the middle, leaving the main frame alone.

- *Vertical Split*—Independent right and left frames.

Selecting a frames template causes each of the frames to be created in the Page view of FrontPage 2000. Unlike with other templates, no new pages are created. Instead, each frame contains three buttons: New Page, Help, and Set Initial.

The New Page button creates a new page and places it in the frame. The Help button opens the frames section of FrontPage 2000's built-in help system. The Set Initial button opens a dialog that enables you to place an existing page in the frame. This page can be an existing part of your Web or an address on the World Wide Web.

Although it isn't readily apparent, every group of framed pages contains one more page than it would appear to need. The extra page holds all of these frames and the information that's needed to determine their size, whether scrollbars are displayed, and similar details. For a two-frame template like Horizontal Split, for example, there's a top page, a bottom page, and the extra page.

When you save a group of pages that are placed within frames, you must save the extra page also or lose all frame information.

In the FrontPage 2000 Page view, you work directly on the pages that are contained within frames. A blue border appears around the frame that's currently being edited, and menu commands that apply to pages—such as the Save button—apply to the current frame instead.

Modify a Frame

Because frames are created from standard templates, you will probably need to make adjustments as you're working on a frame-based Web.

To make changes to a frame, right-click anywhere within its boundaries and select Frame Properties from the menu. The Frame Properties dialog box, shown in Figure 8.3, will open.

FIGURE 8.3

The Frame Properties dialog.

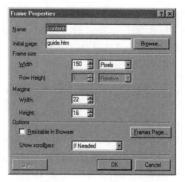

Every frame is given a name by default, and this name is referred to by hyperlinks that load pages into the frame.

You can adjust a frame's width or row height, but not both. Vertical frames are measured according to their width, and horizontal frames are measured according to their row height.

These measurements can be specified in three ways:

- Pixels
- A percentage
- A relative value

Pixel measurements are the most exact, of course. If you set a frame to 100 pixels in width, it will be displayed at that size whenever possible.

Percentages indicate how much of the browser window will be taken up by the frame.

Relative values are arbitrary numbers that only have meaning when compared to the relative values of other frames. For example, consider a Web page containing two frames, one with a relative value of 2 and the other with a relative value of 8. The first frame will be four times as small as the other frame because its relative value is four times as small.

Create an Alternative to Frames

Although frames were introduced by Netscape in late 1995, people who use text-based browsers and old versions of popular browsers won't be able to use a Web that's reliant on frames. For this reason, many Web developers create an alternative way to view their Webs that doesn't require frames.

In FrontPage 2000, an extra tabbed view called No Frames is available within Page view. This tabbed view displays the alternative page that will appear on non-frame browsing software. The default text for this page states that the Web requires frames in order to use it. No alternative presentation is offered.

You can use the No Frames window to launch a separate navigational route through your Web.

Depending on how a frame page has been designed, you may be able to use it in a Web's non-frame alternative. Its suitability will depend on whether it has hyperlinks of its own rather than relying on another frame page's links.

Open Linked Pages into Frames

When you're using hyperlinks on a framed Web, you must decide which frame will be the target frame. When the hyperlink is selected, the linked page will be opened into this target frame.

Hyperlinks can open a document within its own frame, a different frame, or in a new browser window entirely.

You can designate a target frame whenever you create or edit a hyperlink. The Edit Hyperlink dialog box includes a Change Target Frame button that opens the dialog box shown in Figure 8.4.

You can specify the target frame by name, or you can use one of five alternatives:

- *Page Default*—The frame that all hyperlinks open into when no target frame has been specified.
- *Same Frame*—The same frame as the page containing the hyperlink.
- *Whole Page*—A new page takes up the entire browser window.
- *New Window*—A new page in a new browser window, leaving the existing browser window alone.
- *Parent Frame*—The page that contains the hyperlink's frame and any others created at the same time.

FIGURE 8.4

Selecting a hyperlink's target frame.

8

These alternative targets are useful when you want to break out of the currently displayed frames in some way, either to open new frames or to remove frames entirely.

All of the frame templates in FrontPage 2000 set a default target for each page contained in a frame. You can change this by editing one of the properties of that framed page—right-click the frame, choose Page Properties, and modify the Default Target Frame value.

You can use most of these target frame options with any hyperlink, regardless of whether your Web contains frames. The Whole Page target is useful when you want to make sure a page in your Web is displayed in a full browser window, and the New Window option opens a separate browser window.

Workshop: Create a Personal Web with Frames

During Hour 2, "Use Templates to Quickly Create a Web," you developed a site that used the Personal Web template. Themes, with their coordinated color schemes and built-in graphics, are the fastest way to create a visually attractive FrontPage Web.

One thing you will learn about frames in FrontPage 2000 is that they don't benefit much from themes. The navigation bars and page banners usually require a lot of space in the browser window, so they can't all fit into a page's main frame.

In this hour's workshop you'll re-create the workshop from Hour 2, but with frames and a graphical navigation bar. The only other requirement is that the Banner and Contents frame template must be used.

Don't overwrite the Web you created during the previous workshop. If you make a mistake while you're working with frames, you could accidentally wipe out pages you need to convert to frames.

Solution: Framing Someone

This is one of the more ambitious projects you have tackled so far in this book, although you may not have realized it from the brief description of the workshop. Your own solution was probably much different, but this alternative will give you some guidance about the process.

The first thing to do is make a copy of the Hour 2 workshop Web by publishing it to a new folder on your system. This keeps a clean copy of the original version around.

Next, open the copied Web and rename `index.htm` to `main.htm`. Later you'll see how this makes the conversion process a bit easier.

Add a new page from the Banner and Contents template. Three frames will appear in the Page view. Create new pages for the top frame and the left frame, and save them with names such as `banner.htm` and `navframe.htm`, respectively.

As for the last frame, it should load an existing page: the recently renamed `main.htm`.

At this point, your personal Web will be somewhat similar in appearance to its non-frame version. The biggest difference is that the page banner and navigation bars are squeezed into a frame that doesn't have room for them.

Free up some room by dragging the Page Banner component to the top frame and the navigation bar to the left frame. The navigation bar will cease to work, and a message will appear suggesting that you add the left frame's page to the Navigation view.

Drag the left frame's page into the Navigation view and drop it to the upper-left or upper-right corner of the Web's main page. You don't need to give the page any parent-child relationships because the navigation bar should be set to display Child Pages under Home and the Web's home page. While you're setting this up, switch the bar to graphical buttons.

Also drag the top frame's page to the Navigation view without giving it any relationships. Rename this page "Misery Loves Company."

To finish off the workshop, adjust the top and left frames so that they can't be resized or scrolled. You also may want to adjust the width or row height of the frames to make more room for the Page Banner and Navigation Bar components.

Figure 8.5 shows a redone version of the Annie Wilkes Web from Hour 2.

FIGURE 8.5

The frame-based Annie Wilkes Personal Web.

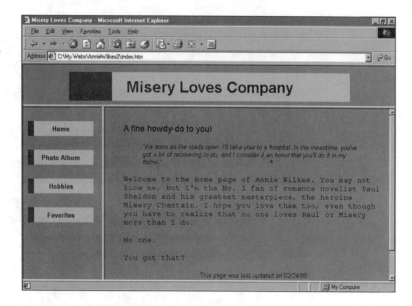

Summary

Now that you have framed someone that you know, you should be relatively comfortable with the way frames are offered in FrontPage 2000. Frames are a good example of the manner in which software such as FrontPage can simplify Web development by handling things behind the scenes.

During this hour, you added frames to a Web and explored how they can be used instead of shared borders. You learned how to change a frame's size, yank out its scrollbars, and determine whether people should be able to move its borders around while viewing the page.

Frames take up a lot of real estate on a browser window, so there's definitely a tradeoff when you use them instead of shared borders or tables.

Q&A

Q Why aren't frames created using cells, as tables are?

A Unlike tables, frames must be defined strictly in one direction: horizontal or vertical. It's a different way to subdivide a rectangular area than tables use, but it can be
just as effective.

A page with multiple frames is crafted one frame at a time. The first two-page
frame is loaded, one of those frames splits into two, and so on, until all frames
have been developed.

**Q Why doesn't the Location field change in a Web browser when I navigate to
different pages in my Web?**

A The Location field, which displays the Web address of a document, shows the page
that contains all of the frames in a framed Web. As you open hyperlinked documents in these frames, the Location field does not change because the page containing these frames is still being displayed.

Also, if you add a bookmark while visiting a framed Web, your bookmark will
refer to the address in the Location field rather than a document within a specific
frame.

Exercises

Challenge your knowledge of FrontPage 2000 frames with the following exercises:

- Create a Web similar to the search engine example from this hour. Place all of your
  hyperlinks in one frame and load the pages they link to into another.

- Change the name of the main frame of a page to something new and test its hyperlinks to see the results. To fix this problem, cause hyperlinks to open in their own
  frame.

PART III

Using Graphics in FrontPage 2000

Hour

Hour 9

Display Graphics on a Page

One of the easiest things to do in FrontPage 2000 is add a picture to a page. This is fortunate because images are an essential part of the World Wide Web experience. Without them, the Web might still be a little-known Internet service, scanners would be far less popular, and people really would visit the *Playboy* site to read the articles.

After you add the pictures to a page, arranging them with other parts of the page is a little trickier.

During this hour, you'll become an image-conscious FrontPage 2000 user. You'll lay out large pictures with paragraphs of text, and you'll line up smaller pictures with text and other page elements.

To feed the World Wide Web's enormous appetite for imagery, you'll also explore the FrontPage 2000 clip art gallery. This archive includes dozens of icons, buttons, drawings, and photographs you can use on your own FrontPage Webs.

Add a Graphic to a Page

In FrontPage 2000, you can add pictures to a Web page with the Insert, Picture, From File command. The image will be displayed in the Page view, enabling you to see how it looks immediately.

Most pictures that are displayed on the World Wide Web are in the GIF or JPEG formats, because they're supported as a built-in feature of Netscape Navigator and Microsoft Internet Explorer. A newer format, an improvement on GIF called PNG, is becoming the third-most popular choice for Web imagery.

One way to work with picture files is to import them into your Web before you add them to any pages. FrontPage 2000 automatically creates an images subfolder with every Web template that can be used to store these files.

You also can add an image that isn't a part of your Web. It can be on any folder on your system or any address on the World Wide Web. Use the FrontPage 2000 File Open dialog to both select local files and specify a file by a URL address.

If you've added images from folders on your system, copies of these images will be made when you either save the Web or preview it with a browser. A dialog box will open that lets you determine where these copies should be saved and what names they should be given. This enables you to create folders on your system that contain commonly used graphics. FrontPage 2000 will copy these graphics into Webs when they are used, effectively importing them for you.

> Another good reason to work with copies of common images is that FrontPage 2000 can make changes to images. As you'll see later, FrontPage can edit images directly to alter their quality and size. By keeping originals outside of any Webs, you prevent them from being modified.

Align a Picture on a Page

After you add a picture to a page, you can determine how it should be displayed in relation to everything else on the page. This is handled in the Picture Properties dialog, shown in Figure 9.1.

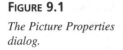

FIGURE 9.1

The Picture Properties dialog.

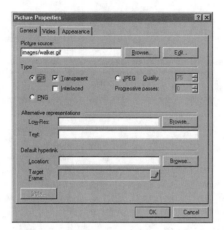

9

The Appearance tab enables you to set the alignment of the image. Large pictures are generally aligned in one of three ways:

- The picture appears to the left of the text and other page elements that follow.
- The picture appears to the right of the text and other page elements that follow.
- The picture appears above everything that follows.

The easiest of these three to lay out is the third option: placing the picture above the following part of the page. To do this, the picture is added and a new paragraph or line break is inserted right after it. FrontPage 2000 places the Page view cursor at the lower-right corner of a picture after it is added to a page.

Figure 9.2 shows two Web pages. They're identical in every way but one: the picture of a city square has been set to a different alignment.

The pictures are set to either right or left alignment on these pages. This alignment controls where the text that follows is laid out.

As you look at the Web page with the text to the left, you may be confused about how it is that the text follows the picture. Anyone using a language that is written from left-to-right, like English, may think the *picture* follows the *text* because it appears to the right.

On a Web page, text follows a picture if the picture was inserted in one of two places:

- A cursor position closer to the top of the page than the text.
- A cursor position to the left of the text on the same line.

FIGURE 9.2

Two versions of the same Web page.

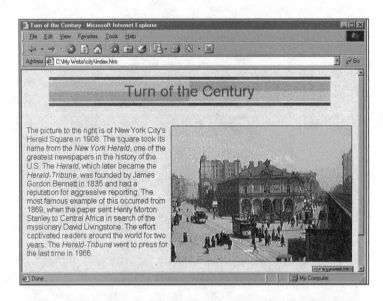

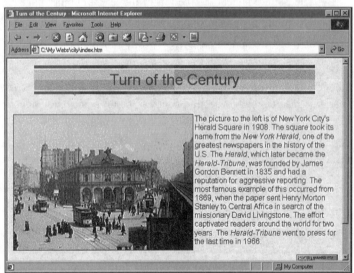

If you become confused about the cursor position where a picture has been added, the easiest remedy is to move it using cut-and-paste. Press Ctrl+X to delete the picture and add it to the Windows Clipboard, place your cursor in front of the text that should follow the picture, and hit Ctrl+V to paste it back to the page.

The remaining picture alignment options are most useful with small pictures, such as icons and menu buttons. Options such as Top, Middle, Absolute Middle, and Bottom determine how the picture is vertically aligned with the page elements that follow. By default, and when you're using left or right alignment, the top edge of a picture will be lined up with the top edge of whatever follows: text or another picture.

Figure 9.3 shows four "walking man" icons followed by lines of text. A box surrounds each icon to show exactly how big the picture is.

9

FIGURE 9.3

Aligning a picture vertically.

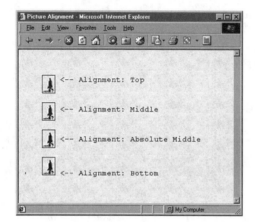

These alignments control layout as follows:

- Top alignment lines up the picture with the top of the following text.
- Bottom alignment lines up the bottom of the picture with the bottom of the text.
- Middle alignment lines up the middle of the picture with the bottom of the text.
- Absolute Middle alignment lines up the middle of the picture with the middle of the text.

You can use these and other vertical alignment options with text, images, or anything else that is narrow enough to be displayed on a page side-by-side with a picture.

If using these alignments to arrange text and pictures isn't sufficient, you can also place page elements within the cells of a table, as described during Hour 7, "Organize a Page with Lists and Tables."

Add Hyperlinks and Descriptions to a Picture

The Picture Properties dialog can be used to add a hyperlink to a picture and to add alternate text that describes a picture.

Add a Hyperlink

Hyperlinks are added in the same manner that they're associated with elements of a Web page. You can specify the URL of a site on the World Wide Web or pick a file that's on your own system.

You also can associate a hyperlink with a picture in the same manner that you would add a link to any element on a Web page. Select the picture and then either choose Insert, Hyperlink or click the Hyperlink button on the Standard toolbar.

Remember that the linked files on your system should be part of your Web if you're going to publish it.

Add Alternate Text

Providing a text description of each picture is important for making your Webs more usable. When a page is being downloaded, the text description is shown in the area that will be occupied by the picture. If the picture is a menu button or part of a navigation bar, this text enables people to use the picture's function before the picture is down-loaded. If you're using a 28.8Kbps or slower Internet connection, you've probably done this many times to get to the page you wanted before the pictures finished loading at glacial speed.

Also, text descriptions are the only way a nonvisual Web browser can make any sense of hyperlinked images. If images are required to navigate your Web, each image should have text that describes its purpose.

Figure 9.4 shows how a Web page looks before the images have been loaded to replace the text descriptions. The text for "Interests," "Photo Album," and "Favorites" is shown next to icons with a square, circle, and triangle. These are all part of a navigation bar—FrontPage 2000 automatically creates descriptions for them—and they have active hyper-links associated with them.

> You can make all your Web pages look like Figure 9.4 by telling your browser not to dis-play any images. In versions 4.0 and 5.0 of Microsoft Internet Explorer, you can do this by clicking Tools, Internet Options and then clicking the Advanced tab. One of the check boxes on this tab controls whether pictures are displayed.

FIGURE 9.4

A Web page with picture descriptions.

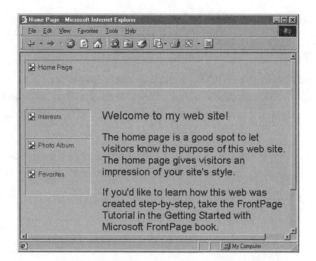

Choose Between GIF, JPEG, and PNG Graphics

Most images on the World Wide Web are in the GIF or JPEG formats, although PNG has become more popular in recent years as a substitute for GIF.

JPEG files, which usually have the `.jpg` file extension, use a data-compression algorithm that shrinks the file size (and more importantly, the download time) at the expense of image quality. When you save a JPEG file, you must decide how to balance these two factors.

Because of the data compression, JPEG is usually the format chosen to display complex images with a large number of colors. JPEG files are often good for displaying scanned photographs that don't have large areas of solid colors, even when the file sizes of the images have been greatly compressed.

GIF files have the `.gif` file extension and are often the best choice for simpler images with fewer colors. You can't display more than 256 colors in a GIF picture, so if a photograph is to be displayed as a GIF, it must first be reduced so that no more than 256 different colors appear in the image.

Despite the reduction in colors, GIF pictures often look much better than JPG files for photographs and other images. The problem with displaying a large, multicolor GIF file on the Web is that it takes much longer to download than a corresponding JPEG of the same image. For this reason, GIF files are normally used with small images that don't have a large number of colors, sometimes even eight or fewer.

GIF is much better than JPEG at handling images with large areas of a single color. Because of the way the JPEG data-compression algorithm saves file space, wavy lines will appear along the edges of any solid blocks of color, making the image appear more blurry.

The navigation bar buttons in each of FrontPage 2000's themes are GIF files. Many of them use solid colors and do not take up a lot of room on a page, so GIF is the better choice.

> The Reports view will keep track of the download time required for the pages on your Web. You can use this to see when a page might need some JPEGs instead of GIF files to speed things up.

A third format that's becoming more popular on the World Wide Web is *PNG*, which stands for *Portable Network Graphics*. PNG was introduced as an enhanced alternative to the GIF format.

> The PNG format was created in response to a 1994 announcement by CompuServe that it would begin charging royalties for some uses of the GIF format. Unisys claimed that the GIF format violated a file compression patent it owned, so PNG was created to be a legally secure public standard for image files.

PNG images have the .png filename extension. They're often used in the same way as GIF files, but PNG also can support thousands of colors and can be used as an alternative to the JPEG format.

Past versions of PNG were supported by Web browser plug-ins—programs that are downloaded and installed separately from a browser and that enhance its functionality. Versions 4.0 and later of Netscape Navigator and Microsoft Internet Explorer can display PNG files without a plug-in.

Another way to enhance the display of pictures on your Webs is to offer low-resolution versions of the pictures. These versions should be extremely small in file size so they load quickly, and they can be specified in the Picture Properties dialog.

Add Clip Art to a Page

FrontPage 2000 includes a gallery of clip art—images you can freely use on your own Webs. To browse through the gallery, select the Insert, Picture, Clip Art menu command.

Clip art is arranged according to more than a dozen section headings. If you know what you're looking for, you can use the search feature to view only the clip art related to that topic. For example, a search for "letter" would produce the images shown in the Clip Art Gallery dialog (see Figure 9.5). A thumbnail drawing of each picture is shown. You can view a full-size version of each image and add it to a page as if you loaded the picture from a file.

FIGURE 9.5

Searching the Clip Art Gallery.

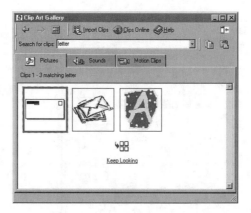

Adding a picture from clip art instead of another source requires an extra step: You must select the format in which to save the graphic in your Web. You don't actually work with the graphic contained in the Clip Art Gallery. Instead, you make a copy in one of three formats: GIF, JPEG, or PNG. This choice is made in the Picture Properties dialog.

When you select a GIF file, you can configure the picture to be displayed in an interlaced pattern. *Interlacing* displays a picture as a series of more focused images. If that definition is itself a little blurry, think of a set of binoculars that are completely out of focus when you first look into them. As you adjust the focus, the thing you're looking at changes from a blur of colors into an increasingly sharp image. Interlacing is similar to this, because it displays an image as if you were bringing it into focus. On the other hand, a *non-interlaced* GIF displays the image in successive horizontal lines as it downloads them, so you'll see the top half of a picture in full before the bottom half arrives.

Clip art that's saved as a JPEG file must have a Quality percentage indicated. The scale ranges from 1 (compressed as much as possible) to 100 (no compression at all). The default is 75 percent.

A JPEG file that is compressed loses quality every time it is compressed again. Whenever you create JPEG graphics, you should keep an original file that isn't compressed at all—as the FrontPage 2000 Clip Art Gallery does. This enables you to return to the original and compress it at a different quality.

One thing you'll want to do often with clip art is resize it. All the pictures on a Web page can be displayed at different sizes, whether it's larger, smaller, or even distorted so that the width is at a different scale than the height. You can make these changes on the Appearance tab of the Page Properties dialog (see Figure 9.6).

FIGURE 9.6

Altering a picture's display size.

You can change the picture's size in pixel increments or as a percentage of the original. This does not alter the actual picture, so an image displayed at 10 percent of its normal size still takes the same amount of time to download.

If you can't find a suitable picture in the Clip Art Gallery that's included with FrontPage 2000, you can find more pictures, photographs, and movie files in Microsoft's online version of the gallery. After connecting to the Internet, choose the Clips Online button on the Clip Art Gallery dialog to open Microsoft's Web site of clip art. You'll be able to browse through it and search for specific keywords, and the clip art you select will be imported automatically into FrontPage 2000.

Add Page Banners and Navigation Bars

Page banners and navigation bars are specified with all of FrontPage 2000's themes, so you should already have experience working with them. Page banners look like giant navigation buttons (if they're graphical), and they provide a way to give a page a title. Navigation bars are related groups of hyperlinks that are represented as graphical buttons or text. Both of them are FrontPage 2000 components—special interactive elements that can be used on your Webs. They combine editable text and pictures.

You can add these components to pages with the Insert, Navigation Bar and Insert, Page Banner commands.

A page banner contains a single line of text and can have a graphical background. The picture used as the background is defined by the Web's theme—Webs without a theme cannot have graphical page banners.

The text of a page banner will be the same as its title in the Navigation view window. If the page isn't in the navigational structure of the Web yet, it must be added before a banner can be displayed.

When you save or publish a Web, FrontPage 2000 creates pictures for each graphical page banner and navigation bar on your Web. The text is displayed over the component's background image.

All of this takes place behind the scenes, so you work with these components differently than you do with pictures.

Workshop: Use Clip Art in a Business Report

This hour has introduced you to FrontPage 2000's gallery of clip art, so it's only fitting that the workshop uses it in the production of a company's annual report. Produce the first page of the annual report using the following:

- A graphical page banner.
- A main image to the left of the introductory text.

9

- A secondary image that's placed somewhere to the right of a paragraph of text in the body.
- A list, with small pictures to the left lined up with each item on the list to the right.

The images you choose aren't important, although searching for "business" and "money" is likely to yield better results in the Clip Art Gallery than "whipped cream" or "Tyra Banks." (Better in the sense of being more businesslike—neither the author nor Macmillan Publishing means any slight towards Ms. Banks or the makers of dairy dessert toppings.)

The text isn't important either. Although you're free to research a company and summarize its financial condition as of the most recent year, you're even freer to copy the same text over and over again into several different paragraphs.

Solution: Get Down to Business

Figure 9.7 shows one solution to this workshop. The page has four pictures: a large image of increasingly smaller men at increasingly smaller desks, a compass star, and a few miniature George Washingtons. Because most clip art in the gallery is large, the Picture Properties dialog was used to shrink each image to different degrees.

FIGURE 9.7

The annual report of Quick Brown Fox, Inc.

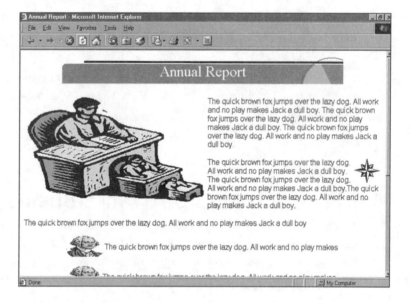

The Picture Properties dialog also was used to set the desk men to the left, the star to the right, and the Georges in the absolute middle.

Adding the page banner as a graphic required a theme. Pie Graphs, one of the additional themes you can install with FrontPage 2000, seemed like a good choice for this strict-bottom-line company.

All of the pictures were saved as GIF files. Download time could have been reduced by making the desk men image a JPG file, but in the image has enough solid colors to cause a fuzzy image after compression.

Working with clip art in this way makes it easier to produce a page. The biggest drawback is the size of many pictures. If you have an image editor on your system, you can resize the images after they've been copied into your Web's `images` folder.

Summary

This hour enabled you to set your sights higher on your FrontPage Webs.

By looking into the subject of image handling, you've learned how to make pages and entire Webs more visually compelling. You saw how to add pictures, align them with other parts of a page, and change how they're displayed. You took a gander at the three most common formats for graphics files: GIF, JPEG, and PNG. Finally, you found a sight for sore eyes in the FrontPage 2000 Clip Art Gallery, a collection of pictures you can easily add to your own pages.

During the next hour, you'll take more than a passing glance at a special type of Web picture called an *image map*.

Q&A

Q Is there a limit to how much you can expand a graphic? I'd like to create a tiny, all-brown GIF and stretch it to cover a large part of a page.

A There's no reason you can't do that. One trick that Web designers do is to use small, one- or two-color GIFs as vertical or horizontal borders, stripes, and other parts of a page. They load almost as quickly as the text does.

Exercises

Challenge your knowledge of FrontPage 2000 pictures with the following exercises:

- Add a few images into FrontPage 2000 from Microsoft's World Wide Web version of the Clip Art Gallery. Create a Web page that contains these images, which may need to be displayed at a smaller size to fit on a page.

- Experiment with different alignments for several different small pictures on the same line, such as arrows, icons, or symbols taken from clip art.

HOUR 10

Add Links to a Graphic with Imagemaps

A saying you have probably heard is that "a picture is worth a thousand words." It's an expression that was doubtlessly coined by a photographer, but writers are likely to have a different view. From my own vantage point as an author, I have to wonder why the photographer invented that expression using words, considering that pictures are so much more expressive. (Angry pictures of complaint can be sent by photographers to the author in care of Sams Publishing.)

Regardless of where you stand on the issue, you'll learn how to make pictures more expressive during this hour.

In your efforts up to this point, pictures have been worth a single hyperlink. Using a new type of Web element called an imagemap, you can make a picture worth a *thousand* hyperlinks.

Imagemaps enable you to associate specific portions of a picture with different hyper-links. You can use them to create menus, maps, and other complex navigational features. They're created in FrontPage 2000 using some special drawing tools.

Although it may be hard to believe that "a thousand links can be associated with an image," it's a much catchier saying than "a picture is worth anywhere from six to more than a dozen hyperlinks, in most cases."

Create an Imagemap

There are two kinds of imagemaps you can use on a Web page: client-side maps and server-side maps. A client-side map is handled by the Web browser, while a server-side map is handled by the browser and a Web server working together.

FrontPage 2000 supports client-side maps, which can be handled entirely by adding an imagemap to a Web page. Server-side maps require special access to the server that will deliver the page.

When you select an existing image in the Page view, a Picture toolbar is added to the FrontPage 2000 interface. Normally, this toolbar appears along the bottom edge, but like all Microsoft Office toolbars, it's highly mobile. You can drag it to any edge of the inter-face or even off it entirely.

Figure 10.1 shows the Picture toolbar as a separate window.

FIGURE 10.1

*FrontPage 2000's
Picture toolbar.*

Several of the buttons on the Picture toolbar have shapes on them, including a rectangle and an ellipse. This group of buttons is used to create imagemaps, in which each special hyperlink is associated only with a portion of a picture instead of the whole thing.

Imagemaps are commonly used for the following purposes on a Web page:

- To add hyperlinks to an image that serves as a navigation bar.
- To add hyperlinks that describe a specific part of an image.
- To add hyperlinks that pinpoint specific regions of a graphic, such as a map.

When you're associating an imagemap with a picture, you designate specific regions of the picture that will be associated with hyperlinks. These regions—also called *hotspots*—are created using those buttons on the Picture toolbar: rectangular hotspot, circular hotspot, and polygonal hotspot.

After clicking a hotspot button, you click the picture to begin defining the hotspot's region. With rectangular and circular hotspots, you drag your mouse over the area of the picture that the hotspot will occupy. Once the hotspot takes up the desired part of the picture, click again to complete it.

FrontPage 2000 will draw all hotspots as thick borders as overlays on a picture in Page view. Figure 10.2 shows a hotspot over the word "News" on a picture.

FIGURE 10.2

Defining a hotspot on a picture.

10

A polygonal hotspot requires one click for every intersection of the polygon. When you finally define the last intersection, finish the hotspot with a double-click.

After you've defined a hotspot of any kind, a dialog will open that enables you to associate a hyperlink with it. You can choose a file in your Web, one on your system, or a URL address on the World Wide Web.

Some imagemaps will have a default hyperlink that is used if a visitor clicks the picture in an area that doesn't have a hotspot. You can change a hotspot's hyperlink by right-clicking the hotspot and choosing Hotspot Properties from the pop-up menu that appears. To set a default hyperlink, right-click the picture and choose the Picture Properties dialog.

If two hotspots overlap each other, only the most recently created hotspot will be used in the overlapping area. A hotspot on an imagemap is limited to a single hyperlink.

The currently selected hotspot can be deleted by clicking the hotspot and pressing the Delete key.

In a picture with several different hotspots, you may have trouble determining which hotspot is currently selected. The Picture toolbar has a Highlight Hotspots button that makes the picture invisible, leaving the hotspots behind. All hotspots show up as black outlines except for the currently selected one, which appears in solid black, as shown in Figure 10.3.

FIGURE 10.3

Viewing hotspots on an imagemap.

The Highlight Hotspots view can be used to select different hotspots for editing or deletion.

Workshop: Use Imagemaps to Describe a Picture

This is one of the shorter hours in the book, so it's a good opportunity to tackle a more challenging project.

Imagemaps can be an informational tool in addition to a navigational one. Up to this point, you've learned how to use these maps to provide linked routes through a Web. For this project, you'll use an imagemap in conjunction with frames to provide additional information about a picture.

In printed media, it can be hard to make much sense of an image that contains many different things that must be identified. Consider the example of a class photograph. My high school had around 900 students overall (and I would have been valedictorian if 412 people had not overachieved). Our class photo was a giant panoramic photo, and the list of names from top to bottom and left to right was enormous.

Using imagemaps, you can create a hypertext version of a class photo. Each person's head can be linked to a page that names the person.

Jumping back and forth from the photo to the person's name can be cumbersome, however. This can be solved by using a two-frame Web page. The larger frame, which is on top, contains the picture. This can be a group photo or a map—both have numerous elements that can use further attribution. The smaller frame, which is on the bottom, is used to load a page associated with each hyperlink on the picture's imagemap.

All you need to finish this workshop is a scanned photograph or map with at least five or more things to identify. You can spruce up the project by selecting a theme for all of the pages—Expedition's a great one if you're working with maps.

This project will probably be more challenging if you find your own image to work with. If you can't find any, there's one you can use on this book's World Wide Web site at http://www.fp2k.com/24, in the Hour 10 section. There's also some information you can associate with each hyperlinked area on the image.

10

Solution: Combine an Imagemap and a Map

By combining frames and imagemaps, you can make a lot of information available on your Webs in an easy-to-use format.

Figure 10.4 shows a Web page that displays information about points on a map.

FIGURE 10.4

An interactive map Web page.

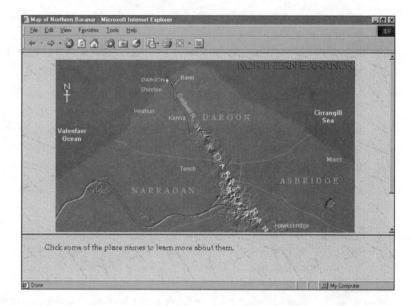

The frame template chosen for this solution is Footnotes, which contains a large upper frame that has links to the bottom frame.

When the two frames are created, new pages are added to both frames and saved as `map.htm` and `notes.htm`, respectively. The Expedition theme is applied to both frames.

At this point in a frame project, it's useful to save the whole thing so you can name the main page that holds the frames. For this solution, it's called `index.htm` because the Web only contains this interactive map.

If you're adding an interactive map or photo to an existing Web, don't overwrite `index.htm` as the main page of this map. Give it a new name that isn't already being used on another page.

Once all three pages have been saved and named, the map's picture is added to the top frame and text is added to the bottom frame. This text explains how to use the map—click places to see their descriptions.

The next step in the project is to create a page for each description, which will appear in the bottom frame. The easiest way is to change the existing text and save the page under a new name. This is the same as creating a new page, selecting a theme, adding the text, and saving it—minus a few steps.

Before any of these pages are created, open the bottom frame in a new Page view by right-clicking that frame and selecting the Open in a New Window command. This is necessary because you can't have a single frame under a new name if other frames are open—FrontPage 2000 will save all frames under that name instead.

When all of these description pages are created, the map picture is turned into an imagemap. Every place that has a description page is associated with a hotspot and a hyperlink.

10

The finished product can be viewed on the World Wide Web at `http://www.fp2k.com/24/dargonmap`.

Summary

Now that you've read more than a thousand words on the subject, you should have a much better idea of how many hyperlinks a picture is worth in FrontPage 2000.

By adding hotspots to regions on a picture, you have learned how to create groups of hyperlinks called imagemaps. They're useful for site navigation and other visual ways to request information on a Web page. You create them in FrontPage 2000 using buttons on the Picture toolbar, which appears when you select an image for editing.

A picture is worth a lot on a page when it's associated with an imagemap.

Q&A

Q I've seen imagemaps that display the cursor's position on the browser's status line. How is this done?

A Those imagemaps rely on an older form of Web imagemaps that were handled by the Web server. The imagemaps you created during this hour are called *client-side* maps because the Web browser that displays the map does all the work of identifying hotspots with hyperlinks.

The other type of imagemap is the *server-side* map. The Web server that sends the page to a browser must receive mouse clicks on the image and must know what to do with them. Client-side maps are much easier to create and maintain because they don't require special access to a Web server.

Exercises

Challenge your knowledge of FrontPage 2000 imagemaps with the following exercises:

- Explore the images folders of some past FrontPage Webs you have created. When you find one that contains an image used for a navigation bar, copy this image to a new folder and use it to manually create a navigation bar using an imagemap.

- If you have a photo of yourself that's in electronic form, create a Web page in which your various body parts are all hotspots (hubba hubba!). The hyperlinks you associate with these body parts are up to you, but remember that there might be children visiting your page.

Hour 11

Create and Edit Graphics for Your Web

For most of the World Wide Web's development, images displayed on the Web have been created with drawing and editing software, and Web pages have been created in an entirely different manner, such as with Web editing software like FrontPage, Macromedia Dreamweaver, Claris Home Page, and others.

FrontPage 2000 blurs the line between the two types of software by offering image-editing features. Many tasks that used to require specialized graphics software, such as Adobe PhotoShop, can now be done within FrontPage.

You can make several changes to an existing image file, including its size, contrast, and brightness. If the image is in the GIF format, you can make part of it transparent and add editable text to the image. You can also crop the image, keeping the parts you want while discarding the rest.

Although these are some of the simplest features of a professional graphics tool, when you combine them with the images that are available in the Microsoft Clip Art Gallery, you can quickly improve the look of your own FrontPage Webs.

Work with Graphics

Most of FrontPage 2000's image-manipulation features can be found on the Picture toolbar, which shows up whenever you select a picture in Page view. (You also can make it appear by clicking View, Toolbars, Picture.) This toolbar is shown in Figure 11.1.

FIGURE 11.1

The Picture toolbar.

Hover your mouse over each of the buttons to find out its purpose. These buttons are organized into several different groupings. One group contains four buttons with pairs of right triangles on them. These buttons are used to rotate or flip the picture. You can rotate a picture to the left or right, and flip it horizontally and vertically.

Another group of four buttons contains icons that look like either a half moon or the sun. These control the contrast and brightness of the picture, two things that any television owner should be familiar with (unless you have a much better TV than mine).

The black and white button turns a color image into a monochrome one, and the bevel button makes a photograph or other picture look like a 3-D button by giving it shadowed edges.

Because these buttons cause instantaneous changes to a picture, you may get the impression that they just change the way it's displayed. (During the last hour, you altered a picture's display size without actually changing the picture itself.) However, these buttons do make permanent changes to a picture. You can undo these changes before the page or your Web have been saved, and then use the toolbar's restore button to return it to its last saved version.

You also can use this toolbar to permanently change the size of a picture. If you have resized a picture's display area and you want to make this the actual size of the picture, click the Resize button.

Crop a Picture

As you're working with drawings, photographs, and other images in FrontPage 2000, you might decide that the shape of a picture doesn't fit with the layout of a page. You can reshape a picture either by changing its dimensions and clicking Resample or by cropping it. *Cropping* is a photography term for keeping a portion of an image and discarding the rest.

To crop a picture, select it in Page view and click the Crop button on the Picture toolbar, which is identified in Figure 11.2. A thin border will appear that's similar to the one used for imagemap hotspots. In Figure 11.2, a cropping border appears on a drawing of a violinist.

FIGURE 11.2

Cropping an area of a picture.

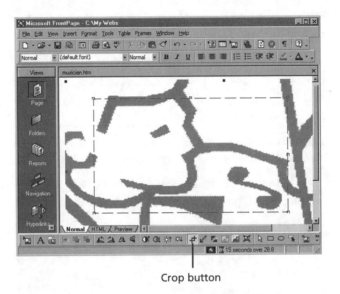

Crop button

When the picture is cropped, everything within the border will be saved and the rest will be deleted. In Figure 11.2, the cropping removes the violinist's ear and most of his hair and bow.

When you have established a border that you like, click the Crop button again and the cropped area will become the full picture.

Add Text to a Picture

Whenever you create a graphical navigation bar, FrontPage 2000 combines a background picture with the text of each item on the bar. This happens automatically, but you can manually add text to any picture that's in GIF format. This text appears on top of the picture, so you'll need one of the image-editing buttons on the Picture toolbar.

To add text to a picture, start by clicking the picture so that the Picture toolbar appears, and follow with the Text button—an icon with the letter "A." A border will appear on top of the picture, and you can begin entering text with your keyboard. You can do all of the following to format this text:

- Adjust the borders so that there's more room for the text.
- Use all of the text-editing buttons on the Standard and Formatting toolbars, including the font selection, font size, and bold/italics/underline buttons.
- Click Format, Font to select a font, color, size, and special effects.

If you try to add text to a picture that isn't in GIF format, FrontPage 2000 will ask if you want to convert it to a GIF file. This may not be feasible with some large pictures that are in JPG format, because GIF files of comparable height and width take up much more disk space. However, there's no way in FrontPage to add text to JPG or PNG files.

Text that you add can be moved and resized at any time. It will be combined with the background GIF when the Web is saved or published.

Figure 11.3 shows text being added to a drawing of a globe from the FrontPage 2000 Clip Art Gallery, and the text button that was used to add it.

FIGURE 11.3

Adding text to a picture.

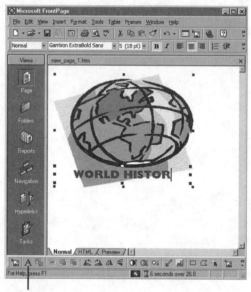

Text button

To add transparency to a picture, select it in Page view and click the Set Transparent Color button. FrontPage 2000 will ask whether the picture should be converted to GIF, if it isn't already in that format. After you click the Set Transparent Color button, the cursor will turn into an eraser-tipped pencil with a small arrow at one end. Place this arrow over the color that you want to make transparent and click once. This color will vanish as if it was deleted from the picture.

> To remove transparency, you can click Set Transparent Color and select the invisible area of the picture. You also can open the Picture Properties dialog and uncheck the Transparency check box on the Appearance tab.

Making a color transparent doesn't actually change the picture's colors—it just uses a feature supported in the GIF format. If you remove all transparency later, you'll see that the original color has been retained.

Transparency is especially useful when you're working with graphical page backgrounds. For example, Figure 11.4 shows two images of lions over an intricate background. The lion on the left has a white background that covers up the page's background. The lion on the right uses transparency to more closely blend in with its surroundings.

FIGURE 11.4

Working with non-transparent and transparent pictures.

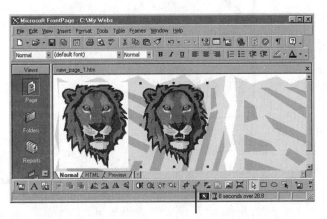

Set Transparent Color button

The Set Transparent Color button shown in Figure 11.4 can be used to set or change the current transparent color. If you try to use transparency with a graphic that isn't in the GIF format, FrontPage 2000 will convert it to GIF before enabling a transparent color to be selected.

Interlace a Picture

Now that you're working with graphics on your Webs, you'll have to face one of the biggest issues for any Web designer: download time. Striking the right balance between a graphically appealing Web and one that loads quickly is a challenge.

As a GIF file is being downloaded, you can provide a preview to Web visitors by making it an interlaced graphic. Interlacing, as you learned during Hour 9, "Display Graphics on a Page," is the process of displaying an image as a series of increasingly focused images. Figures 11.5, 11.6, and 11.7 show three steps in the display of a magazine's interlaced, scanned-in cover logo.

FIGURE 11.5

Interlacing at 20 percent.

FIGURE 11.6

Interlacing at 60 percent.

FIGURE 11.7

The final picture.

There isn't an interlacing button on the Picture toolbar. To add or remove interlacing from a picture, open its Picture Properties dialog. The General tab has a check box for interlacing.

The JPEG graphics format has its own version of interlacing called *progression*, which offers more control over the process. You can set the number of progressive passes that will be displayed as the JPEG is being loaded. The more passes you establish, the more images will be displayed as the JPEG progresses from a blurry image to a sharp one.

Did your mother ever tell you not to make a funny face or it will get stuck that way? Some Web designers frown on the practice of interlacing people's pictures because it makes their faces look funny during intermediate stages of downloading the image. The White House's official World Wide Web site at http://www.whitehouse.gov has numerous interlaced graphics at the time of this writing, so go see President Clinton, Vice President Gore, and other top officials making faces at you.

Workshop: Create Graphical Menu Buttons

Two features of FrontPage 2000 make it easy to turn graphics into buttons: beveling and adding editable text.

This hour's workshop is to create three graphical buttons for a Web. Each button should have the same shape, whether rectangular or square, and there should be enough room to place a text label on each one.

To find images for these buttons, search the Microsoft Clip Art Gallery. If you're connected to the Internet, you can extend the search to include the World Wide Web portion of this gallery. Images selected from the online gallery will be stored in FrontPage 2000's version for permanent use. Pick three buttons with the same theme—animals, business, sports, the business of animal sports, or whatever you choose.

In addition to the Bevel and Text buttons, use any of the other elements on the Picture toolbar that can help make the graphics look appealing.

When you're done, put these three buttons together in a shared border for a new Web, and create pages that are linked to each button.

Solution: Turning Graphics into Buttons

Figure 11.8 shows a Web page containing three buttons from the Microsoft Clip Art Gallery's online archive. Native American images were added recently to the gallery, which is updated monthly with new material.

As you've worked on your own buttons, you've probably learned one of the limitations of the bevel feature: It doesn't work well with pictures that are either too dark or too light.

By adjusting the contrast and brightness of a picture, you can make it more suitable for the bevel effect. In the Native American buttons shown in Figure 11.8, only the middle button didn't require any changes to its colors. The top and bottom buttons both needed to be brightened before the bevel effect could be applied.

After the pictures were resampled at their new size, a text label describing a page on the Web was added to each of them. The buttons were placed within a shared border to make them accessible throughout the site.

FIGURE 11.8

A menu of beveled picture buttons.

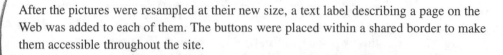

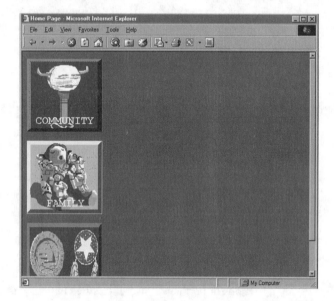

Summary

Now that you've beveled some buttons and cropped some clips, you've seen what FrontPage 2000's image-editing features can accomplish. Although the resizing, editing, and conversion features of FrontPage aren't on a par with professional image-editing tools, they place some of the most common tasks within easy reach.

Making a transparent GIF, which wasn't even offered in most graphics software packages a few years ago, is immediately available from the Page view.

By combining editing with the Clip Art Gallery and the many graphics packaged with each theme, you can create a fully graphical Web without ever leaving FrontPage 2000.

Q&A

Q I've been working with a graphic for a while and the edges are starting to look jagged. What can I do about this?

A Any picture you edit within FrontPage 2000 is going to change each time you save or resample it. If you've altered the size several times, you'll lose some clarity each time as FrontPage tries to anti-alias the picture.

Anti-aliasing is a graphic design term for adjusting the edges of an image so it blends in more smoothly with the background. FrontPage can't always anti-alias smoothly if pictures are repeatedly resized. If possible, revert to the original version of the picture and redo your edits to get better clarity.

Exercises

Challenge your knowledge of FrontPage 2000's image-editing features with the following exercises:

- Using the Clip Art Gallery as source material, create buttons, a background picture, and other graphics that can be incorporated into your own modified theme.
- Paste a picture onto a Web page four separate times, and then crop each one so they combine to form a single copy of the picture. Try to line the pieces up with each other so they look like a single picture.

11

HOUR 12

Animate a Web Page

When you're viewing pages on the World Wide Web, few things grab your attention better than animated graphics. It can be difficult for static text and still pictures to compete with the moving graphics on banner ads and other trickery, like spinning logos and dancing hamsters.

FrontPage 2000 helps to level the playing field by making it easy to animate your own Webs.

During this hour, you'll learn how to create animation effects, such as transitions that appear when a new page is loaded and buttons that change when a mouse passes over them. You'll use Dynamic HTML to make text and pictures on your pages swoop down from above, hop into position one piece at a time, and bounce elastically into place. You'll also learn how to place animated graphics on your pages and control the way they're displayed.

The material should be fairly… well… moving.

Add Animation and Other Special Effects to a Page

You may not realize it, but you've already learned how to work with one type of animation in FrontPage 2000. Adding an animated GIF file to a page is no different than adding any other picture.

Animated GIFs are the primary form of animation on the Web. Almost all non-static banner ads are in this format, as are many of the moving images you see on personal pages, like spinning envelopes and other small graphics.

These GIF files are created by software that combines several GIF pictures into a single file. This file also contains information that determines the order in which to display these pictures, how much time to pause between each picture, and how often to cycle through all the pictures.

The final product is treated like a GIF within FrontPage 2000 and has the same filename extension: .gif. You can import this graphic, add it to pages, and resize its display area.

One thing you can't do within FrontPage is edit it. You can't add beveling, adjust its contrast, or use any of the other image-editing features you learned about during the previous hour. This is because any changes to the GIF will remove its animation and reduce it to a single picture. FrontPage prevents this from happening by graying out everything on the Picture toolbar that would damage the animated GIF.

You can use the Picture Properties dialog to determine how often the animation should be displayed. By default, a GIF animation that's loaded into FrontPage will display each of its pictures once—a single loop. You can determine the number of times it should loop or set it to loop forever.

"Forever" meaning "for as long as you sit there looking at it." Does the animation continue after you leave the page and go to a new one while keeping the browser open? That's one of those questions for the people who try to figure out whether a falling tree makes a sound when nobody's around to hear it.

Creating most of the animation in this hour is only slightly more difficult than working with these animated GIF files.

Create a Transition Effect Between Pages

One of the easiest special effects you can add to a page in FrontPage 2000 is a *page transition*. This displays something out of the ordinary when you either load a page in your browser or leave it to load another page.

In movies, transition effects have been a staple of adventure serials like the original *Star Wars* trilogy and *Raiders of the Lost Ark*. To move from one scene to another, filmmakers use transitions such as the wipe, which replaces a new scene for the old one as if it was wiped on with a rag.

Figure 12.1 shows a Web page in mid-transition. Two Web pages are visible: a "Turn of the Century" title page and a page from the exhibit it's announcing. This is called a *circle transition* because the old page is shown in a shrinking circle until it disappears.

FIGURE 12.1

A circle transition between two Web pages.

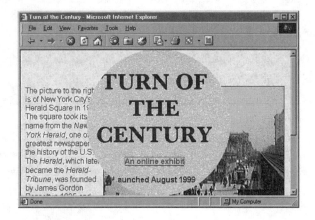

Click Format, Page Transition to add transitions to or remove them from a page. You can associate transitions with four different events:

- When the page first loads.
- When the page is exited.
- When the Web first loads.
- When the Web is exited.

There are many different page transitions you can use, and most have self-explanatory names like Circle, Checkerboard, and Wipe.

A transition also may be associated with a direction, as with Wipe Right, which wipes the new page onscreen from left to right. The Random transition loads one of the other transitions at random each time the event occurs.

12

When you select a transition, you also can select its duration, measured in seconds. This determines how long it will take to display the effect. You can choose longer transitions, such as a 10-second or 20-second effect, but keep in mind that this slows down people who are using your Web. They may not want to wait that long between page loads.

> The easiest way to see all of the transitions is to apply a Random page transition to the loading and exiting of a test page.

Animate Page Elements with Dynamic HTML

FrontPage 2000 offers another group of special effects that you apply to specific elements of a page instead of the entire thing. These effects can be associated with text, hyperlinks, and images, animating them upon such events as the loading of a page, the clicking of a link, or a mouse hovering over text or a picture.

Dynamic HTML, an extension of HTML that offers additional support for animation and interactivity, is supported by FrontPage.

> Actually, it's more accurate to say that Microsoft's version of Dynamic HTML is supported by FrontPage 2000. The two leading browser developers, Netscape and Microsoft, have developed competing implementations of Dynamic HTML. You'll have to test the FrontPage-created effects thoroughly in Netscape Navigator to make sure they work.

To animate something on a Web page, highlight it and click Format, Dynamic HTML Effects. A toolbar will appear that enables you to pick the special effect that will be used on the selected item.

Many Dynamic HTML effects can be applied to text. You can cause it to move into its correct place onscreen in a variety of different ways:

- *Elastic movement*—The text moves from offscreen to a little bit beyond the destination, and then snaps back to the correct place.
- *Drop in*—The text drops into place one word at a time.
- *Fly in*—Words fly in from several different directions.
- *Hop in*—Words move into place one at a time in a leisurely circular motion.

These effects, and others, are set to occur when an event takes place. One of these events is the loading of the page that contains the text. For hyperlinks and pictures, you can also trigger an effect based on mouse actions. You can animate a text hyperlink when it's clicked or double-clicked, and cause a picture to react when the mouse hovers above it.

Figure 12.2 shows the Dynamic HTML toolbar being used to associate a special effect with the headline "New York Newspapers 1850-1900."

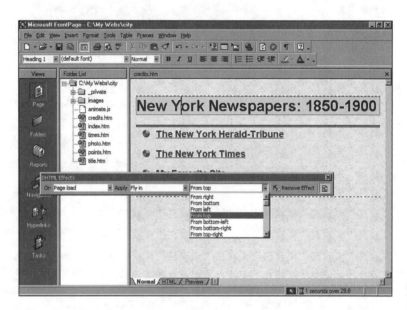

Create a Mouseover Picture

One of the most popular Dynamic HTML effects on the World Wide Web is the *mouseover picture*. The name comes from the way a picture changes when a mouse is moved over it.

If you select the Active Graphics option when you apply a FrontPage 2000 theme, all graphical navigation bars function as mouseover pictures. The buttons on the bars change appearance when a mouse is in position to click them.

Before you can create this effect, you need two pictures—the original image and the changed version that will appear in response to a mouseover event. This changed version can be a modified copy of the original or a different image entirely.

The easiest way to incorporate these pictures into your Web is to import them first. The original version of the picture will be displayed when the mouse is not hovering over it. This picture should be added to the page in the same way any other picture is added.

The second picture is specified as a Dynamic HTML effect. Select the original picture and bring up the Dynamic Effects toolbar. The event is a mouseover, the effect is Swap Picture, and the third pull-down menu on the toolbar enables you to select the swapped picture.

Figure 12.3 shows the dialog used to select a picture, which is previewed.

FIGURE 12.3

Selecting a swapped image for a mouseover effect.

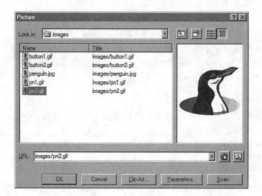

The swapped picture should be the same size as the original. If it isn't, FrontPage 2000 will resize the picture's display area so that it fits the space available to it.

The Swap Picture effect also can be associated with a mouse-click, which enables you to create a three-image sequence of pictures: original, mouseover, and click.

Paint a Format Around a Page

Using Dynamic HTML can be a tedious process when you're applying the same effect to several different elements of a page, such as a row of navigational buttons. FrontPage 2000 has a feature that makes it much easier to copy one page element's formatting to any other: the Format Painter.

Figure 12.4 shows the Format Painter button on the Standard Toolbar.

Format Painter stores the fonts, colors, special effects, and other formatting associated with a page element. To use it, select the item that has the formatting you want to duplicate and then click Format Painter. The button will be highlighted to show it can be used for painting. Click the item that should receive the stored formatting information.

There's only enough "format paint" for a single item, so you'll have to click the button once between every copying operation.

12

FIGURE 12.4

The Format Painter button.

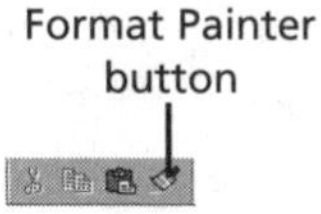

Format Painter button

Workshop: Make a Mess of Your Web

Dynamic HTML may not yet be an accepted standard like HTML, but there's a good reason not to ignore it entirely while Microsoft, Netscape, and other organizations try to reach common ground: It's fun to putter around with. After hours of working on Web pages that stay exactly where you leave them, moving animated pictures and text around ought to be an entertaining change of pace.

This hour's workshop is to do exactly that. Create a Web using one of the templates that has around 5-10 pages, such as the Personal Web template. Give each page its own theme, preferably one that looks remarkably different than all the others. Add clip art to any pages that look a little plain to you, and pay absolutely no attention to whether the graphics look good in relation to everything else.

When you're done with this task, create transition effects that are triggered when each page is entered.

As a last step, use at least two Dynamic HTML effects on each page, and then preview the whole thing in a Web browser.

Solution: Another Fine Mess

Dynamic HTML effects are one of the more entertaining features of FrontPage 2000, offering you a chance to surprise visitors to your Webs who may not have encountered these kinds of effects before. By experimenting with the effects it offers, you should get a better idea of which ones may be suitable for your own projects.

You also should get a much better idea of how many special effects are too many.

Summary

Now that you've gone through all the motions, you shouldn't have any doubt that your FrontPage 2000 Webs can compete visually with other animated offerings on the World Wide Web.

You can use several different kinds of animation on your Webs: animated GIF pictures, page-to-page transition effects, and Dynamic HTML tricks like elastic text, zooming pictures, and mouseover graphics.

This hour's workshop showed you many, if not all, of the animation effects that are possible in FrontPage. These effects are much livelier in person than can be conveyed in the pages of a book. No one has invented Dynamic Print yet, so the text of this chapter will remain the same. (Just imagine this paragraph flying in from the shadows of the binding and hopping into place, doing the two-dimensional version of the hokey-pokey dance…)

Q&A

Q **FrontPage 2000 won't let me use Format, Dynamic Effects or any other features like it—the Dynamic Effects toolbar is all grayed out and inactive. What's causing this?**

A You should check whether Dynamic HTML has been deselected as a feature your Web can use. FrontPage 2000 enables developers to target a Web to a specific audience by specifying some features they can't use. Since Dynamic HTML won't work on older versions of Netscape Navigator and Microsoft Internet Explorer, you can disable it from being used on a specific project.

To check this and similar options, click Tools, Page Options, Compatibility.

Exercises

Challenge your knowledge of FrontPage 2000 animation with the following exercises:

- Place the same picture (from the Clip Art Gallery or another source) on a Web page three times. Use FrontPage 2000's image-editing features to create three slightly different versions of the picture, and use them for normal, mouseover, and click effects.

- Copy an animated banner ad from this book's Web site at `http://www.fp2k.com/24`—the Hour 12 page has several ads from some of the World Wide Web's best-designed sites. Incorporate the ad into one of the Webs you have already created to see how it works as a part of the Web's design.

PART IV

Publishing and Maintaining Your FrontPage 2000 Web

Hour

HOUR 13

Publish Your Web

All of the Webs you have created so far were viewed locally on your own system. After 12 hours of dress rehearsal, you may be wondering when this production is ever going to open to the public.

It's showtime.

During this hour, you'll learn how to publish a FrontPage 2000 Web on the World Wide Web. The same techniques can be used to put it onto a corporate intranet. You'll be able to publish Webs and partial updates to a server, set up a Personal Web Server on your own system, and save Webs directly to a server.

The curtain opens on a lonely FrontPage Web, eager to see—and be seen by—the world...

Publish Your Web to a Server

FrontPage 2000 can publish Webs to three different places:

- A hard drive on your system or local area network
- A server on your system such as the Microsoft Personal Web Server
- A server on the World Wide Web

Saving a Web to your hard drive is a form of publication. You can view each of the pages, test the hyperlinks, and try out many of the features supported by FrontPage 2000.

You won't be able to test some of the features that rely on FrontPage Server Extensions—special programs that run in conjunction with a Web server to offer extra functionality to FrontPage Webs. To test these before you publish on the World Wide Web, you must install a Web server on your system and equip it with FrontPage Server Extensions.

One server that's well-suited for this kind of testing is the Microsoft Personal Web Server. You also can publish to the World Wide Web and test it there, if you have an account with a Web hosting service.

Installing the Personal Web Server

The Personal Web Server is one of the options you can install with Windows 98 and NT. If you don't have it on your system, you can install it from the original CD-ROM. Open the Control Panel and select Add/Remove Programs to find your Windows setup options.

 If you installed a past version of Microsoft FrontPage before upgrading to 2000, you may already have Personal Web Server on your system. Windows 95 users can download the current version for free from http://www.microsoft.com/ie/pws.

Once Personal Web Server has been installed on your system, it should show up on the Start Menu in an Internet or Internet Tools folder.

If you're running the server for the first time, an installation wizard will ask several questions about how you want to configure it. The defaults should be sufficient if you only need it for testing—FrontPage Webs should function normally under either the minimum or typical installation options.

The installation wizard will ask you to designate a folder on your system as the root for your Web server. The root folder will contain all FrontPage Webs that you publish to the Personal Web Server. An easy way to organize the root folder is to create a new sub-folder there for each Web that you publish to it.

The last step required by the installation wizard is to reboot your system. After you do, the Personal Web Server will automatically run at boot-up and an icon will appear in the service tray—the area on the Windows taskbar near the current time.

When Personal Web Server is running, your root folder can be accessed in two ways:

- By its real name, such as `C:\InetPubs\wwwroot`
- By the URL address `http://localhost`

You can test out the second address in your Web browser once Personal Web Server is running. The name `localhost` is an alias—a nickname—for your machine, in the same way that `www.fp2k.com` is a nickname for a machine installed somewhere on the Internet.

Publishing to a Web Hosting Provider

The only real difference between publishing on your system and to the World Wide Web is in the way you specify the destination. Publishing on your system requires the name of a folder. Publishing to the World Wide Web requires the name of a machine, and possibly the name of a folder where your FrontPage Web can be stored. In both cases, you're copying files from one location to another.

Before you can publish a FrontPage Web to another machine on the Internet, you need a username and password that grant you permission to store files on that machine. You also may need the name of the folder where the Web can be stored, depending on how the Web hosting service is configured.

The location where you can store your Web is indicated by a Web address. Here are some fictitious examples:

- `http://www.fp2k.com/~yourusername`
- `ftp://ftp.fp2k.com/users/yourusername/public_html`

Both of these examples specify a machine name (either `www.fp2k.com` or `ftp.fp2k.com`), followed by a folder name. The folder name tells the Web hosting machine where the files should be stored when they're published by FrontPage 2000. It also can be used after publication to load the site in a Web browser.

13

Choose Where to Publish a Web

When you're ready to publish a FrontPage 2000 Web, select File, Publish. Your first choice will be to publish the Web to the last place a Web was published, which will probably be a folder on your own system. Click the Browse button to use an Open Web dialog, as shown in Figure 13.1.

The Open Web dialog includes a column of icons that resembles the Views bar. Click the Web Folders icon to list shortcuts to Web servers where you have previously published sites.

The Folder name field can be used to enter the full Web address and folder name (if necessary) where the site should be published.

GeoCities, a free hosting service that can be used as a place to publish FrontPage Webs, does not require a folder name at this time. To publish a Web to GeoCities, ftp://ftp.geocities.com should be entered in the Folder Name field.

Another free host, Tripod, requires a folder name as part of the Web address. If your username is palmetto, the folder name should be http://members.tripod.com/palmetto.

If you're publishing a Web to the main folder of a Personal Web Server, http://localhost should be entered as the folder name. However, this address publishes the Web in the root folder of a Personal Web Server. Publishing to a subfolder requires a two-step process:

- Click the Browse button and open the localhost Web folder.
- Click the New Folder button to give this subfolder a name.

Click the Open button when you've selected the place where your Web should be
published.

> The Personal Web Server places a default home page in the root folder
> when it is installed, and it's no comparison to the kind of Webs you can cre-
> ate with FrontPage 2000. To get some practice with publishing to a server,
> create a new Web for the server's home page and publish it to
> `http://localhost`.

Publish Your Web to a Server

The last step in the Web publishing process is the moment of truth: Connecting to the
server so that files can be published on it.

Figure 13.2 shows the Publish Web dialog.

FIGURE 13.2

Publishing a Web.

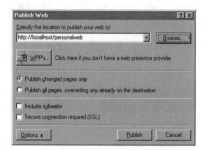

You can choose to publish an entire Web or just the files that have changed since it was
last published, if this is applicable. If the Web hosting service requires an SSL connection, put a check mark in the Secure connection required (SSL) box.

The Publish button begins the transfer of files. You must be connected to the Internet
before you can publish to a server that's on the World Wide Web. If FrontPage 2000 can
make a connection to the Web server and it requires a login, a dialog will appear requesting your username and password.

Barring any login problems, FrontPage will then begin copying files from your system to
the Web server. This process can take five minutes or more, depending on the speed of
your Internet connection and the number of files in your Web. (Publishing to a Personal
Web Server is much quicker, of course.)

13

Unlike some file transfers, this one doesn't give you an excuse to take care of any tasks you've been neglecting while you learned how to use FrontPage 2000, such as food, drink, taxes, and yelling at the kids who drive past the house too fast. FrontPage 2000 may have questions as it transfers files to the server. If it encounters a file on the server that isn't in your Web, it will ask whether to delete it. Also, if a file has been changed on the server since you last published it, FrontPage will warn you about this before over-writing the changed file.

A successful transfer ends with a happy dialog box that invites you to click a hyperlink to the newly published Web.

Solve Any Publishing Problems

When you're just learning how to publish a Web, there are several different problems that can stymie the process. You may begin to suspect that there's no happy dialog box and that Web publishing is a myth, like the 40-hour work week, the Wizard of Oz, and tax refunds.

The following suggestions may help you bring up this wonderful dialog, and none of them involve clicking your ruby slippers together while wishing you could return to Kansas.

Wearing ruby slippers can't hurt, but be warned that I cornered the market on them in a Men's 14 when I was preparing this book.

Try the following when good Web transfers go bad:

- If you're publishing to a Personal Web Server, make sure it's running. Click the server's icon on the taskbar to see its current status.

- Double-check your username and password to make sure they're correct.

- If you're specifying a Web address and folder name, such as http://www.fp2k.com/~yourusername/, load this address in your Web browser. In most cases, a test page or file listing should appear because Web hosting services often create the folder before you ever publish to it.

- If you're specifying a folder name, try taking it out and specifying only the machine name, as in http://www.fp2k.com. Some Web hosting services will find the right folder for your username automatically.

These examples cover the most commonplace problems that may occur as you're publishing a Web. In some instances, you may encounter problems because the hosting service doesn't offer FrontPage 2000 Server Extensions, although this normally doesn't prevent pages and files from being transferred to the Web server.

One of the buttons on the Publish Web dialog is labeled WPP's—Web presence providers. Click this button to go to Microsoft's list of hosting services that are specifically tailored to FrontPage Webs. Many of these services will have guidance and support for your publishing problems.

Workshop: Take Your Web Online

During the first 12 hours of this book, you've had the chance to create several different Webs. This hour's workshop is to publish one of these Webs to a World Wide Web server and load your site in a browser.

Instead of using the Personal Web Server, you should publish the Web to a server over an Internet connection. If you don't have a hosting service yet, you can sign up with either of the following free home page providers:

- GeoCities at `http://www.geocities.com`
- Tripod at `http://www.tripod.com`

These services give you a username, a password, and an address where your Web can be loaded with a browser. They also provide additional information on how to publish FrontPage 2000 Webs to their servers, including the address you should use when publishing your site.

All you need to sign up for either service is a valid email address.

These services are suitable for publishing a FrontPage Web, but they may not have implemented FrontPage 2000 Server Extensions yet at the time you try this workshop. You'll be able to browse through your Webs, but some interactive features like feedback forms may not function.

13

Solution: Publishing Your Web to GeoCities

When you go through the GeoCities sign-up process, you'll choose your own username and the folder where your home page will be located. GeoCities organizes folders as a group of neighborhoods, and each home page has an address number. If you're at address number 1000 in the PicketFence neighborhood, your Web page is located at this address:

```
http://www.geocities.com/PicketFence/1000
```

Your password will be mailed to the email address you specified during signup. This generally arrives within an hour after you join, but it may take longer.

Once you have the password, you can publish a Web. The folder name you should publish to is simply `ftp://ftp.geocities.com`, with no folder specified. GeoCities will ask for your username and password, and will publish your Web to the folder associated with that account.

One quirk of publishing on GeoCities is that the service only allows approved filename extensions. If you're trying to publish a file with an unapproved extension, you'll get an error message and the Web won't be fully published.

This shouldn't affect any of the files created by FrontPage 2000 to support a Web, nor will it prevent Web pages or most file formats, such as GIF, JPEG, or WAV, from being published.

What it will affect are which files you may import into a Web. The most notable example of a forbidden extension is `.exe`. GeoCities does not allow executable programs to be stored on its Web servers as part of a site.

When you've published a Web and the happy dialog appears to note this achievement, try it out in your Web browser.

Solution: Publishing Your Web to Tripod

As of this writing, Tripod offers support for FrontPage Server Extensions, unlike GeoCities. For this reason, it may be a better free-hosting choice for your Web.

After you go through Tripod's sign-up process for a free home page, Tripod will give your Web an address that's based on your username. If you selected palmetto as your username, for example, your Web's main address would be this:

```
http://members.tripod.com/palmetto
```

If your site requires FrontPage Server Extensions to operate features such as discussion Webs or feedback pages, you must enable these extensions on Tripod before publishing your Web. This can be done from the following Web address:

```
http://homepager.tripod.com/tools/frontpage
```

When you enable the extensions, Tripod will create several new folders in your Web that contain files used by FrontPage. Don't delete these files and folders, or some features of your Web may cease to function.

After your Web is published successfully to Tripod, you'll get a chance to try it out in your browser immediately.

Summary

The curtain closes on your FrontPage Web, which has fulfilled its lifelong dream of being published, met a nice girl, and saved the town's building-and-loan from being closed by mean old Mr. Potter. The production should be viewed as a success if you've published a FrontPage 2000 Web to a server.

During this hour, you learned how to set up and use a Personal Web Server—software that makes Webs on your machine accessible from a browser. You also learned how to publish on other servers—Web hosting providers on the Internet.

Publishing a Web in FrontPage 2000 is one of those tasks that's easy once you've done it successfully. It becomes as simple a task as saving files from one folder to another. Getting to that point can be a challenge sometimes, depending on how FrontPage 2000 and your Web hosting provider work in conjunction with each other.

Q&A

Q If a Web hosting provider doesn't offer FrontPage 2000 Server Extensions, should I use them?

A The answer depends on two things: whether your Web is reliant on server-specific features, and whether you can live without some FrontPage 2000 maintenance features.

You'll learn about Web maintenance during the next hour. To see whether a Web is reliant on the extensions, publish it to the hosting provider and try all of its features. Some of them, such as forms, can be rewritten to use an alternative. Others, such as threaded discussions, require the extensions and can't be replaced easily.

13

Exercises

Challenge your knowledge of FrontPage 2000 publishing with the following exercises:

- Use the WPP's button in the Publish Web dialog to see the list of FrontPage 2000-friendly hosting services. The directory is organized by area, so you may find that your own Internet provider (or one near you) is on the list.
- Publish a Web to a service you didn't use during this hour's workshop—GeoCities, Tripod, or another hosting provider.

HOUR 14

Keep Your Web Up-to-Date

FrontPage 2000 offers numerous features for creating content for the World Wide Web—hyperlinked pages, interactive programs, and multimedia such as pictures, audio, and video. Creating a useful, functional Web is only part of the challenge, however. Unless your Web is a one-shot that you don't intend to update, you've still got a lot of work to do.

Most Webs require regular maintenance, much like a car, spouse, friend, or Chia Pet. Web pages must be edited to keep them accurate. Hyperlinks must be checked to make sure they still lead to real Web addresses. Tasks must be assigned to the folks who actually do all this work—or in some cases, to a single, overworked person.

FrontPage offers features to make these site-management chores easier. During this hour, you'll learn how to automatically verify hyperlinks and how to break a Web project down into the tasks that must be accomplished. You'll also find out about some FrontPage enhancements called add-ins, which make it easy to rate your Web's content and enhance its usability.

Every maintenance chore that you have FrontPage 2000 perform is one you won't need to assign to someone, so it's worthwhile.

Keep Hyperlinks Current

Hyperlinks are the backbone of the World Wide Web, creating instant association between millions of Web pages and other files. During a typical session, you might circle the globe to chase down information, using hyperlinks to surf through seven different sites in seven different countries.

If your FrontPage 2000 Web contains a lot of links to other places on the World Wide Web, one of your continuing maintenance tasks will be to keep these links current. FrontPage makes this task easier by automatically verifying links for you. In the Reports view, you can list hyperlinks by the following criteria:

- All hyperlinks
- Unverified hyperlinks
- Verified hyperlinks
- Broken hyperlinks

To verify a hyperlink in one of these lists, right-click the link in the Reports view and select Verify from the pop-up menu that appears. If the link is to a World Wide Web address rather than your own system, you must be connected to the Internet before you can verify the link.

To verify all of the links in a report, first open the Reports toolbar with View, Toolbars, Reports. The Verify Hyperlinks button on this toolbar enables you to verify one or all hyperlinks in a Web.

FrontPage 2000 will attempt to connect to the Web address associated with each hyperlink, so the verification process can take quite a while if a number of links are being verified. An "OK" will be reported for every address that contains a page or file. Otherwise, "Broken" will be reported. This status will remain as long as the Web is open—when you close it, all hyperlinks are switched back to "Unverified" status.

Figure 14.1 shows a group of hyperlinks being verified.

FIGURE 14.1

Verifying a Web's hyperlinks.

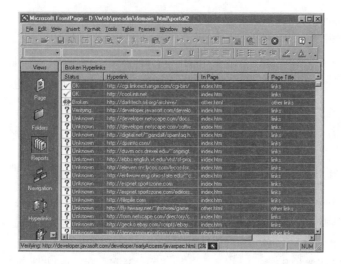

Some broken links may be the result of a temporary problem connecting to the Web address, so you may want to keep a broken link around for a little while before deleting it.

In general, a Web server must respond with a "Page not found" error or be offline entirely for a hyperlink to be reported as broken. Some Web hosts send an alternative page if a hyperlink isn't working. For example, if a GeoCities-hosted page is no longer available, GeoCities responds with one of its main navigational pages instead.

You can revise a hyperlink directly from the Reports view by right-clicking the link and selecting Edit Hyperlink or Edit Page. Selecting Edit Hyperlink brings up the dialog box shown in Figure 14.2.

FIGURE 14.2

Editing a hyperlink from the Reports view.

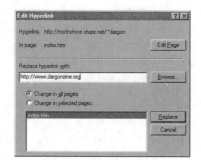

14

The Edit Hyperlink dialog also has an option for editing the page, which opens the page on your Web that contains the hyperlink so you can edit it in Page view.

 FrontPage 2000 makes it easy to keep the links to pages within a Web current. If you rename a page, a dialog will ask if this new name should be reflected in all pages of the Web that link to it.

Use Plug-ins to Accomplish Tasks

Web browsing software often is enhanced with *plug-ins*—separate programs that run when the browser encounters information it can't normally handle.

The streaming audio and video player from Real Networks is a popular plug-in, enabling Web pages to broadcast files in Real's proprietary format. Once Real's player program is installed, it functions as if it was always a part of the browser. Without a plug-in, the Netscape Navigator and Microsoft Internet Explorer browsers can't do anything with Real files.

FrontPage 2000 also offers new features through *add-ins*—its own name for pluggable software. Microsoft and other software companies will be offering plug-ins to extend the functionality of FrontPage. Two of the first to become available will be the RSAC Ratings and Accessibility add-ins. To see which add-ins are present on your copy of FrontPage 2000, and to add new ones, select Tools, Add-ins.

Rate Your Web's Content with RSAC

To address concerns about objectionable content on the World Wide Web, the Recreational Software Advisory Council (RSAC) has established a voluntary ratings system that judges the level of sex, nudity, language, and violence on a Web. The RSAC rating for a Web is determined by the person or group who published it, and uses the PICS guidelines for rating content that were established by the World Wide Web Consortium (W3C), the group that shepherds the development of HTML and other Web publishing technology.

The system is entirely voluntary, so your FrontPage Webs don't have to be rated by RSAC or any other organization before you can publish them.

Some Web browsers can be configured to lock out all Web sites that don't have a rating from RSAC or another group.

The purpose of RSAC ratings is to provide information for consumers who want to filter what appears on their browsers, such as parents, corporations, and libraries. If you publish a Web that contains offensive language, you can use an RSAC rating to provide a warning about this content.

You can rate a site or Web page manually by visiting http://www.rsac.org. The RSAC ratings add-in makes the process easier by turning it into a FrontPage wizard, which asks a series of four questions. Your answers are used by RSAC's system to assign a numerical rating from 0 (either non-offensive or mildly so) to 4 (Katie, bar the door) in four categories: sex, language, nudity, and violence.

The wizard creates the HTML coding needed to establish the RSAC rating for your Web and adds it to the rated page or an entire Web. It also prepares an email that will be sent to the RSAC about the newly rated Web.

Figure 14.3 shows how Internet Explorer can be configured to block content based on its RSAC rating.

FIGURE 14.3

Filtering a browser by using RSAC ratings.

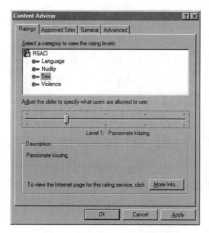

14

As you might expect, the subject of content ratings is a controversial one on the World Wide Web, so the RSAC ratings add-in may not be a wizard you call on for your own Webs. More information about the development of these systems is available from the RSAC Web site, and from the World Wide Web Consortium at `http://www.w3.org`.

Make Your Web Accessible

The Accessibility add-in makes it easier for Web publishers to expand the audience that can view their sites. Differently abled people can use non-visual Web browsers, spoken text, and other technology to surf the Web.

Some of the tips for making a browser work without pictures apply to accessibility. If you add alternate descriptions to your hyperlinked pictures, accessibility software can use this information. For example, if your Web relies on an imagemap for navigation, the alternative text of that map can provide a reference to text links on the same page that can be used instead.

The Microsoft Accessibility add-in will evaluate how navigable your Web is. You determine how stringent the evaluation should be and some of the things that should be checked, and the add-in highlights anything that might be a problem. It also suggests solutions.

If the add-in has not been distributed with your copy of FrontPage 2000, you can find some of the same features at the Bobby Web site:

`http://www.cast.org/bobby`

Bobby is a wizard of sorts that can load any page on the World Wide Web and offer tips for making it more accessible. Bobby also looks over the HTML coding of the page to see if there are any problems with its composition.

Establish a To-Do List of Tasks

Publishing a Web can be a complex process, especially if it involves a large number of pages, a large number of people working together, or both. FrontPage 2000 includes a task management system to better organize the work that's involved in developing and maintaining a Web.

As you've explored features of FrontPage 2000, you probably noticed several places where you had a chance to add a task. For example, right-click a filename in the Folders view. One of the options that appears is Add Task.

A task in FrontPage 2000 is any job that needs to be done to a Web. It's given a one-line title, with room for a longer description if needed. It can be assigned to a specific person or groups of people, if you're collaborating with your colleagues on a project, and given a priority of Low, Medium, or High.

Given the nature of today's working world, Microsoft should consider renaming these priorities Urgent, Extremely Urgent, and Tomorrow Morning Or You're Back in the Mailroom.

Tasks can be sorted by their priority in the Tasks view. So if your boss leaves on a week-long business trip, you can downshift tasks to low priority and take your own unplanned sabbatical. Figure 14.4 shows the New Task dialog.

FIGURE 14.4

Describing a new task.

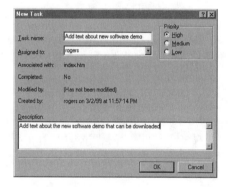

When you add a new task, it shows up in the Tasks view with a description of its status: Not Started, In Progress, or Completed.

Tasks can be associated with several different things in FrontPage 2000, including pages and pictures. All work on these tasks must begin from the Tasks view in order for FrontPage to track what you're doing. You can double-click a task in this view to find out more about it and tell FrontPage you're ready to work on it.

For example, consider a new task that has been associated with a picture: "Make portrait brighter so visitors stop sending me fruits that are high in vitamin C." Double-clicking this task brings up a Task Details dialog like the one shown in Figure 14.5.

14

FIGURE 14.5

Working on a task.

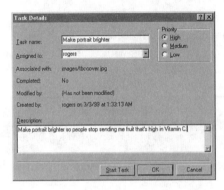

The Start Task button on the Task Details dialog enables you to begin work immediately. If the task is associated with a Web page, it will be opened in Page view. If it's a picture or another file type, FrontPage 2000 will open the software identified as its editor.

If there's no editor configured for a task's file type, an error message will be displayed. To configure editors, click Tools, Options and click the Configure Editors tab.

FrontPage 2000 keeps track of the tasks you begin using the Start Task button. When it looks like you might have finished this task and are saving your changes, a dialog box will ask whether the task is complete. The task's status will be listed as In Progress or Completed, depending on your answer.

Organizing Tasks by Category and Review Status

If you're collaborating on a project, another way to manage tasks is to assign a category and review status to the files that make up your Web. You can establish both of these by right-clicking a file, selecting the Properties command, and clicking the Workgroup tab (see Figure 14.6).

Categories are used to group files together because of some common connection they share. If your Web is divided into editorial and marketing pages, you could create categories for each of these and use them to prevent people from editing pages outside their departments.

You can add your own categories, delete existing ones, and assign multiple categories to a file. A Web's files can be listed in the Reports view, according to their category, with View, Reports, Categories.

FIGURE 14.6

Assigning categories and review status reminders.

Review status is a more specialized category that establishes who must review a page or file. There are default review status categories for Legal Review, Manager Review, and others, and they also have a corresponding report command: View, Reports, Review Status.

Workshop: Verify Your Favorite Links

Although task management is useful no matter how many people work with you on a FrontPage Web, it's most needed on collaborative projects. FrontPage 2000's hyperlink verifier is useful even if your Web publishing endeavors are a one-person production.

This hour's workshop is to create your own Web with links to all the sites you visit regularly. You're probably using your browser's bookmark feature for this purpose, but placing these links on a Web gives you much more control. It also provides some nice usability features, such as frames, tables, and lists.

When you're done, verify all of the Web's hyperlinks. You can either delete the ones that don't work or leave them in to check again later (in case the problem is temporary).

After you've created this Web, make it your browser's default home page. You've just entered the portal business, although you may not be ready to go head to head with Yahoo!, Snap, Go.Com, or Lycos—at least not until you've finished this book.

Solution: Your Own Personal Portal

After you've designed a personal portal and placed all of your favorite hyperlinks on it, they can be verified in the Reports view. If you don't see some hyperlinks reflected in this view, close the Web and save all open files. FrontPage will update the Reports view when you reopen the Web.

14

As you're going through a hyperlinks report to test the ones that show up as broken, you can load a link in a Web browser by holding down the Ctrl key as you click the link in Page view. In most cases you'll get an error or a "Page Not Found" warning, but this is a useful way to double-check before deleting a link permanently.

Summary

If you're using a task-management system that's monitoring your progress through this book, you can change the status of one item. Revise the "Maintain a Web" item from "In Progress" to "Done Once I Finish the Q&A and Exercises sections."

FrontPage 2000's task- and hyperlink-management features make it easier to maintain your Webs on an ongoing basis. Add-ins like the RSAC and Accessibility wizards also offer some time-saving benefits. You can use the software to keep your hyperlinks current, break down your work into manageable tasks, and assign tasks to specific people or groups. You can also organize your Web into categories, making it easier for different parts of the Web to be maintained by the appropriate people.

Although there's still plenty that FrontPage 2000 can't do for you, if you use these features, you'll be left with more time for the other things you need to maintain—relationships, friendships, and plantships.

Q&A

Q Where does FrontPage 2000 get the names that appear when tasks are created, such as my own?

A FrontPage 2000 looks at the name that was used when you logged on to your system during bootup. If you're the only person who uses the computer, you may have configured Windows to log on automatically.

The name you assign to a task doesn't have to be a valid user of the system. However, anyone who shares your system to use FrontPage 2000 should have their own username and login. This way, they'll show up under that name in the Tasks view so you can monitor each other's progress at any time.

Exercises

Challenge your knowledge of FrontPage 2000 maintenance with the following exercises:

- Go task-happy on the next Web you create, assigning tasks to everything you must do prior to actually tackling any of the work. Start every part of the project in the Tasks view, creating a new task if you've overlooked something that must be done.

- Assign the pages and pictures on a Web to different categories based on how frequently they require updates. View the categories report to see how this could be used to manage the frequency of required tasks.

14

HOUR 15

Extend a Web's Capabilities with FrontPage Server Extensions

As you start to deal with more advanced features of FrontPage 2000, you'll run headlong into the subject of FrontPage Server Extensions.

FrontPage 2000 extends the capabilities of a Web by offering special components that must be supported by the Web server hosting the site. This support is provided by implementing FrontPage Server Extensions. As the name indicates, the extensions are added onto an existing server. Although you might expect the support to be offered only for Microsoft servers, extensions can be added to a variety of server programs and operating systems.

During this hour, you'll discover the benefits of publishing to a server that supports FrontPage 2000. You'll also discover how to create Webs that don't rely on these extensions, in case you choose a hosting service that doesn't offer them.

Use FrontPage Server Extensions

In earlier hours of this book, you've used special FrontPage components that aren't a part of standard Web development. These components add functionality like navigation bars, graphical banners with editable text, and timestamps.

A few FrontPage 2000 components require a Web server that can support them through FrontPage Server Extensions.

FrontPage Server Extensions aren't limited to server software developed by Microsoft, such as the Internet Information Server or Personal Web Server. They've also been made available to administrators running Apache, a free Web server for Linux and other operating systems based on UNIX. Apache is presently the most widely used server program on the Internet.

At the time of this writing, FrontPage 2000 Server Extensions were only available for Microsoft's Web server software. Microsoft has announced that extensions will be available for Apache but has not yet released them.

To find Web presence providers that support FrontPage Server Extensions, choose File, Publish Web and then click the WPP's button. This brings up a Microsoft site with a searchable database of companies that support these extensions on their Web servers, organized by name or location. There are hundreds of these companies.

FrontPage components that require server extensions include the following:

- *Form handler*—Collects information from a form on a Web page.
- *Hit counter*—Counts the number of times a page is loaded.
- *Search form*—Searches a Web for specific text and returns a results page.
- *Confirmation field*—Responds to information collected by a form handler.

With the exception of the form handler, you can find these components by choosing Insert, Component.

You can temporarily disable all features of FrontPage 2000 that require server extensions. Choose Tools, Options and then click the Compatibility tab, shown in Figure 15.1.

FIGURE 15.1

Disabling features that require server extensions.

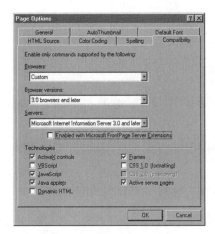

The Compatibility tab can be used to restrict FrontPage based on Web browser, browser version, and server. If the Enabled with FrontPage Server Extensions box is unchecked, you won't be able to add hit counters or other extension-reliant features to your Web.

Publish to a FrontPage-Enabled Server

FrontPage Server Extensions also give you more control over how a Web is published. For starters, you can publish a Web using HTTP instead of FTP as the transfer protocol.

If you try to publish a Web using an address beginning with `http://` and the server doesn't have extensions, you'll see an error message like the one shown in Figure 15.2. FrontPage 2000 won't publish a Web through HTTP unless it can find its extensions on the destination server.

FIGURE 15.2

An unsuccessful attempt to publish using HTTP.

If you're having difficulty publishing a Web using HTTP, many Web hosts allow you to use FTP publishing as an alternative. A Web address that begins with `ftp://` uses this transfer protocol.

FrontPage Server Extensions have been improved as of version 2000 of the software, but you may encounter Web servers that support an older version of FrontPage.

If you're working on a Web that has been saved to a server, you can find out more about that server within FrontPage. Choose Tools, Web Settings and then click the General tab. The following items will be displayed:

- The server software and version number.
- The FrontPage Server Extensions version number, if extensions have been installed.
- The IP address of the server.
- The address of the proxy server, if one is in use.

Track Changes to a Web

Another advantage of publishing to a FrontPage-enabled server is that FrontPage is better able to keep the Web current. Server extensions can be used to make sure that two copies of the same Web are kept in sync.

This works as follows: If you have a Web stored on your system and you also publish it to a Web server, sometimes they won't match. For example, you could rename one of your Web's pages that's on your system, and FrontPage would immediately change all hyperlinks to it on other pages within the same Web. If you publish changed pages to this Web later, FrontPage 2000 can use server extensions to make sure that all changes made on your system are made on the server as well.

You also can use the extensions to edit a Web directly on the server.

> If you're trying to keep two versions of a Web in sync, you should not make changes directly to the version on the server. FrontPage 2000 does not make sure that those changes are duplicated on a second copy of the Web that's stored on your system.

Control Access to Your Webs

If the server that's hosting your Web supports it, you can use FrontPage 2000 to restrict access to folders, pages, or files.

Unless you're creating a private Web for a corporation or similar organization, most of the material you publish on a Web should be publicly accessible. But when something has been restricted, a user must enter a username and password (if he has one) to get access to it.

15

Because most Web surfers expect information on the World Wide Web to be publicly available, you should have a good reason before you restrict something. An example would be a file that contains a user's personal information collected by a form. Something like that should be kept away from prying eyes for privacy and security reasons.

Choose Tools, Security, Permissions to add and remove users who have special access to your Web. If you can't choose Tools, Security because it's grayed out, you can't adjust security features on the server that's hosting the current Web. Your Web will be publicly available on the World Wide Web without any restrictions, which is the norm.

> If you're saving your Web to a folder on your system, you can't use FrontPage 2000's security features on that Web. You must open a Web directly from a server to edit security features for the Web, and this is possible only if the server is equipped with FrontPage 2000 extensions.

When it is permitted, FrontPage 2000's security feature enables you to choose two levels of access:

- Everyone can view the Web.
- Only permitted users can view the Web.

If you limit a Web to permitted users, they can have one of three security levels:

- *Browse access*—Can view the Web only.
- *Author access*—Can view the Web and make changes to it.
- *Administrator access*—Can view the Web, change it, and add and remove permitted users who have access to it.

A Web passes down its security permissions to all of its sub-Webs unless they have their own permissions set up. If you set up the root folder on a Web server so that a user named Mitnick has author access to it, Mitnick will have the same access to all other folders that host Webs.

On servers that are running under Windows NT, users are set up by the operating system and not from within FrontPage 2000. Also, all members of the NT system's Administrators group and the SYSTEM account will have Administrator access to Webs hosted on that machine.

The current version of Personal Web Server does not allow security measures—everyone can view the Webs it hosts, and author and administrator functions are limited to the computer that is running the server.

> If you're running a Personal Web Server and you're connected to the Internet, people can view your pages if they know your current IP address. By preventing people on other computers from doing anything but viewing Webs, the Personal Web Server keeps these files from being changed.

Workshop: Publish a Page That Requires Extensions

This hour's workshop requires a Web server that supports FrontPage 2000 Server Extensions. If your hosting service does not provide this support, use FrontPage to visit the page at Microsoft's Web site that lists companies supporting these extensions. You must be connected to the Internet to reach the site.

If you haven't worked with any components that require extensions, you can add a hit counter to a page on one of your existing Webs. This counter will keep track of the number of times the page has been visited. These visits are also called *hits*.

Add a hit counter by clicking Insert, Component, Hit Counter. You can use the Hit Counter Properties dialog, shown in Figure 15.3, to configure the counter in three ways:

- Choose the graphical numbers that will be displayed.
- Choose the current value of the counter, which will start at 0 if no value is chosen.
- Limit the number of digits that will appear in a counter.

FIGURE 15.3

Configuring the hit counter component.

When you add a hit counter to a page, the text "[Hit Counter]" will appear. This text is a placeholder for the real counter graphic. You can use it to determine where to display the counter on the page and how to align it in relation to other page elements.

Add a counter to a page on a new Web, or one you've already created. Choose one of the graphical styles for this counter, and then publish this page to a Web hosting service that supports FrontPage Server Extensions.

Solution: Use Extensions on Your Web

The hit counter is a simple FrontPage 2000 component that requires FrontPage Server Extensions. When you reload a page that includes a counter, FrontPage Server Extensions will increase the counter's value by 1. The file that stores the amount on the hit counter is stored in the _private folder of the Web.

Figure 15.4 shows a hit counter on a Web page that has been loaded more than 400,000 times.

FIGURE 15.4

Counting hits on a FrontPage Web.

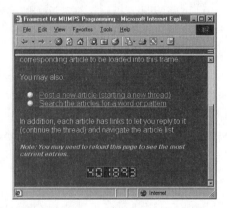

One problem you may have run into during this workshop is a grayed-out menu item that doesn't let you choose Insert, Component, Hit Counter. FrontPage 2000 will prevent you from using any feature that won't work on the Web server you're storing the Web on. Therefore, you can't add a hit counter to a Web page if you've configured it not to use any features that require FrontPage Server Extensions.

To correct this problem, choose Tools, Page Options, Compatibility. One of the check boxes indicates that FrontPage Server Extensions will be available to your Web.

Summary

You can get a good feel for the usefulness of FrontPage Server Extensions by configuring FrontPage 2000 to disable all features that rely on them. They provide substitutes for some of the most advanced Web page features, including form handling, search pages, and a way to count visits to your Web.

Some of these are available through alternate means. Although you can use the FrontPage hit counter to keep track of visits to your Webs, companies such as LinkExchange offer hit counters that anyone can use on any Web. (See `http://www.fastcounter.com` for details—it's the free counter service offered by LinkExchange.)

Extensions also give you more control over a Web's publication. You can keep two copies of a Web in sync—one on your system and one live on the World Wide Web.

They're also the only way you can publish using HTTP, the same protocol that delivers Web pages to your browser.

In the coming hours, you'll find out about other features that are reliant on FrontPage Server Extensions.

Q&A

Q Is there an advantage to publishing using the HTTP protocol instead of FTP?

A HTTP may be slightly faster and more reliable, but the difference between the two is negligible. As you use a Web browser, you can alternate between several HTTP- and FTP-transferred pages and probably won't know the difference without looking at the Web pages' addresses.

The main issue with a protocol is whether your hosting service supports it. Some hosts restrict Web publishing to HTTP or FTP only, so you should read a provider's documentation to see what restrictions they have in place.

Exercises

Challenge your knowledge of FrontPage 2000 Server Extensions with the following exercises:

- Save a Web to a folder on your system, and then publish it to a Web that supports FrontPage Server Extensions (if you have access to one). Rename a page on the local copy, and then publish all changes to the version on the World Wide Web. Make sure all changes are reflected in the second version.

- Add a hit counter to a page on one of your Webs and publish it to a FrontPage-enabled server. Load the page a few times to verify that the counter is working.

15

Hour **16**

Make Your Web Compatible with Multiple Browsers

A word that's often used in conjunction with the World Wide Web is "standards." There are standards in place for most of the languages and protocols used to exchange information on the Web: HTML, FTP, ActiveX, CSS…the list grows every month. The Internet thrives because of open standards like TCP/IP for communication, SMTP for sending mail, and NNTP for Usenet messaging.

Unfortunately, if you're a Web designer who's trying to make a page look the same on all browsers, the only standard that you can count on is chaos.

Trying to make a Web page work in all leading Web browsers is a challenge. The audience is split mostly between Microsoft Internet Explorer and Netscape Navigator, and each browser has non-standard Web features that make it challenging to create a Web that works on both browsers.

FrontPage 2000 makes it easy to add many of these non-standard features to your Webs. Fortunately, it also makes it easier to sort through the chaos and decide which features to use and which to avoid.

During this hour, you'll learn how to create a FrontPage Web that's targeted to a specific audience and designed with your Web hosting provider in mind.

Handle Differences Between Web Browsers

The World Wide Web Consortium has been entrusted with creating a standard version of HTML, the language used to create Web pages. You can visit the group's site at http://www.w3.org to learn about the current version of the standard and proposed improvements for the next version. The consortium also develops other standards that affect Web development.

For the past four years, the consortium's standards have often been at odds with the two companies that are most involved in following them: the browser developers Netscape and Microsoft. The fierce competition between the two has prompted both companies to introduce their own enhancements to HTML, Web page scripting, and Cascading Style Sheets.

Many of these new features are appreciated by Web users. Adding images to a page was once a non-standard enhancement, and many designers have been calling for new solutions like Cascading Style Sheets to be adopted. However, it has been standard practice at both companies to introduce new features in their browsers without waiting for them to become standards.

One of the simplest examples of this involves blinking text. For an early version of its browser, Netscape added a way to make text on a Web page blink on and off like a "VACANCY" sign outside a motel. It's a simple, eye-catching effect that calls attention to a word, sentence, or more.

Making your text blink is easy in FrontPage 2000. Choose Format, Font and then select the Blink option, shown in Figure 16.1.

You're likely to find that the Blink tag has been disabled and can't be selected. By default, FrontPage 2000 is set to create Webs that work in both Navigator and Internet Explorer, and Navigator is still the only browser to support blinking text (send your thanks to Lou Montulli at http://people.netscape.com/montulli/).

FIGURE 16.1

Making text blink.

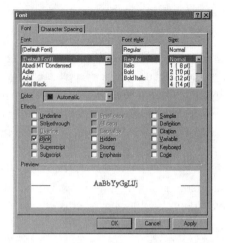

It's likely that Navigator will always be the only browser to support blinking text. The World Wide Web Consortium, faced with widespread sentiment that blinking text should be banned by the United Nations, has kept it out of the standard for HTML.

"To blink or not to blink" is only one of the questions you must ask when you design a FrontPage Web. The software includes more than a dozen different features that are affected by differences between the popular Web browsers.

Select an Audience for Your Web

One of the goals of FrontPage 2000 is to shield you from many of the complexities of Web design. At this point you may not be too familiar with technology like HTML, Dynamic HTML, and JavaScript because FrontPage uses these things behind the scenes as you work on a Web. You can focus on the effects and presentation that you want on your page, not the techniques used to make it happen.

The easiest way to keep it like this is by answering four questions before you start a FrontPage Web:

- Which Web browsers will be used by my target audience?
- Which versions of those browsers will they use?

16

- Which Web server will my Web be published on?
- Does it have FrontPage Server Extensions?

Although there isn't a definitive source for Web usage statistics, a look at several different surveys provides a pretty good picture of what people are using to browse the World Wide Web. As of this writing, it appears that approximately 85 percent of all Web surfers use either Netscape Navigator or Microsoft Internet Explorer, each of which has around 42 percent of the audience. Roughly 80 percent of all Navigator and Internet Explorer users have upgraded to version 4.0 or higher of the software, and another 15 percent are using version 3.0, according to the surveys.

Although Navigator and Internet Explorer have the browsing audience largely to themselves, a third browser is developing a following: Microsoft's WebTV, the consumer device that displays Web pages on a television.

Most Webs are developed for Navigator and Internet Explorer users with version 4.0 or later. This means that Web designers can take advantage of the newest features in these browsers. Some designers have taken the more conservative approach of aiming at version 3.0 or later of these two browsers.

You can also choose to design a Web for a specific browser, such as Navigator, Internet Explorer, or even WebTV. This enables you to use specific features, like the oft-maligned blinking text, that aren't available in any other browser.

Another thing you can determine when you're selecting a browser's target audience is whether you'll be relying on FrontPage 2000 Server Extensions. Several of the features of a FrontPage Web rely on these extensions, including some of the feedback submission options and discussion Webs.

The Web server you use to host a Web affects browser compatibility to a much lesser degree, because few features offered in FrontPage 2000 rely on a specific Web server.

Use Technology on a Web

Once you've chosen the audience for your Web, you can configure FrontPage 2000 to reflect this decision. To set your Web's target compatibility, choose Tools, Page Options and click the Compatibility tab, shown in Figure 16.2.

The choices you make in the Compatibility tab don't change existing features of a Web. They simply disable some features in FrontPage 2000 because your target audience won't be able to use them.

FIGURE 16.2

Choosing a Web's target audience.

16

For example, page transition effects rely on Dynamic HTML, which is not supported in version 3.0 of either popular browser. If you want to include the folks who are still happy with Navigator 3.0 in your target audience, FrontPage 2000 won't allow you to add page transitions unless you change the selected audience in the Compatibility tab.

You can change the Compatibility settings as often as you want during the development of a Web. However, you may end up with features on your Web that aren't suited to your intended audience.

The Compatibility tab shown in Figure 16.2 has a set of check boxes that represent different kinds of technology that can be applied to a Web. Some of them are covered in other hours of this book, such as frames, Dynamic HTML, and Cascading Style Sheets. You might not be as familiar with the following:

- *ActiveX controls*—Programs that run as part of a Web page using a programming standard developed by Microsoft.

- *VBScript*—A scripting language developed by Microsoft that enables some interaction between a user and a Web page.

- *JavaScript*—Netscape's Web scripting language, which preceded VBScript and is still the most commonly used and widely supported in browsers.

- *Java applets*—Interactive programs, written with the Java programming language, that run as part of Web pages.

- *Active Server Pages*—Web pages that use features handled by a Microsoft Internet Information Server.

The check boxes will be selected or deselected depending on the browser, browser version, and server you select.

If you're writing a Web only for Microsoft Internet Explorer version 4.0 and later, all the Technologies check boxes will be selected. As you might expect, FrontPage 2000 works best when you're aiming directly for the most recent versions of Internet Explorer. Every one of these technologies works in Microsoft's most current browser.

If you're writing for both popular browsers, or only for Navigator 4.0, ActiveX controls and VBScript technologies will be deselected while everything else is selected.

Losing the use of VBScript doesn't make much impact on a Web. JavaScript is so similar that you can achieve almost all of the same effects with it.

ActiveX was developed by Microsoft and has never been adopted by Netscape's browsers. Without ActiveX controls, you can't use Insert, Advanced, ActiveX to add any of these programs to a Web. Nor can you use three Office 2000 components: Chart, PivotTable, and Spreadsheet. All three of these are implemented with ActiveX, so they only work with Internet Explorer. You'll learn more about them during Hour 24, "Use Office Components and Launch Your Web."

Writing strictly for Internet Explorer 3.0 or later makes two of the technologies unusable: Dynamic HTML and CSS 2.0, which stands for Cascading Style Sheets 2.0. You'll learn more about style sheets during Hour 20, "Format Your Web Through Cascading Style Sheets."

Writing for both browsers at version 3.0 excludes an additional technology: CSS 1.0.

Without Dynamic HTML, you can't use any of the following on your Web:

- Page transitions
- Hyperlink rollover effects on a page's background
- Collapsible outlines

Writing only for WebTV restricts you from using any of the technologies shown in Figure 16.2, although this may change as WebTV adopts more of Internet Explorer's functionality in its new versions. WebTV's browser isn't as sophisticated as either

Navigator or Internet Explorer, so you're limited to the basics of Web page design and cannot have any frame-based pages.

Several Web elements can be used only in FrontPage 2000 if your target audience is limited to Internet Explorer users:

- The Marquee and Video components
- Background pictures that are displayed under a table instead of an entire Web page
- Borders around table cells, background colors for specific cells, and background pictures for cells

16

Restrict Specific Technology on a Web

The check boxes on the Compatibility tab enable you to override the selections that were determined when you picked a browser audience. If you do this, you may spend time on features that aren't really usable by your audience. For example, if you enable ActiveX controls for a Web, you'll be able to add things like Office 2000 components. However, if you're targeting an audience that includes Navigator users, they won't be able to see or use that Office component.

However, you may find it handy to disable a technology simply because you don't want to use it anywhere. For example, some Web developers choose not to place any Java applets on their pages. Although these programs can be a compelling way to present interactive content on a Web page, Java can reduce the speed with which a page loads. A Web browser must load an applet into a special environment called a *virtual machine* before it can begin running.

If you disable Java technology on a Web, none of the following FrontPage features can be used:

- Java applets
- The Banner Ad manager component
- The Hover Button component

FrontPage 2000 themes use JavaScript to create mouseover graphics on navigation bars, so if this scripting language is disabled, you can't select the Active Graphics option when applying a theme. The graphics on navigation bars will not change when a mouse hovers over them.

Deal with Server Compatibility Issues

The last compatibility-related factor is the one you may have the least control over: the Web server that's hosting your site.

If your Web is hosted on Microsoft Internet Information Server, you can use Active Server Pages no matter which browser or browser version you're targeting, even WebTV. On the other hand, an Apache server running on Linux or another operating system doesn't support Active Server Pages.

The effect of server extensions was discussed during the previous hour, "Extend a Web's Capabilities with FrontPage Server Extensions."

Use Browser-Specific Features

As you start to deal with the issue of browser compatibility, you're more likely to restrict yourself than to expand the possibilities of your FrontPage 2000 Webs. This is because, like most people, you probably want to reach both Navigator and Internet Explorer users as your primary audience.

> "Both" as in "both groups," not as in "two guys who are using these two browsers." If the latter were the case, you could handle compatibility by going to their houses and upgrading their software yourself.

Using FrontPage 2000, there are two routes you can take to use browser-specific features on a Web aimed at everyone.

The longer route: Duplicate some of the pages in your Web and create two navigational structures, one for Navigator users and one for Internet Explorer users. Visitors can click hyperlinks on one of the Web's main pages to select the Web that matches their browser, and each one can have different compatibility options.

The shorter route: Put browser-specific features on separate pages and provide hyperlinks to those pages for people with the right browser.

For example, if you have a page that uses an ActiveX control, you could provide a link to it indicating that it requires Internet Explorer. This prevents visitors from wasting time loading a page that they can't use.

These two techniques expand the amount of work you have to do, especially if there are a lot of duplicated pages.

Given the present statistics on browser usage, anything that's limited to one of the popular browsers will be usable by less than half of the Web's audience. This may not be a problem in some cases—a corporate intranet Web could be limited to the Web browser that's installed on all desktop machines.

 This book's official Web at `http://www.fp2k.com/24` is another example of a site that can count on a big audience that's using a specific browser, so there are plenty of FrontPage-specific features on it.

16

Workshop: Install Additional Browsers

The easiest way to sort through the chaos of multiple browsers is to test a Web thoroughly with each of them.

This hour's workshop is the quickest to describe and takes the longest to accomplish: download your target audience's Web browsers.

Solution: Download Navigator and Internet Explorer

If your primary audience is Navigator and Internet Explorer 4.0 and later, install the current versions of each browser. Internet Explorer is probably already set up because the FrontPage 2000 installation wizard offers to install it along with FrontPage.

Download and install the current version of Navigator, if you haven't already. The quickest way to find it is by visiting the Web address `ftp://ftp.netscape.com`. You also can visit `http://home.netscape.com`, although you'll have to dig around the site a little bit longer to find the browsers page.

The most up-to-date version of Internet Explorer is available from `http://www.microsoft.com/ie`.

When multiple browsers are installed on your system, choose File, Preview in Browser to test your Web on each of them.

Summary

Over the past few years, there have been numerous articles in business and computer magazines about the "browser war" between Netscape and Microsoft. After sorting through the material in this hour, you may believe that the first casualty of this war is your sanity.

At present, there are three HTML standards being used on the World Wide Web in any significant numbers: Microsoft's standard, Netscape's standard, and the real standard determined by the World Wide Web Consortium. As you can tell, it's standard operating procedure in the Web browser business to create non-standard additions to HTML.

FrontPage 2000 makes it simpler to do two things on your Webs:

- Stick with the features that different browsers share with each other.
- Avoid using features that your audience can't use anyway.

By determining your Web's audience before you develop the Web, you can concentrate on the features offered in FrontPage 2000 rather than thinking about the technology that makes them possible.

Q&A

Q What's the point of having an HTML standard if neither Netscape nor Microsoft follows it?

A The idealist's answer is that these companies can be persuaded to begin complying with the standard. If enough developers insist on following the HTML standard and Web users support sites that adhere to it, the browser developers will start following the standardization process instead of trying to stay ahead of it.

The pessimist's answer is that the browser companies are using these new features to gain a competitive edge over each other, and HTML's standard will always be underutilized until one of the browsers takes over the market.

Frustrated Web developers who want to stop spending so much time dealing with incompatibilities have been lobbying both companies to standardize. One such effort is the Web Standards Project at `http://www.webstandards.org`.

Exercises

Challenge your knowledge of FrontPage 2000 browser compatibility with the following exercises:

- Configure FrontPage 2000 for a WebTV audience on an Apache server. Create a personal Web and see which elements you can use in FrontPage's most restrictive configuration.
- If you've installed both Internet Explorer and Navigator, add a page to a Web that includes page transitions and Dynamic HTML animation. Test it in both browsers to see whether it's fully supported in each.

PART V

Enhancing a FrontPage 2000 Web

Hour

Hour 17

Communicate on Your Web with Forms

One of the easiest mistakes to make as a World Wide Web publisher is to treat this medium like its older siblings: television, radio, and print. For the most part, those media are a one-way street because the audience can't immediately respond (with the possible exception of Elvis Presley, who once registered his displeasure with a television by shooting it). Nor can they do anything to change the presentation as it's occurring—no matter how many times I yell "Look out, iceberg!", my favorite character in the movie *Titanic* still ends up in several pieces at the bottom of the ocean.

At its best, the World Wide Web is a collaboration between the people who publish sites and the people who visit them. As a Web publisher, you can collect information from the visitors to your pages, present it on your site, and use it in other ways to create a more engaging experience.

When you collect information on your FrontPage 2000 Web, you'll be using a Web page element called a *form*. Forms are made up of text boxes, lists, and other means of gathering information from visitors.

Today, you'll learn how to work with forms in the following ways:

- Using the Form Page Wizard to quickly create a new form.
- Adding questions to a form.
- Customizing a form.
- Saving the information collected on a form to a text file or a Web page.

Create a Form with the Form Page Wizard

If you've never created a form before, the easiest way to start is by asking the Form Page Wizard to do it.

Like other wizards in FrontPage 2000, the Form Page Wizard asks a series of questions to determine what you'd like to add to your Web:

- What questions do you want to ask?
- What kind of answers are acceptable?
- How should the questions and answers be formatted on the Web page?
- What should happen to the answers afterward?

When all of this has been determined, the wizard will create a new page in the current Web and add the form to it. You can either use this page or transfer it to another page using copy and paste.

Call on the Wizard

The first step in using the Form Page Wizard is to add a new page to an existing Web by clicking File, New, Page. A list of templates and wizards that can be employed on the new page is shown.

When the Form Page Wizard is selected, you can immediately add questions to the form. You also can either remove or modify existing questions, which makes it easy to change things on-the-fly as you're working with the wizard.

The wizard requires two things in order to add questions to a form: a prompt and an input type. A *prompt* is a succinct line of text that asks a question or describes a group of related questions. The *input type* represents the structure of the information collected in response to the prompt.

Ask a Simple Question

Several of the wizard's input types determine how a single question can be answered. They include the following:

- date—A calendar date.
- time—A time.
- number—A numeric value.
- range—A number from 1 to 5 that's used to rate something.
- string—A single line of text.
- paragraph—Text that can be longer than a single line.
- boolean—A response limited to one of two options, such as yes or no, true or false, and on or off.

Figure 17.1 shows the Form Page Wizard being used to add the question "Have you ever been convicted of a crime?" The input type for this question has been set to boolean, which limits responses to an either/or proposition such as yes or no. The string or paragraph input types could have been used instead, giving someone a chance to provide a more unstructured answer such as "Not since I quit using illegal drugs."

FIGURE 17.1

Adding a boolean *question to a form.*

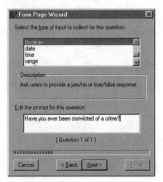

Each of these questions can be customized once the input type and prompt have been defined. You can limit date and time answers to specific formats, restrict a string answer to a specific number of characters, and make other decisions that affect how the form will be used.

One of the things you must customize about a question is the name of its *variable*, which is a place in a computer program where information can be stored for later use. Variables are used in Web forms to keep track of how questions have been answered. Each variable is given a name that can be used to retrieve or modify its value.

17

A variable's name should describe its purpose. You can use any combination of letters, numbers, and the underscore character (-) when you're naming variables. For example, three appropriate names for the "convicted of a crime" question are `Convictions`, `Any_Convictions`, or `CriminalRecord`.

Choose from a List of Options

There are two input types in the Form Page Wizard that enable answers to be selected from a list of possible choices:

- `one of several options`—A single item can be picked from the list.
- `any of several options`—An unlimited number of items can be picked (including none).

The prompt should identify what the list is being used to answer.

Each choice in a list must be a single line of text. Single-choice lists can be presented in three different ways on a Web page: a drop-down menu, radio buttons, or a list. All of these are shown on the portion of a Web page displayed in Figure 17.2.

FIGURE 17.2

Three ways a list of options can be presented.

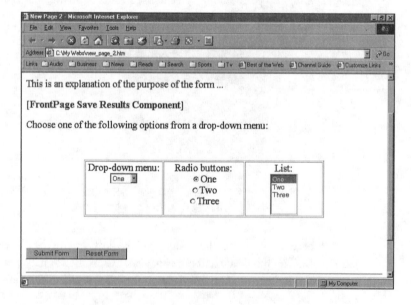

As shown, a drop-down menu shows only one possible answer at a time. If you click the arrow next to the answer, a menu of other answers will appear. Radio buttons and lists show several possible answers.

To make a drop-down menu easier to understand, use the visible answer to provide explanatory text such as "Click to make your selection." This also prevents the visible answer from being picked more often than other answers simply because it is automatically displayed.

A multiple-choice list enables the user to select more than one answer from a list. Each possible answer is shown next to a check box. A single-choice list restricts the answer to a single item in the list. Both types of lists must have a named variable to store answers in.

Multiple-choice lists require a group of variables—one for each possible choice that can be selected. Instead of providing a name for each of these variables, you provide a *base name*. This will be combined with the text of each answer to form variable names.

Figure 17.3 shows the Form Page Wizard being used to create a multiple-choice list. The list is used to answer the question "Which of the following languages do you speak?" One of four answers can be selected: English, Spanish, German, or Esperanto.

FIGURE 17.3

Providing answers and a base variable name for a multiple-choice list.

The base variable name is `Speaks`. The answers to this question will be saved in the variables `Speaks_English`, `Speaks_Spanish`, `Speaks_German`, and `Speaks_Esperanto`.

Ask Multiple Questions at Once

The remaining input types in the Form Page Wizard are used to ask several related questions at the same time. They include the following:

- `contact information`—Name, title, address, phone number, and other identification.

- account information—Username and password.

- product information—Product name, product version, and serial number.

- ordering information—Products to order, billing information, and a shipping address.

- personal information—Name, age, physical characteristics, and related information.

The Form Page Wizard automatically provides a prompt for each question in the group. If you provide your own prompt, it will be used to introduce the entire group rather than for any specific questions.

These combined input types make it easy to add some of the most common questions to a form. You can customize these questions by removing any questions that you don't want to ask.

In Figure 17.4, the Form Page Wizard is being used to customize a group of questions after the contact information input type was selected. The figure shows all of the customization options offered with the contact information input type. The Name and E-mail address questions are selected.

FIGURE 17.4

Selecting which contact information questions to use on a form.

For some of these input types, the variable names will be provided by the wizard. Otherwise, a base variable name must be provided for the group of questions. This will be used by the wizard to associate a variable name with each question.

Determine How the Form Will Be Presented

After you've finished adding questions to a form, you can choose how the questions will be presented on a Web page. You can lay out the form as a series of paragraphs or as one of three different lists:

- A numbered list.
- A bulleted list, in which each question is indented with a bullet character (like the list you're currently reading).
- A definition list.

A definition list is a standard Web page element that's ideal for displaying a group of words and their definitions. The formatting varies depending on the browser being used. Generally, words are presented flush-left, and definitions are indented below the word they define. The following text is presented in the style of a definition list:

```
Do
    A deer; a female deer
Ra
    A drop of golden sun
Mi
    The name I call myself
Fa
    A long, long way to run
```

On a form that's displayed as a definition list, questions are presented flush-left and possible answers are indented.

Another presentation decision you must make is whether to use tables when laying out your form. Tables can be used to arrange elements on a page. If you decide to use a table, the Form Page Wizard will place questions and answers into their own cells on the table, making the form appear more organized. The borders of this table will not be visible when the form is created.

If you decide not to use a table, questions and answers will be arranged more loosely as a series of paragraphs.

The main reason not to use tables is that a small percentage of the audience—from 1 to 2 percent, according to most estimates—is still using Web browsers that don't support them. Tables have been supported since version 1.1 of Netscape Navigator and the comparable version of Internet Explorer, so anyone who has downloaded and installed one of these browsers in the past three years can view tables.

A browser that doesn't support tables will display them in a manner that's confusing for the visitor.

17

Most people who can't view tables are using Lynx, a text-only browser that was originally developed by the University of Kansas Distributed Computing Group. If you're developing a site aimed at Lynx users or visually challenged people, you should create forms that aren't presented as tables.

Figure 17.5 shows a Web page that contains two versions of the same three-question form—a survey for owners of a company's bread-makers. The upper version of the form is formatted with a table, which lines up the questions and possible answers evenly in two columns. The lower version does not use a table.

FIGURE 17.5

Arranging a form with and without a table.

Save the Information Collected on a Form

The last step in creating a form with the Form Page Wizard is to decide how a user's answers will be saved. The following three options are available:

- save results to a web page
- save results to a text file
- use custom CGI script

To save a form's answers to a Web page or text file, you must be publishing your Web on a server that is enabled with FrontPage Server Extensions.

All answers submitted using the form will be saved to the same page. A question is identified on this form using its variable name followed by a semicolon. The answer to that question is presented on the following line. Figure 17.6 shows two sets of form results saved to a Web page.

Figure **17.6**

Viewing a form's results that have been saved to a Web page.

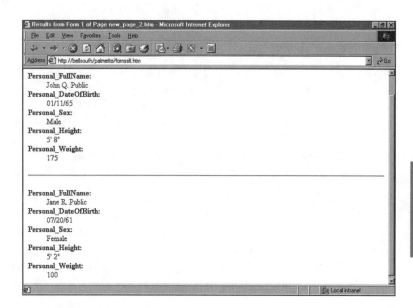

Displaying results as a Web page is useful when you want to view the answers in an easy-to-understand format.

If you're going to use form results with other software (such as Microsoft Access or another database program), they should be saved to a text file. This file can easily be imported into a database program. The first line of the file will identify each of the form's variables, and each subsequent line will contain a set of results.

The following output contains the same form results shown in Figure 17.6, saved to a text file instead:

```
"Personal_FullName"    "Personal_DateOfBirth"    "Personal_Sex"    "Personal_Height"
"Personal_Weight"
"John Q. Public"    "01/11/65"    "Male"    "5' 8"""    "175"
"Jane R. Public"    "07/20/61"    "Female"    "5' 2"""    "100"
```

This text file uses Tab characters to separate each field: "Personal FullName", "Personal DateOfBirth", "Personal Sex", and "Personal Height". A format like this is less readable to humans than HTML, but much more readable to database software.

When you save form results, you must name the file that will be used to store them. The Form Page Wizard will provide an .htm or .txt file extension for you, so all you'll need to choose is the name that precedes the extension. Results are saved in the same folder as the Web page that contains the form, unless you specify a different one along with the filename.

A FrontPage Web's _private subfolder is a useful place to save form results that shouldn't be viewed by the people who visit your site. To save results to this folder, precede the filename with the text "_private/". Also, make sure that access permissions for that folder have been established correctly.

The file that contains form results can be loaded within FrontPage 2000. If you'd like to delete all existing results, delete the file. A new file will be created automatically when new results are submitted using the form.

The final option for saving form results is to use a custom *Common Gateway Interface (CGI)* script. CGI refers to the use of special programs—also called *scripts*—that are run in conjunction with Web pages. A Web server that supports FrontPage 2000 offers a lot of the same functionality as a CGI program. The main use of CGI on the World Wide Web is to handle the results of Web forms.

CGI programs require special access to the Web server that's hosting your Web. You'll need to know the name of the CGI program to run and its location on the Web site.

Workshop: Survey Visitors to Your Web

To test how familiar you've become with the Form Page Wizard, use it to create the form shown in Figure 17.7. This form is used to conduct a survey related to a popular theme park. Visitors are asked their name, email address, number of visits to the park, favorite attraction, and favorite restaurant. The results are saved to a text file on the Web.

The user answers the first three questions by entering text into a box on the page, and answers the last two questions by choosing an option from a drop-down list of possible choices.

The favorite attraction and restaurant questions should each include several of the most popular places at the park. If you're not familiar with the theme park shown in Figure 17.7, replace it with one you're more familiar with or make up an imaginary one.

Save the form's results to a text file, giving it a name that describes its purpose.

FIGURE 17.7

A form that conducts a survey over the World Wide Web.

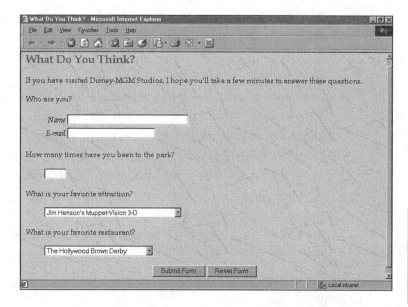

When you're done, give the page a title and a descriptive headline, such as "What Do You Think?". You can also add a theme and some introductory text if you want to create a more presentable page. Then name it and save it to your Web.

A description of one possible solution follows.

Solution: One Way to Use the Wizard

There's more than one way to use the Form Page Wizard to create a form, so the steps you took may be different from those offered in this solution. The most important thing is to ask the same kinds of questions, collect the same kinds of answers, and save the results in the same manner.

The form shown in Figure 17.7 was created using the following steps in the Form Page Wizard:

- A question was added with the input type `contact information` and the prompt "Who are you?".
- Only two of the `contact information` questions were selected: Name and E-mail address.
- A question was added with the input type `number` and the prompt "How many times have you been to the park?".
- The question was given the variable name `Visits`.

- A question was added with the input type one of many options and the prompt "What is your favorite attraction?".
- Labels were provided for several attractions at the park, and the base variable name was set to FavoriteAttraction.
- A question was added with the input type one of many options and the prompt "What is your favorite restaurant?".
- Labels were provided for park restaurants, and the base variable name was set to FavoriteRestaurant.
- The wizard was told that no more questions would be added.
- The default presentation options were used: normal paragraphs and the use of tables to arrange questions and answers.
- Results were saved to a text file named parksurvey.txt, and the wizard created the form on a new page.

To see this form on the World Wide Web, visit the book's official Web site:

http://www.fp2k.com/24

Summary

By using the Form Page Wizard, you can easily add interactive features to your FrontPage 2000 Web. As you explored the wizard's capabilities and created your own form in this chapter, some ideas on how to use this Web page capability probably sprang to mind. Forms can be employed to offer user surveys, visitor feedback, polls, questionnaires, tests, and many other interactive features.

Elvis Presley, not having a satisfactory way to communicate with television programmers, shot one of the devices in his home. Forms give visitors to your Webs a satisfactory way to communicate with you that do not involve possible violations of federal, state, or local law.

During the next hour, you'll learn how to create forms without using the wizard and how to extend an existing form's capabilities.

Q&A

Q **Using the Form Page Wizard, I created a form and chose not to lay it out using tables. Some parts of the form extend beyond the right edge of the browser instead of wrapping around to the next line. Why is this happening?**

A In order to line up forms without using tables, the Form Page Wizard uses the HTML formatting tag <PRE>, which is an abbreviation for *preformatted text*. This tag causes text to appear exactly as shown rather than applying the normal rules of Web page formatting, which is useful when you want to use spaces to line up text. Load the form into the FrontPage 2000 editor and click the HTML tab to see how <PRE> is used.

The disadvantage to this approach is that preformatted text will be shown exactly as it appears, even if it scrolls off the side of a page. To avoid this problem, create forms that don't use tables within the FrontPage editor rather than relying on the wizard.

17

Exercises

Challenge your knowledge of FrontPage 2000 and the Form Page Wizard with the following exercises:

- Create a form that surveys people's opinions about at least five controversial political issues, providing multiple-choice answers. Ask a question to determine the person's political party affiliation, and save the results in a form that a database program can handle.

- Add a feedback form to one of the Webs you have already created. Save the results to a Web page so you can easily review the answers that have been submitted.

HOUR 18

Collect Information from Users with Forms

During the previous hour, you learned how to make information flow in two directions on a FrontPage 2000 Web—outward as Web pages and other files, and inward as answers collected on a form.

Forms gather information from the people who visit a Web. You can use forms to solicit feedback, conduct surveys, play games, and interact with an audience in ways that aren't possible with other media.

The Form Page Wizard is well-suited to many of the forms you might want to use on a Web. For the times that it isn't, you can create a form manually by designing it on a Web page.

During this hour, you'll learn how to design a form by using text boxes, check boxes, radio buttons, drop-down menus, and more. You'll create these elements, add labels that describe their purposes, and limit the visitor's answers to a range of possible choices.

When the form is completed, you'll determine how to use the information it has collected—saving it to a text file, sending it as email, or calling special Web server programs that can decode the form.

You'll also be able to modify existing forms, which is useful even if they were originally created by a FrontPage 2000 wizard.

Create a Form by Hand

Choose Insert, Form to add a form element to a Web page. Forms are made up of the following elements:

- One-line text boxes
- Scrolling text boxes
- Check boxes
- Radio buttons
- Drop-down menus
- Labels
- Pushbuttons
- Pictures

Figure 18.1 shows all of these elements on a Web page, except for pictures.

FIGURE 18.1

Elements of a form.

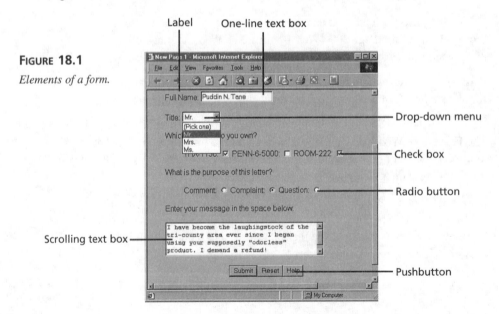

Create a new Web page and add any of these form elements to it. When you add your first form element to the page, FrontPage 2000 creates a form border and puts the element within this border. It also adds two extra elements:

- A Submit button for transmitting the information collected on the form.
- A Reset button for clearing out all answers on a form and starting over.

These two buttons are placed at the bottom of a form, but you can move them anywhere within the form's border.

All information that is collected on a form must come from elements located within its border in Page view. This border is used *only* for that purpose, and it does *not* show up when the page is displayed in a browser.

Form elements can be arranged within a border, just like anything else on a Web page. You can put them into tables, add pictures, and other things, as long as the form elements stay within the border.

You can add additional forms to a page by dropping form elements outside of a border. FrontPage 2000 will automatically border the elements and add Submit and Reset buttons.

Add Text Boxes

Text boxes enable the visitor to enter keyboard input on a Web page—a single line in a one-line box, and an unlimited number of lines in a scrolling box.

Add a text box to a form by choosing Insert, Form, Text Box, and remember to place the text box within the form's border. FrontPage 2000 assigns it a default width that approximates the number of characters that can be displayed in the box. More characters can be entered, but they won't all appear within the box. Scrolling text boxes also have a default number of lines that are displayed.

FrontPage also gives each box a default name and value, just as is does with all other form elements. To change these things after the element has been added to a page, double-click it to bring up the Text Box Properties dialog, shown in Figure 18.2.

FIGURE 18.2

Editing a text box.

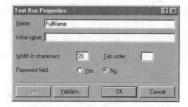

18

Every form element should be given a descriptive name that explains its purpose. This name will be used when the element's information is transmitted, and it also can be used by a scripting language such as JavaScript to get the element's value.

The name given to a form element should contain only alphanumeric characters and the underscore character ("-"). If you use anything else, such as spaces, FrontPage will warn you that the form might not work correctly in a browser.

If you give a text box an initial value, it will appear when the form is first loaded or the Reset button is clicked. This can be used to give the text box a default value. For instance, the Internal Revenue Service could put a default value of 100 in the Percentage of Your Income To Pay This Year in Taxes text box. Taxpayers would have to edit this initial value to pay less than 100 percent of their income in federal tax.

Select the password field option to hide all input entered into a one-line text box. Asterisks will appear in place of what's really being typed as a way to protect against snoops.

Add a second one-line text box to a form and select the password field option for that element. Although asterisks appear in that box when you type into it, the real text you're typing will be sent when the form is submitted.

Add Labels

A *label* is text that describes the purpose of another form element. Since elements are often used to answer questions, labels are used to actually ask the questions.

To add a label to a form, begin by typing the text for the label. This text should be on the same line as the form element it's associated with. Enter the text of a label next to a one-line text box, and then highlight both of the text and the form element and choose Insert, Form, Label. A border will appear around the text to indicate that it's now a label.

Turning text into a label makes it easier for people to use a form. In many cases, they can click the label in addition to the form element. Clicking a check box's label is the same as clicking the check box, for instance.

Labels provide assistance to Web users with non-visual browsers and other technology for the differently abled. Assistive software can use the label to explain the purpose of a form element. For example, a nonvisual Web browser could speak each label aloud before enabling the user to enter information into the form element that's associated with the label.

Add Radio Buttons and Check Boxes

Radio buttons and check boxes are form elements that have only two possible values: selected or not selected. You can set these elements to either value when the page is first loaded.

A check box appears with a check mark if it's selected and appears empty otherwise. Each box is given a name and a value—ON by default—that is sent for each selected check box when the form is transmitted.

One way to use check boxes would be to ask people what political parties they voted for in the past decade. There could be check boxes for the Republican, Democratic, Libertarian, and Reform parties. Between 0 and 4 boxes could be checked, depending on how often the person jumped across party lines at the ballot box. An appropriate value for these boxes would be YES, because it's only transmitted for boxes that are selected.

A radio button is a circle that has a dot in it if it's selected. You group radio buttons together by giving each of them the same name, which should also contain only alphanumeric characters and underscores.

Add a check box and a series of radio buttons to a form by choosing Insert, Form, Check Box and Insert, Form, Radio Button, respectively. Only one radio button can be selected in any group, so if you select one of them, the others will all be deselected. This is where the name *radio buttons* comes from—buttons on a car radio function the same way, limiting you to one station at any time.

The value given to a radio button should describe what selecting the button means. Consider radio buttons with the group name CustomerSatisfaction and the labels Ecstatic, Happy, Undecided, Displeased, and Enraged. These labels could also be used as values for the buttons—so if someone picks the Enraged button, CustomerSatisfaction will be transmitted with a value of "Enraged".

Add Drop-Down Menus

Drop-down menus serve a similar purpose to radio buttons: They enable the user to choose from several possible responses. However, instead these possible choices being divided into buttons, they're placed in a menu. Drop-down menus also differ in another way—they can be configured to allow more than one choice to be selected.

When you add a drop-down menu to a form, it doesn't have any possible responses. You add these responses by editing the menu. Double-click it to open the Drop-Down Menu Properties dialog, shown in Figure 18.3.

18

FIGURE 18.3

Editing a drop-down menu.

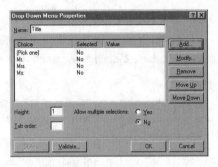

The Add button is used to add new responses to the menu. Each response has a Choice value that will appear on the menu, and the Selected value is transmitted with the form unless you specify an alternative.

The default behavior of a drop-down menu is to allow one choice to be selected and to display the menu on a single-line when it isn't being used. Both of these things can be changed in the Properties dialog—double-click the form element to make these changes.

After you've added all possible responses to a drop-down menu, you can rearrange them with the Move Up and Move Down buttons.

The first choice in a drop-down menu is sometimes used like a label. A value such as "(Pick one)" or "(Click here to select)" is used as the topmost choice. This has the added advantage of preventing the first real choice from being selected simply because it appears when the page is loaded.

Add Pushbuttons and Pictures

Pushbuttons are form elements that look just like the Submit and Reset buttons incorporated into every FrontPage 2000 form.

If you delete the Submit or Reset buttons from a form, you can put them back by inserting a pushbutton for each and editing its properties. Otherwise, there isn't a way to use a pushbutton to transmit a value without writing your own interactive programs in a scripting language such as JavaScript.

Pushbuttons can be associated with hyperlinks, so you can add them to a form as links to other pages. One possible use: a Help button that loads a page describing how to use the form.

Pictures on a form, which are added by choosing Insert, Form, Picture, are used for two purposes:

- Replacing the Submit button with a graphical version.
- Creating an imagemap that is handled by a Web server.

A picture element is placed on a form as a FrontPage imagemap component. This component, unlike other imagemaps, requires a Web server that includes FrontPage Server Extensions.

When the picture is clicked, the form is submitted with some extra information: the exact location on the picture where it was clicked. Neither FrontPage 2000 nor its server extensions do anything with this location information. Because of that, the only thing you can do with a picture label is use it as an alternate submit button—if your server has FrontPage extensions.

Receive Information from a Form

The last step in creating a form is deciding where to put all the information you've gathered. Your choices are the following:

- Send it in an email to a specified address.
- Store it as a file on your Web.
- Store it in a database on your Web.
- Send it to a form-handling program on your Web server.

The first three options require a Web server that supports FrontPage Server Extensions. Form data that is mailed will arrive like any other email. The name and value of each form element will be displayed in the body of the email, as in the following:

```
FullName: Puddin N. Tane
Title: Mr.
THX-1138: Own
ROOM-222: Own
Purpose: Complaint
```

To save a form to a file, you specify the filename and folder where it should be stored. If this file doesn't exist when someone uses the form, it will be created.

If you don't restrict access to the form results file by using FrontPage 2000's security feature, anyone who visits your Web will be able to read the file by loading its address directly with their browser.

Saving forms to a database is introduced during Hour 23, "Add a Database to Your Web."

The last way to handle forms is to call up a program on your Web server that can take in form data and do something with it. (Most of these programs simply email the data to a specified address.)

Form-handling programs rely on the Common Gateway Interface (CGI), a protocol that determines how a Web server exchanges information with other programs on the same computer. CGI programs require special access to a Web server, and most Web hosting services don't grant it to their customers for security reasons. Some hosting services install CGI programs that can be shared by all customers.

If you have a CGI program that handles forms, all you need to do in FrontPage 2000 is specify the name and location of the program and its delivery method. The method is either POST or GET, and the documentation for the CGI program should specify which one to use.

Figure 18.4 shows how this information is configured in FrontPage 2000.

FIGURE 18.4

Calling a CGI program to handle a form.

Workshop: Create a Feedback Form

Anyone who believes that there's no such thing as a stupid question, as I do, should get a chance to test that theory with the hour's workshop. Your project is to create the world's most intrusive Web feedback form.

Many sites on the World Wide Web include a form for sending feedback to the publisher. They ask for your name, email address, and some comments about the site. Some might ask other questions, such as the subject of your message, but usually the requests are kept to a minimum.

With this in mind, take one of the Webs you've created and add a new feedback page to it. Instead of relying on the Form Page Wizard or the Feedback Form template, add it as a blank page and develop the form by hand. Ask for as much personal information you can possibly think to ask: name, email address, mailing address, phone number, birthday, birthplace, mother's maiden name, blood type, weight, height, allergies, gender, current net worth, most painful childhood memory, number of past broken bones, phobias, and so on.

Try to add questions that require every one of the form elements, except pictures—it isn't easy to intrude on someone's personal life with a question that requires an imagemap.

Also, give every form element (except for labels) a name that describes its purpose. This will make it easier to decipher form results that are mailed to you or published as a Web page.

When you're done, save the form responses using a method that's supported by your Web hosting server, and then publish the Web. If you're hosting Webs on a server that supports FrontPage Server Extensions, have the form results mailed to an email address.

Solution: Use Each Form Element

Figure 18.5 shows a Web form that includes every element but pictures.

FIGURE 18.5

An intrusive Web form.

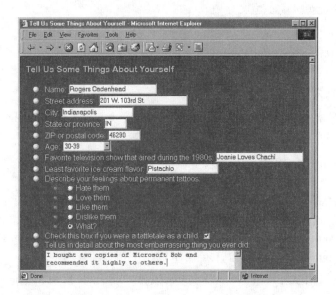

18

Creating this form took the following steps:

- Text was added to a Web page for use as a label.
- A form element was added adjacent to the text.
- The form element was double-clicked and given a name using its Properties dialog.

An extra step was involved in the creation of the radio buttons—all of these buttons were given the same group name.

After the drop-down menu was placed on the form, items were added to it by double-clicking the menu and using its Properties dialog.

If the form shown in Figure 18.5 was submitted to an email address, it would arrive looking like the following:

```
*************************************************************************
Name:                        Rogers Cadenhead
StreetAddress:               201 W. 103rd St.
City:                        Indianapolis
StateOrProvince:             IN
ZipOrPostalCode:             46290
Age:                         30-39
Favorite80sTVShow:           Joanie Loves Chachi
LeastFavoriteIceCreamFlavor: Pistachio
Tattoo:                      What?
Tattletale:                  ON
EmailAddress:                frontpage24@prefect.com

MostEmbarrasingThing:

I bought two copies of Microsoft Bob and recommended it
highly to others.
```

Summary

Forms are an essential feature of the World Wide Web because they immediately connect a publisher with the people who visit a Web.

You can create forms quickly with FrontPage 2000's Form Page Wizard. You also can take more control over a form by adding its elements to a Web page directly.

By using text boxes, check boxes, radio buttons, and other parts of a form, you can ask questions in a variety of different ways. A multiple-choice question can be limited to a single answer with radio buttons or multiple answers on a drop-down menu. More open-ended answers can be typed in as one or more lines of text.

After two hours on the subject of Web forms, you should be able to ask the visitors to your FrontPage 2000 Webs anything. Getting them to actually *answer* is another matter.

Q&A

Q **Why would an imagemap be a form element?**

A There are a number of useful purposes for a picture on the World Wide Web that tells a form handler where it was clicked. One of the most common is a street map that can be clicked to center the map at a new location.

There also are games in which visitors must click a specific place in a large picture to win a prize. Because the imagemap handler is on the Web server, the contest organizers can successfully hide the location. Using these imagemaps requires CGI programs and special Web server access.

Exercises

Challenge your knowledge of FrontPage 2000 forms with the following exercises:

- Create a Web survey in which each answer is a number on a scale from 1 (strongly dislike) to 10 (strongly like). Ask at least 10 related questions that can each be answered by picking a number on the scale.

- Add a Help button to the form you created during this hour's workshop. Use it to either apologize to people in advance or simply to help them understand how to use the form.

18

HOUR 19

Use HTML on Your Web

All World Wide Web pages are created by using Hypertext Markup Language (HTML), a set of formatting commands that are added to text documents. These formatting commands, which are called *tags*, turn normal text into headings, hyperlinks, paragraphs, and anything else you can put on a Web page.

When you apply formatting to part of a page, FrontPage 2000 marks that section with the corresponding HTML tag. FrontPage acts as an interpreter between what you want to do and how HTML does it. None of this is shown in the Page view, because you work with the page as it's going to look in a browser. For this reason, you can avoid learning HTML entirely.

Well, almost entirely.

During this hour, you'll learn how to edit a Web page using HTML and see the markup tags that make up the document. This skill will come in handy when you're given some HTML-tagged text that should be added to your Webs. It also provides insight into how pages are created in FrontPage 2000 and enables you to create and edit Web pages directly with HTML.

Tag a Page with HTML Commands

A Web document is actually an ordinary text file that you can load with an editor, such as Windows Notepad. HTML tags are added to the text to achieve different effects, such as the following:

- Creating a hyperlink.
- Turning text into a heading.
- Making several lines of text into a list.
- Displaying a picture of your 1970 Dodge Dart.

All HTML tags begin with the < character and end with the > character. The following tag adds a horizontal line to a Web page:

```
<HR>
```

"HR" stands for "horizontal rule." You can place an <HR> tag on a Web page anywhere you want a line to appear.

There are two kinds of tags: opening tags and closing tags. An *opening tag* indicates where some kind of formatting should begin. A *closing tag* indicates where it should end.

Consider the following marked-up text from a Web page:

```
<H1>Today's Top Story</H1>
```

This text uses the HTML tag <H1> to turn the text "Today's Top Story" into a size 1 heading. There also are <H2>, <H3>, <H4>, <H5>, and <H6> tags for headings with five additional sizes.

There are two HTML tags in this example: the opening tag, <H1>, and its closing tag, </H1>. The names of all closing tags are preceded by the slash character (/).

Most HTML tags require opening and closing tags in order to function correctly. For headings, you must use both tags to show where the heading begins and where it ends.

The <HR> tag is one of several opening tags that do not require a corresponding closing tag. The horizontal line appears on a page exactly where the <HR> opening tag is placed.

HTML tags aren't case sensitive, so you could place <h1>, </h1>, and <hr> on a Web page and achieve the same effects.

An HTML tag begins with the < character and the name of the tag. It also may contain extra information to control two things:

- How the tag is displayed on a page.
- What the tag can be used to do.

All of this extra information is placed before the > character at the end of a tag, as in the following example:

```
<HR WIDTH="50%">
```

This `<HR>` tag has the added text `WIDTH="60%"`. This is an attribute of the tag that causes the horizontal rule to be displayed 60 percent as wide as it would appear normally. A tag can have more than one attribute as long as they're set apart from each other by blank spaces.

Once you understand the way HTML tags are structured, it becomes easier to understand what they're being used to accomplish. Even if this is your first exposure to HTML, you may be able to figure out what the following does:

```
<A HREF="http://www.mcp.com">Visit Macmillan's Site</A>
```

This turns the statement "Visit Macmillan's Site" into a hyperlink pointing to `http://www.mcp.com`, which is the URL for Macmillan Computer Publishing's site. The `<A>` tag stands for "anchor"—another term for a link—and the `HREF` attribute is named for "Hypertext Reference."

Work with HTML in Page View

19

The normal mode in FrontPage 2000 is to convert what you do in Page view into HTML. For this reason, if you added the `<HR>` tag to a page, FrontPage would assume you wanted to display these four characters, not a horizontal rule—which you add by choosing Insert, Horizontal Rule.

To work directly with HTML in FrontPage, click the HTML tab at the bottom of the Page view window. There are three tabs for three different editing modes:

- *Normal*—For letting FrontPage write its own HTML behind the scenes.
- *HTML*—For writing your own HTML.
- *Preview*—For looking at the page as it will function in a Web browser.

You can click the HTML tab at any time to see a Web page's HTML formatting. If you're looking at a page that was created in FrontPage 2000, don't expect to make much sense of it unless you're experienced with HTML. The software uses some complex HTML to achieve many of the effects you can use on Web pages.

The easiest way to experiment with HTML in FrontPage is to first create a new Web with no pages and no theme. When you add your first page and view it in the HTML mode of Page view, the document should resemble Figure 19.1.

FIGURE 19.1

Viewing a Web page's HTML formatting.

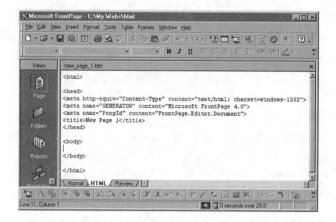

FrontPage 2000 starts every Web page with a minimal amount of HTML formatting:

- <HTML> tags to show where the Web page begins and ends (in other words, the entire document).
- <HEAD> tags to indicate the page's header—information about the page that isn't displayed in the main browser window.
- <TITLE> tags to give the page a title in the browser's title bar.
- <BODY> tags to indicate the page's body—the area that will show up in the main browser window.

FrontPage also uses several <META> tags in the header of the page that describe the document and how it was created.

One of these tags shows that "Microsoft FrontPage 4.0" is the Web editing software being used to work on the page. This is probably an internal version number, since FrontPage 2000 is the fourth major release of the software and Microsoft is a strong believer in naming software using the same tradition as almanacs (*World Almanac 1999*) and aviation disaster films (*Airport '77, Airport '79*).

You can change the title of a page by editing the text between the opening and closing <TITLE> tags. The text will appear on the title bar of the Web browser when the page is loaded.

Anything you want to display on a Web page should be placed between the existing <BODY> tags.

Paragraphs of text are formatted with the <P> tag in HTML, as in the following:

```
<P>For years, researchers and politicians have been saying
that the amount of violence on television causes children to
behave more violently in real life.</P>

<P>I've been watching around 7-10 hours of TV every day for
the past 15 years.</P>

<P>When I read things about how TV makes you violent, it
makes me so angry I could hit someone.</P>
```

The <P> tags control how this example is formatted when it appears on a page. Adding blank lines after each paragraph and hitting the Enter key at the end of each line does not affect how it is displayed—in an HTML document, tags control all of the formatting.

Figure 19.2 shows how this text appears in a Web browser.

FIGURE 19.2

Paragraphs of text on a Web page.

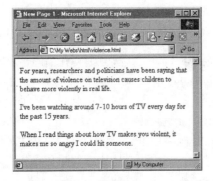

This text behaves like the paragraphs you've been working with in FrontPage. It fills the available space and moves around if you resize the browser window. You can switch back and forth between normal and HTML mode in Page view, editing the page in both views.

A good way to discover things about HTML is to create a simple page using HTML (like the one displayed in Figure 19.2), make a change to it in normal mode, and switch back to HTML mode so you can see what was changed.

The following output shows the TV violence text after a few changes have been made in Page view:

```
<P>For years, researchers and politicians have been saying
that the amount of violence on
<a href="http://www.tvultra.com">television</a> causes children
to behave more violently in real life.</P>

<P><i>I've been watching around 7-10 hours of TV every day for
the past 15 years.</i></P>

<P>When I read things about how TV makes you violent, it
makes me so angry <b>I could hit someone</b>.</P>
```

Three things are different:

- The word "television" is a hyperlink to TV Ultra, a World Wide Web site recommending the day's best show (whether violent or non-violent).
- The second paragraph uses the <I> tag to italicize the text.
- The words "I could hit someone" are surrounded by the <B> tag, which makes them appear in boldface.

Appendix A, "HTML 4.0 Quick Reference," describes each tag in HTML 4.0 and its attributes. You can use it to better understand how FrontPage 2000 implements HTML.

Workshop: Add a Hit Counter Using HTML

It's possible to use FrontPage 2000 entirely as an HTML editor. You can take advantage of its Web management and maintenance features while you mark up pages, as if you were using Windows Notepad or another plain-text word processor.

However, it doesn't take a psychic friend to figure out that most FrontPage 2000 users will be content to let the software write its own HTML. If you're one of them, the main reason you'll need HTML mode is to add HTML-tagged text to a page.

The World Wide Web has numerous services that can enhance your Web, including free hit counters, guest books, and banner advertising exchanges. Many of these programs offer their services through HTML tags that you must place on your pages.

One of these services is FastCounter from LinkExchange, a company acquired by Microsoft in 1998. FastCounter is a hit counter that you can place on any Web page, or even on each page in a Web. The service is free, in exchange for a hyperlink to FastCounter's Web site.

Full details on how to join FastCounter are at `http://www.fastcounter.com`. When you sign up, you receive HTML-tagged text that must be placed where you want the counter to appear on a page.

For this hour's workshop, add a FastCounter hit counter to one of your FrontPage Webs.

Solution: Try Out Your Hit Counter

The specific HTML tags for FastCounter will be different depending on the account ID you receive when you sign up. (LinkExchange may also have altered the HTML tags by the time you try the service.) The following is an example of FastCounter HTML for account number 956167:

```
<!-- BEGIN FASTCOUNTER CODE -->
<a href=
"http://member.linkexchange.com/cgi-bin/fc/fastcounter-login?956167"
target="_top">
<img border="0"
src="http://fastcounter.linkexchange.com/fastcounter?956167+1912341">
</a>
<!-- END FASTCOUNTER CODE -->
<br>
<!-- BEGIN FASTCOUNTER LINK -->
<font face="arial" size="1">
<a href="http://fastcounter.linkexchange.com/fc-join" target="_top">
FastCounter by LinkExchange</a>
</font><br>
<!-- END FASTCOUNTER LINK -->
```

The HTML text for FastCounter is presented in a scrolling text box so you can cut-and-paste it to your Web. This text can be placed anywhere on a Web page. It's often put at the bottom, right above the `</BODY>` tag that closes out the page's visible contents.

If you have trouble finding the right place within the HTML view, switch to Page view's normal mode before pasting the code. Click your cursor exactly where you want the counter to be placed, and then switch back to HTML mode. Your cursor will be at the same place you clicked.

Figure 19.3 shows a Web page with account number 956167's FastCounter placed at the bottom.

19

FIGURE 19.3

*Counting hits using
FastCounter.*

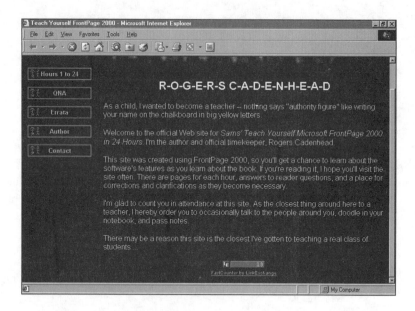

You can see this counter on the World Wide Web at `http://www.fp2k.com/24`, this
book's official site.

Summary

It doesn't take long to become an old fogey, by World Wide Web standards. If FrontPage
2000 is your first experience creating Webs, you'll probably hear some "in my day,
things were different" stories about HTML.

Before the development of software like FrontPage, all Webs were created by marking up
text with HTML tags in text editors like Windows Notepad. Many developers still prefer
HTML because of perceived limitations in software that creates these tags for you. They
feel that you get more control over the finished product by coding it yourself.

You can be both old-fashioned and newfangled with FrontPage 2000. You can view the
HTML when you want to, and hide it when you use the software's graphical user interface to design Webs. You also can use FrontPage 2000 to avoid HTML entirely.

No matter how you do it, things are a lot easier than they were in my day, back in 1995. As an old fogey myself, I should point out that we worked on our HTML while walking uphill 20 miles both to and from school in driving snow, without any of that fancy GORE-TEK insulated coat-lining, and we etched our pages onto rusty shovels with sharp rocks.

And we liked it.

Q&A

Q Why doesn't any of the text from a shared border show up in HTML mode?

A FrontPage 2000 saves the contents of shared borders separately from the rest of each page in a Web. The border elements are saved to their own Web pages in the Web's _borders folder. Everything is combined when you publish.

You can't normally get to the _borders folder within FrontPage—it's one of several folders that never show up when folders and files are listed. To make these folders appear, choose Tools, Web Settings, Advanced and then select the Show Documents in Hidden Directories option. You'll be able to open the borders as individual pages in Page view and edit their HTML directly.

Q Is there any reason I should work directly with HTML instead of using FrontPage 2000 to create the HTML for me?

A One of the main purposes of software like FrontPage 2000 is to make it easier to create Web pages. Many people who don't have a technical background will find it easier to develop Web pages if they don't have to learn the tags and syntax of HTML.

The main advantage of learning and using HTML is that you can implement everything in the language as it's introduced. FrontPage 2000 supports most features that are currently implemented by Netscape Navigator and Microsoft Internet Explorer, but as new features are introduced by the World Wide Web Consortium and browser developers, you may need to rely on HTML to implement them.

19

Exercises

Challenge your knowledge of FrontPage 2000 HTML editing with the following exercises:

- Create a Web page in HTML mode that contains a list of five Web sites you visit regularly. Use the tags you've learned about during this hour and any others you're familiar with.

- Create a page with no themes and no shared borders. Re-create the list of five favorite sites using the Page view's normal mode and the unnumbered list feature. View the page in HTML mode to see if you can figure out what the <UL> and <LI> tags accomplish.

Hour **20**

Format Your Web Through Cascading Style Sheets

The biggest push in World Wide Web design today is to separate the appearance of a page—its fonts, colors, and alignment—from the information it offers.

This is being done for several reasons. First, it will make a Web publisher's life much easier when the site needs to be redesigned. A site in which specific fonts and font styles are entered one page at a time also must be changed in the same manner.

Second, it makes a Web more adaptable to the diverse audience that will view it. Although Netscape Navigator and Microsoft Internet Explorer users constitute more than 85 percent of Web surfers today, many other types of browsing software will be used to visit a public Web—text-only browsers, nonvisual browsers, screen readers, and lesser-known browsers such as Opera.

Third, it gives a Web publisher much more control over how pages are presented.

Earlier, you learned about themes, which are a way to define a Web's visual appearance in FrontPage 2000. During this hour, you'll take that principle one step further by using a developing new Web technology called Cascading Style Sheets.

Define Styles on the Web

Most popular word processors today have a feature called *styles*. They enable you to define the kinds of information that will appear in a document—such as headlines, body text, and pictures—and then give each of them its own specific formatting.

For example, you could establish that all body text in your document will be 12-point Courier New text that is indented .25 inches from the left margin. After you have set up this rule for body text, you can apply the style to all paragraphs that are part of the document's main body. They'll show up exactly as if you applied the font and formatting directly. Later, if you decide to pick a different font or font size, you can modify the body text style instead of changing the document itself. All body text will change accordingly.

This idea has been introduced to the World Wide Web through *Cascading Style Sheets (CSS)*, a new language that specifies how a Web page and its elements should look. Cascading Style Sheets are an extension of HTML, rather than a replacement. A Web page incorporates CSS commands as hidden sections of the page, or on separate pages that contain all CSS formatting information.

Currently there are three versions of CSS, which started to be supported in version 3.0 of Internet Explorer and version 4.0 of Navigator. CSS 1.0 is most widely supported in current browsers, and it contains commands to set the fonts, colors, and formatting of text, hyperlinks, and other parts of a page.

"Most widely supported" is a far cry from "fully supported" when it comes to Cascading Style Sheets. At the time of this writing, neither Microsoft nor Netscape has implemented more than 70 percent of the CSS standard in their version 4.0 browsers, and there are incompatibilities between their two implementations.

Use Styles Instead of FrontPage 2000 Themes

FrontPage 2000 includes a feature that enables you to choose an entire Web's appearance at one time—*themes*. You can modify parts of a theme, like a text font, and all selected Web pages will be updated to reflect the change.

Themes are similar to Cascading Style Sheets, but are much more limited. Everything you use a theme for can be handled manually within Page view. You can set the background, establish all fonts, and create your own navigation bar graphics.

One of the things you can do with CSS is apply a theme. If you choose not to apply a theme using CSS, FrontPage 2000 will apply the graphics, fonts, and colors of a theme using standard HTML. CSS can produce the same effects.

CSS can't be used to apply a theme if you're targeting a browser audience with anything below Internet Explorer 3.0 or Navigator 4.0. Style sheets are not supported by WebTV or older browsers.

Unlike themes, Cascading Style Sheets can be used for techniques that are completely impossible in HTML. Take a look at Figure 20.1.

FIGURE 20.1

A Web page that uses Cascading Style Sheets.

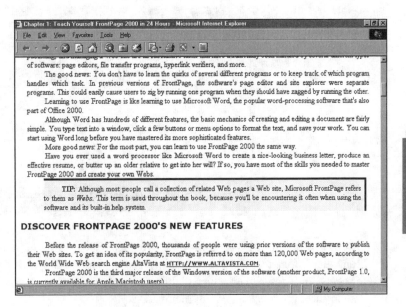

20

This Web page uses CSS to do several unusual things:

- Remove the blank line between paragraphs of text.
- Indent the start of each paragraph.
- Justify paragraphs along the right margin.
- Give one paragraph its own border edge and background color.

Style sheets enable you to take control over formatting decisions that have been automatically handled by the browser until now, like the blank line between paragraphs that has been standard to most browsers for years. They also give you many more options for determining the appearance of the different page elements.

Create a Style Sheet

Style sheets can be implemented as part of a Web page, or on a separate document that's linked to the page. The second method is better because you can attach the same document to other pages, establishing a common style for all of them.

To begin creating a style sheet, choose File, New, Page and then select the Style Sheets tab (Figure 20.2).

FIGURE 20.2

Creating a new style sheet.

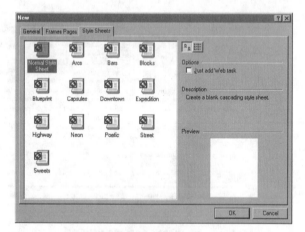

Several of the style sheets from which you can choose have the same names as themes, and they define many of the same fonts, colors, and heading styles. (Cascading Style Sheets don't define navigational buttons or page banners, however.) Choosing a Normal style sheet gives you an empty file to add styles to.

Style sheets should be saved with the .css filename extension. You can place them in the main folder of your Web or any of its subfolders, such as the images subfolder.

Before you make any changes to a new style sheet, save it so you can link it to pages in the current Web. Choose Format, Style Sheet Links to create a link to a style sheet. You can link a page or the entire Web to the .css file that contains the style sheet.

> Themes don't mix well with style sheets, especially when you're working on them for the first time. For the Webs you create during this hour, remove all themes before linking any style sheets.

Once you've established a page's link to a style sheet, the page will automatically display those styles.

Edit a Style

To edit a style sheet, choose Format, Style with either a Web page or a .css file open in Page view. The Style dialog will appear, as shown in Figure 20.3.

FIGURE 20.3

Editing a style sheet.

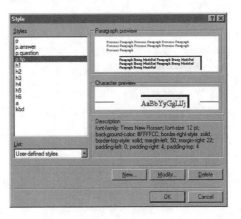

If you edit a style sheet from a Web page, the changes you make will be saved on that page only. Editing styles from a .css file enables you to make changes that apply to all pages linked to the style sheet.

Styles are associated with specific HTML tags. You can take an existing tag and establish a new style for how it is displayed on a Web page.

20

The Style dialog can be used to display all HTML tags or just the user-defined styles—tags that have new styles applied to them.

To see this in action, display all HTML tags in the Style dialog and modify the kbd tag. This tag is used to apply the keyboard effect to text, which is one of the options you can select by choosing Format, Font while editing a Web page.

Clicking the Modify button opens the dialog shown in Figure 20.4.

FIGURE 20.4

Modifying a style.

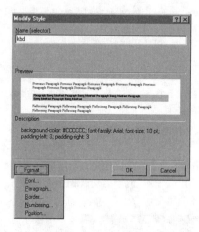

You can use the Format button on the Modify Style dialog to make the following changes to how a tag is displayed on a Web page:

- *Font*—The font, size, color, and other attributes of text.
- *Paragraph*—The spacing and indentation of paragraphs containing this text.
- *Border*—The border and shading that appear.
- *Numbering*—The way lists of this text are numbered and indented.

These formatting changes can be applied to any element, although several options are best suited to text.

Choose a new font, color, and size for the kbd tag, and give it background shading. The changes you make will be reflected in the Preview section of the Modify Styles dialog.

You also can change the positioning of the tag—a feature called CSS 2.0 in FrontPage 2000 that is only supported partially in Internet Explorer 4.0 and higher. The formatting features described during this hour are much more fully supported in current browsers.

When you modify a style directly from a .css page, FrontPage 2000 will display that style using the Cascading Style Sheets language in Page view. Don't edit this document manually unless you're familiar with CSS—if you click Format, Style, you'll be making changes to this file as you work on a style sheet with the Style dialog.

Apply a Modified Style to a Page

Once you've modified the kbd style, you can try it out in one of two ways:

- If you modified the style on a separate .css file, close and save that file. Open a Web page that has been linked to this style sheet.
- If you modified the style on a Web page, you're ready to apply the style to text.

Highlight text on a Web page and choose Format, Font to open the Font dialog. Apply the keyboard effect to this text. On most browsers, the keyboard effect causes text to appear in a smaller, monospaced font such as Courier. The new style that was applied to kbd overrides this formatting in browsers that support Cascading Style Sheets. You'll see the text as it was formatted in the Modify Style dialog.

If you make changes to the kbd style, they will be reflected immediately in all text that has been formatted with the keyboard effect.

Match Tags with FrontPage 2000 Features

Style sheets use HTML tags to identify elements of a Web page. If you're not familiar with HTML, you may not know how these tags are used on a Web page.

When you choose Font, Format to add a special effect, the following HTML tags are used:

- blink: Blink effect
- cite: Citation effect
- code: Code effect
- dfn: Definition effect
- em: Emphasis effect
- kbd: Keyboard effect
- samp: Sample effect
- strike: Strikethrough effect
- strong: Strong effect
- sub: Subscript effect
- sup: Superscript effect

20

- u: Underline effect
- var: Variable effect

Several buttons on the Formatting toolbar can be used to format text. They're associated with the following HTML tags:

- b: The Boldface button
- i: The Italics button
- u: The Underline button
- blockquote: The Increase Indent button

The Formatting toolbar also has a pull-down menu with several formatting options that apply to entire paragraphs. They use the following HTML tags:

- p: Normal
- pre: Formatted
- address: Address
- h1 through h6: Heading 1 through Heading 6
- ol: Before and after a numbered list
- ul: Before and after a bulleted list
- dir: Before and after a directory list
- menu: Before and after a menu list
- li: For each item in a numbered, bulleted, directory, or menu list
- dl: Before and after a defined term list
- dt: For each term in a defined term list
- dl: Before and after a definition list
- dd: For each definition in a definition list

There are other HTML tags that FrontPage 2000 uses as you create Web pages, including a for hyperlinks, img for pictures, and applet for Java applets.

To determine the tags that are being used by FrontPage, create a new page that contains nothing but a single Web element. Switch to HTML mode for that page and you'll see the tag—or tags—used to create it.

Create a New Style

A style sheet can contain new styles that aren't directly associated with an existing HTML tag. These styles often are used to create styles that have been slightly modified from existing tags, as in the following styles:

- p: A normal paragraph.
- p.quote: A paragraph that contains a quotation.
- p.author: A paragraph that identifies the author of the text.
- p.contact: A paragraph that indicates how to contact the author.

You can give each of these styles a different appearance as a way to distinguish them from each other.

In FrontPage 2000, the best way to create a new style is to base it on a paragraph tag that it is similar to, such as p for normal paragraphs or one of the heading tags, such as h3.

To create a new style, choose Format, Style, and then click the New button to give the style a name. The first part of the name should be the tag the style is based on, followed by a period, followed by a unique name that describes what the style is used for. The p.quote, p.author, and p.contact styles are examples of this.

When you name a new style, it will show up on the list of user-defined styles like any other HTML tag you've customized. You can modify how it is formatted, just like any other style.

The best advantage to basing a new style on a paragraph tag is that it shows up in the Formatting toolbar along with the other options to format a paragraph. For example, if you created p.quote, p.author, and p.contact styles, they would show up in the pull-down menu as Normal.quote, Normal.author, and Normal.contact.

Workshop: Add a New Paragraph Style

20

Once you understand the mechanics of how Cascading Style Sheets are employed in FrontPage 2000, working with them is as easy as formatting text in Page view. Most of your time will be spent choosing the right font, and other visual details for each style, and then testing them out on a Web page.

In this hour's workshop, you'll create a new style called p.smallprint. This is a paragraph style, as the first part of its name indicates. It will be used to format text that's part of a legal disclaimer—the kind of thing you see in the teeny-tiny print of a magazine advertisement.

The p.smallprint style should be formatted as 8-point Verdana text with light gray shading and a thin border around it.

Solution: Read the Fine Print

Creating the p.smallprint style involved several options on the Modify Style dialog.

First, the Format button and the Font option were used to select Verdana as the font and set it to a size of 8 points. Second, the Format button and the Borders option were used to choose a background color for the style. (You might need to experiment with some of the available shades of gray to find one that's light enough to make the small print readable.) Third, the Borders option was used to add a thin line around the text. The width of a line is expressed in pixels, so a value of 1 creates the thinnest possible line.

One thing that wasn't required was to add padding around the border, but this helps to set off the text from the border. You can add padding to the top, bottom, left, and right borders, and a value of 1 also is suitable for each of these.

Figure 20.5 shows an example of p.smallprint on a Web page.

FIGURE 20.5

Using styles for special kinds of text.

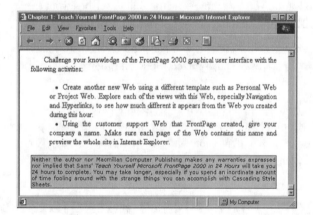

Summary

Cascading Style Sheets provide Web designers with numerous benefits if they're creating a Web for people using current versions of Netscape Navigator and Microsoft Internet Explorer. Style sheets enable you to modify the appearance of a Web in dramatic ways and save all of this information to a single file. Changing the file changes everything in the Web that links to the style sheet.

During this hour, you learned how to create new styles and modify some existing ones. You can extend the visual appeal of your FrontPage 2000 Webs in ways that are not possible through standard HTML.

Another benefit to using CSS is that it provides a way to define the information contained on a page. By creating style sheets with names that describe their purposes, you make the information more coherent and more useful.

For example, a newspaper's Web could define new styles for `p.headline`, `p.author`, `p.date`, `p.dateline`, and `p.lead_paragraph`. Even if all of these looked the same on a Web page, software could be written later to search stories based on author or date by the styles present on these pages.

Q&A

Q **I've created a new style based on the keyboard tag. How do I apply this style to a Web page?**

A FrontPage 2000 only enables you to apply new styles that are based on paragraph tags. They appear as new options on the Formatting toolbar, so you can easily select them.

You can create new styles that apply to text smaller than a paragraph, or even styles that aren't based on an existing HTML tag. However, there's no way to select these styles in FrontPage 2000 without resorting to HTML mode.

Exercises

Challenge your knowledge of FrontPage 2000 style sheets with the following exercises:

- Create a new style for hyperlinks that makes them stand out more from other text.
- Modify styles for each of the six heading sizes so that their prominence is reversed—heading 6 should be the largest rather than the smallest, and so on, down to heading 1.

20

PART VI

Rounding Out Your FrontPage 2000 Expertise

Hour

HOUR 21

Add a Personal Search Engine to Your Web

FrontPage 2000 has several different features that can make your Webs easier for visitors to browse. If you use the Navigation view and navigation bars, most people should be able to quickly find what they're looking for.

For everyone else, you can add a search engine. Search engines, like AltaVista and Google, can be used to scour a large chunk of the World Wide Web for specific text, hyperlinks, and page titles.

You can make a FrontPage Web more useful with the search form component, a searchable text index of the pages on your site.

During this hour, you'll learn how to add a search form component to your FrontPage Web and keep it up to date. You'll also learn how to make your Web pages turn up more often when people are searching the entire World Wide Web for information.

Make Your Web Searchable

FrontPage 2000's search form component requires FrontPage Server Extensions, so you'll need a Web hosting service that supports them in order to use this feature.

The easiest way to add a search engine to your Web is with the Search Page template, one of the standard documents you can choose to create a Web page. This template adds a search page containing the following:

- A search form component with Start Search and Reset buttons.
- Text describing how searches are conducted.

If you change the text on the page, you should keep at least some of the documentation. Every search engine on the World Wide Web has its own rules for how to find things, so visitors to your FrontPage Web will need some guidance on how to compose a search query.

You also can add a search engine to any Web page by choosing Insert, Component, Search Form.

Figure 21.1 shows how the search form looks on a Web page.

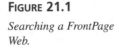
FIGURE 21.1

Searching a FrontPage Web.

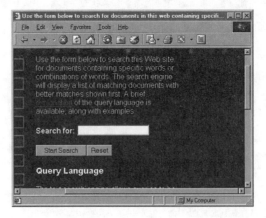

Although this component looks like a standard Web form, you can't add or remove buttons, or do anything else that's possible when you're working with forms. Instead, you edit it the same way as page banners and navigation bars—double-click the component to open a Search Form Properties dialog. This dialog enables you to change several things about the form:

- The label on the text box.
- The width of the text box.
- The text on the two buttons.

FrontPage 2000 supports this component by creating a text index of the words used on each page in your Web. With the exception of 300 common words, such as "a," "an," and "the," this index contains all of the words that appear on the Web. Once you click the button to begin a search, the component will create a results page containing links to the Web pages where the search text is found.

You can also modify this page by editing the properties of the component, as shown in Figure 21.2. The Search Results tab can report several things about the pages it lists: their file sizes, the dates and times they were last updated, and their scores.

FIGURE 21.2

Changing how search results are reported.

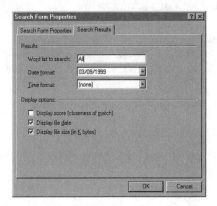

The score represents how often the search terms show up on the page—the form component ranks results based on this figure.

You can also limit a search to a specific folder of your Web. Enter the folder name in the Word list to search text box on the Search Results tab. For example, if you have a Web folder called oops that contains the text of several class-action lawsuit settlements made by your company, put oops in the Word list to search text box. The search form component won't look through the contents of any other part of your Web.

21

If you're publishing a large Web, you can offer several targeted searches by placing more than one search form component on the same page.

FrontPage 2000 automatically creates the searchable text index for your Web and each folder in it. Every new word that shows up on a page will show up in the index, with the exception of the 300 most common words.

One thing FrontPage doesn't do is remove words that are removed from a page after they've been added. To rebuild the search index, choose Tools, Recalculate Hyperlinks after connecting to the Internet.

This feature re-creates the index while simultaneously looking at all hyperlinks on your Web to see if they're still valid. It can take five minutes or longer, depending on how many hyperlinks on your pages link to sites on the World Wide Web.

Figure 21.3 shows how the results of a search are displayed on a Web page.

FIGURE 21.3

Results of a Web search.

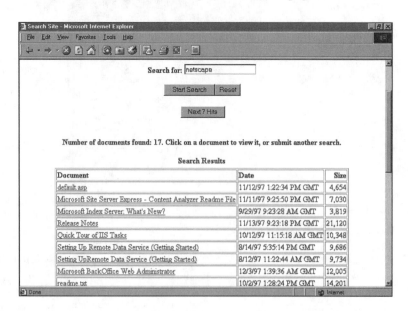

Search results are displayed on a page that's very similar to the search page. It will have the same theme, graphics, and layout, with a table of results below the Search component.

You can modify the format of the table by editing the Search component.

The Search Results tab has different options if you've opened your Web directly from the server that's hosting it, rather than opening a Web stored on your system.

This tab has more options for configuring how the search is conducted, as shown in Figure 21.4.

FIGURE 21.4

Configuring a Search component.

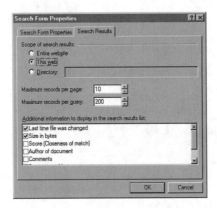

You can configure a search to cover the Web you're editing, all Webs hosted on the same machine, or just a specific folder on your Web. You can also change the number of items that are listed on a search results page.

After you've modified a Search component, be sure to choose Tools, Recalculate Hyperlinks to rebuild the word index that's used during searches.

Make Your Web Easier for Visitors to Find

The other half of FrontPage 2000's search offerings is making your Web easier to locate in other search engines.

Earlier, you gave descriptive titles to your Web pages by right-clicking each page's name in the Folders list and choosing Page Properties. A good title helps your page in two ways:

- Some search engines enable people to look for specific text in titles. Enter the text "title:"FrontPage 2000"" on AltaVista's Advanced Search page and to limit the search to pages with FrontPage 2000 in their titles.

- A few search engines rank words in a title higher than words on the page, causing your page to have a higher score on a results page.

21

You can also add keywords to a Web page that describe its content. Open the Custom tab of the Page Properties dialog (see Figure 21.3). Two different Add buttons are shown—one for system variables and one for user variables.

FIGURE 21.5

Editing a page's hid-den variables.

Variables are places that store information in a computer program. In a Web page, you set up variables by giving them a name and a value.

Add keywords to a page as a user variable with the name `keywords` and the value of a list of keywords that indicate what the page contains. Each keyword in the list should be one to five words that describe something about the page. You can list as many keywords as desired for each page, and they should be separated by commas.

The following text is an example of keywords for a Web page:

```
class action, lawsuit, litigation, sued, sue, defendant, defense,
us, settlement, settled, settle, payment, paid, multi-million,
million, money, moolah, lawyer, law, legalese, plaintiff,
litigant, consumer, customer, apologized, apology, sorry,
contrition, contrite, public relations, public, PR, Pamela
Anderson
```

Although this may read like beatnik poetry, it's a list of several dozen words and phrases that a person might use when looking for the page in a search engine. All of these key-words have something to do with a company's multimillion-dollar class-action settlement and its feelings of genuine contrition.

Actually, the last keyword has nothing to do with the hypothetical page. One quirk of page keywords is that they don't need to have anything to do with a page's real contents. Someone searching the World Wide Web for "Pamela Anderson"—as if anyone would want to do such a thing—could find this example page even if the actress is never mentioned in its text.

Support for keywords varies in the popular search engines. They're fully supported by AltaVista, HotBot, and Infoseek but are not used by Yahoo or Lycos.

 You can find a comprehensive guide to the things that search engines support from Search Engine Watch at http://www.searchenginewatch.com. This site also offers tips for making your Webs appear more prominently in each of the search engines and site directories.

Workshop: Make a Web Search-Friendly

Keywords on a Web page are so useful that they've already been the subject of legal wranglings. The publisher of *Playboy* magazine has sent cease-and-desist letters to numerous World Wide Web sites that use the word "playboy" in their keywords.

Your workshop for this hour is to add keywords to an existing FrontPage Web; preferably one that you plan to publish at some point. Start with a set of keywords that will appear on all pages, and add some to each page that are specific to that page.

If you're adding keywords to a site that was created with the Personal Web template, your main keywords could be about the person who the Web is about. On the page that lists the person's favorite links, these main keywords could be used along with a few extras, such as the names of the sites that are offered as links on the page.

Solution: Find Your Site By Its Keyword

Digital's AltaVista search engine will take recommendations for new pages that should be added to its database. After you've published a Web that includes keywords on a page, submit that page to AltaVista by visiting http://www.altavista.com and clicking the **Add a Page** link.

Normally, you add a Web to AltaVista by submitting its main page to the search engine. Under normal circumstances, this page will show up in AltaVista searches within a week. AltaVista will eventually add the entire site to its database by visiting the links on the Web's main page, but this can take several months.

To more quickly test the keyword feature, add a page to AltaVista that contains keywords, even if it isn't the main page of your Web. Within a few days, you'll be able to enter a keyword from the page to find the Web.

21

If all of your keywords are common words and phrases, you may have trouble finding your Web page among all the other pages containing the same search terms. You may want to use your own name or some other uncommon text as one keyword. That way, you can find the page by that keyword.

Summary

Any FrontPage Web of more than a dozen pages can benefit from a search engine. Even if you create a well-designed site, some visitors will be unable to find what they want and will look for a Search button on your Web's navigation bar.

During this hour, you learned how to create a search engine that's specific to your Web. This is one of the features that makes it worthwhile to seek out a hosting service that offers FrontPage Server Extensions.

You also learned how to make your Web more prominent in the search engines that cover the entire World Wide Web by using keywords. They're a time-consuming aspect of Web design, but they result in more hits from people who are randomly wandering the Web for specific information.

Q&A

Q Is there a way to change the text that appears when my page shows up in a search engine?

A Another user variable you can set up for a Web page is its summary. The summary should be no more than 100 words that succinctly describe what's on the page, in sentence form (rather than a bunch of keywords that identify its topics).

Some Web publishers use a page's main heading and the first few sentences that appear on it for the summary. If you use summaries, it's important to make a different one for each page of your Web. Some search engines will conclude that pages with the same title and the same summary are duplicates of each other, and will only list one of them in their database.

Exercises

Challenge your knowledge of FrontPage 2000's search capabilities with the following exercises:

- Add a search page to a FrontPage Web, even if you aren't necessarily planning to use a host that offers server extensions. Preview the page in a browser to see how FrontPage 2000 handles components in any server that isn't equipped with the extensions.

- Add the keyword "frontpage24hours" to the main page of any Webs that you publish using FrontPage 2000 and this book. This will make it easy for readers to find each other's work in search engines. (If it catches on, we'll develop a secret handshake and award gold watches to each other in 25 years.)

21

Hour **22**

Enable Discussions on Your Web

Keeping a Web from getting stale is a challenge. After you've published it, adding new content that keeps visitors coming back takes continued effort.

Sometimes the best solution is to let your visitors do the work.

Thousands of successful sites on the World Wide Web offer discussion forums where visitors can read and write public messages to each other. Some sites offer nothing *but* this service.

If you're using a Web server that has FrontPage Server Extensions, you can add a discussion forum to a Web and create new all-discussion Webs. During this hour, you'll learn how these Webs are created and maintained.

Create a Discussion Web

Discussions are implemented on a FrontPage 2000 Web through the Discussion Web Wizard. Choose File, New, Web to select this wizard. You can create a new Web that's devoted entirely to discussions, or add discussions to an existing Web.

FrontPage 2000's discussion forum enables visitors to read articles and post their own replies. These replies will become available immediately on the Web. Articles can be threaded so that each article and all of its replies are grouped together. This makes it easier for participants to read about the subjects they're interested in. A non-threaded discussion lists all articles based on the date and time they were written.

The Discussion Web Wizard asks a series of questions about how you want the discussion forum to be structured. One of the first things you must decide is which features to offer, as shown in Figure 22.1.

FIGURE 22.1

Picking your discussion Web's features.

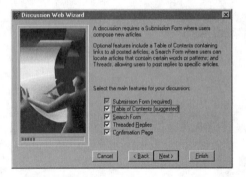

A discussion forum must have a submission form so visitors can post articles. You can also include the following features:

- *Table of contents*—Links to all articles that have been written.
- *Search form*—A search form component for finding articles that contain specified text.
- *Threaded replies*—Articles that are grouped together.
- *Confirmation page*—A page indicating that an article has been posted.

Most of these features are standard for discussion forums on the World Wide Web. The search form component, like the discussion Web, requires FrontPage Server Extensions.

Name the Discussion Web

Next, you must decide what to call your discussion forum and where its messages should be stored. The name will appear atop most pages and articles on that Web. It should be reasonably short. "Everybody Loves Uncle Stan" is better than "A discussion area for all people hoping to get into Uncle Stan's will."

The folder name will determine where articles are placed in the Web. With the exception of the _private folder, all folder names that begin with an underscore character ("-") are normally hidden from FrontPage 2000. They aren't listed in the Folders view or Folder list.

Hidden folders also aren't indexed for searching along with other parts of a Web. If you begin your discussion Web's folder name with an underscore, you'll need a search form as part of the discussion Web or it can't be searched.

> If you'd like to see the hidden folders, choose Tools, Web Settings, Advanced and then select the Show documents in hidden directories option. You'll see all folders you created that begin with the "_" character, along with several that are created by FrontPage 2000 automatically.

Figure 22.2 shows the dialog for selecting a discussion title and folder name.

FIGURE 22.2

Naming and storing a discussion Web.

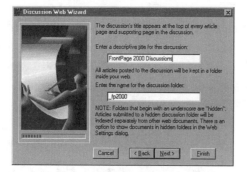

Choose How Postings Are Made

Next, the wizard asks which text boxes should appear on the discussion Web's submission form. You can select one of the following:

- Article subject and comments
- Article subject, category, and comments
- Article subject, product, and comments

You can make your FrontPage discussion Web open to all people who visit your Web, or only to those who have a valid username and password. The second option takes more time up-front because you'll be receiving requests to set up accounts. It also may reduce the amount of participation on the discussion forum—most Web-based discussion areas don't require any user registration before someone can post an article.

Making your discussion forum open to all participants requires more maintenance as the Web is being used. You'll have to remove articles that aren't consistent with your editorial goals for the Web, and there may be articles that contain illegal or objectionable material. For example, the publisher of the Everybody Loves Uncle Stan forum might want to delete all articles that discuss specific details about Uncle Stan's finances and his current state of health. Bad news about the former and good news about the latter could lead to fewer people being nice to Stan.

List Contents and Search Results

If you've added a table of contents to the discussion Web, you can configure it in two ways using the wizard:

- The order in which articles are listed.
- The table's place in the Web.

Articles can be listed in oldest-to-newest or newest-to-oldest order. The latter makes it easier to see what the most recent articles are, but participants are more likely to skip older articles.

The table of contents can be placed as the main page of a Web. If you choose this option, it will be given the name index.htm. So you shouldn't do this if the discussion Web was added to an existing Web.

> Although a discussion Web's articles are posted in their own folder, the pages that are used to post and read articles are stored in the main folder of a Web. When you're using the Discussion Web Wizard, it's easy to accidentally overwrite a Web's main page as you're adding a discussion Web to it.

If you elected to offer a searchable discussion Web, you can use the wizard to configure the search results page. The search can list results in four configurations:

- Article subject
- Article subject and file size
- Article subject, file size, and date
- Article subject, file size, date, and search score

The last configuration displays a score that indicates how often the searched-for text appears in the article.

Complete the Discussion Web

The last question asked by the inquisitive Discussion Web Wizard is how you want to display its articles. This dialog is shown in Figure 22.3.

FIGURE 22.3

Choosing how to display articles.

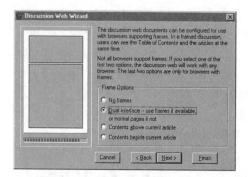

You can present the discussion using frames, no frames, or a combination that supports both. The no frames option places the list of discussion articles and the actual articles themselves on separate pages. Participants must hop back and forth between these pages as they read and write articles. The two frames-only options show the list of articles in a top frame or in a bottom frame. The other frame shows the most recently selected article.

Framing a discussion Web makes it easier to read articles, at the expense of some browser room. The area devoted to each article will be half as large as it would be on a no-frames Web, forcing readers to scroll more often.

A frames-only Web can't be used by people with older browsers, text-only browsers like Lynx, or WebTV.

The dual interface option offers the no-frames discussion Web to people whose browsers don't support them, and one of the frames options to everyone else.

After you answer the wizard's questions, the pages of the discussion forum will be added to the current Web. These pages will be named according to the title of the discussion Web and the purpose of the page. For example, if you're creating a Web called fp24, the following pages could be added to offer discussions:

- fp24_cfrm—The confirmation page, sent after an article is submitted.
- fp24_frm—The main frame of a frame-based discussion Web.

- `fp24_post`—The page where articles are posted.
- `fp24_srch`—The page for searching articles.
- `fp24_toc`—The table of contents page, listing all articles.

Workshop: Create a Discussion Web

The best way to evaluate the usability of a discussion Web is to look at the options that FrontPage 2000 offers.

This hour's workshop is to create a dual interface Web with the Discussion Web Wizard.

The people who visit your discussion Web will be using the interface you choose on a frequent basis. Choosing a good one will go a long way toward establishing your Web as a popular destination on the World Wide Web.

Another way to improve the usability of a Web is to offer plenty of guidance on its submission page, search page, and main page.

Solution: Test a Discussion Web

Before you can test a new discussion Web, you must publish it to a Web server that is enabled with FrontPage Server Extensions or save the Web directly on that server. Figure 22.4 shows a new discussion Web being used to post a message. This Web is devoted to MUMPS, a programming language introduced in the '70s. One use of discussion Webs is to foster communication about a subject that isn't being discussed elsewhere.

FIGURE 22.4

A MUMPS programming discussion Web.

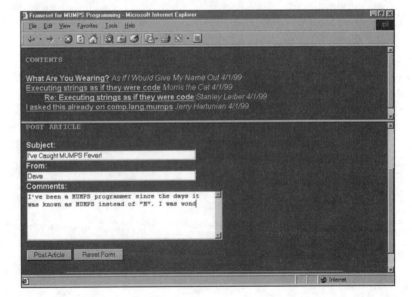

22

Figure 22.4 shows the frame interface for the Web, with a list of messages in the top frame and a place to post a new message in the bottom. If you choose to make the discussion Web's main page the home page for your Web, `index.htm` will contain both of the frames used by the interface.

Click the No Frames tab in Page view to see the other interface for the discussion Web.

Summary

During this hour, you learned one way that visitors to your FrontPage 2000 Web can update it. The Discussion Web Wizard makes it easy to create a place for articles to be read and posted. The real work on your part comes afterward, when visitors start using the forum. A discussion forum is an effective way to attract visitors to a Web, as long as you're willing to do the required maintenance work.

These Webs tend to build their own momentum—the more people participate, the more likely it is that other people will find the place.

Hosting an area for Web-based discussion will give you a close look at the World Wide Web's ability to foster community. As you manage the discussions that take place and the inevitable controversies that will occur in any forum where ideas are freely debated, you may find yourself with a new job title:

Community leader.

Q&A

Q If I put discussion articles in a hidden folder, how can I edit them from within FrontPage 2000?

A You can turn off the feature that hides these folders. To see this option, choose Tools, Web Settings and click the Advanced tab.

Except for _private, all folders in your FrontPage 2000 Web that begin with an underscore ("_") are normally hidden. By revealing these folders, you'll also see the folders that contain shared borders, themes, and other support files used by FrontPage to implement the Web.

It's important not to delete or modify these files unless you know what purpose they serve. You can delete or edit the pages that contain articles without affecting the function of the Web.

Exercises

Challenge your knowledge of FrontPage 2000 discussion Webs with the following exercises:

- If you publish to a server that's equipped with FrontPage extensions, create a discussion Web that's used to offer news updates about a Web. Limit this discussion to four fictitious usernames, and remove links to the submission page. This is one way to enable a select group of people to offer content on a Web.

- Add a product discussion forum to one of the company support Webs you created during a previous hour. Make this a non-threaded Web with a search page for finding text in articles.

HOUR 23

Add a Database to Your Web

FrontPage 2000 is the first version of the Web publishing software to be included in the Microsoft Office family of products. During this hour, you'll get a strong idea of how close-knit this family has become.

FrontPage lets you interact directly with a database from a Web page. Databases are files that are used to store related information together in an organized manner. Each item in a database is called a *record*. Some uses for databases include customer orders, address books, inventory, and the like. You can read records from a database, save records to a database, and even create a new database. All of these features are coordinated with Microsoft Access, the database program in the Office 2000 suite.

You'll create an Access database, populate it with records, and display those records on a Web page. All of these tasks can be conducted entirely within FrontPage 2000, so you can use these features even if you don't own Access 2000.

Work Directly with Database Files

FrontPage 2000 is closely integrated with the other programs in the Microsoft Office 2000 productivity suite. You can easily exchange data between these programs and use some Office 2000 features within FrontPage.

Your FrontPage Webs can interact directly with database files created in Microsoft Access and Microsoft Excel. There are several different ways you can make them interact:

- Create a new Access database to hold the information collected on a Web form.
- Display the contents of an Access or Excel database as a Web page.
- Search an Access or Excel database from a FrontPage Web.

You can create these database connections on any FrontPage Web. To publish a Web that uses database features, you need FrontPage Server Extensions and a hosting service that can support *Active Server Pages (ASP)*. The latter are Web pages that use a scripting language created by Microsoft. While scripts for JavaScript and VBScript run on a Web browser, the scripts on an ASP page are run by the server that delivers the page.

For this reason, you'll have to be on a hosting service that's using Microsoft Internet Information Server or another hosting program that supports ASP in addition to server extensions.

Create a New Access Database

When you collect information from a form on a Web page, you have several ways to store that data. You can send it to an email address, save it as a Web page, or save it as a text file, as you've seen during previous hours.

You also can save the information to a database. To see how this works, add a form to a FrontPage Web using the Form Page Wizard. The wizard doesn't give you a chance to save the form's information to a database (you'll have to change this later), so pick any of the other alternatives.

Once the wizard has created the form page, right-click the page and choose Form Properties to modify how it functions. Choose the option on the Form Properties dialog to save the form to a database.

When you click OK to close the dialog, FrontPage will display an error dialog stating that the form won't work in its present form. This is because you haven't had a chance to specify which database to save the form's information to.

This error dialog lets you immediately fix the problem by clicking Yes. If you do, you'll see the Options for Saving Results to Database dialog, shown in Figure 23.1. This enables you to select the database that will store the form's information.

FIGURE 23.1

Saving results to a database.

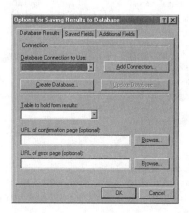

23

You also can use the Saved Fields and Additional Fields tabs to determine which elements of the form will be saved to the database, and which elements will be discarded.

Click the Add Connection button if you've already associated a database with your Web.

The Create Database button will create a new Microsoft Access database to hold the information that's collected from the form. All you have to do is click the button, and FrontPage will use what's on the form to determine how the Access database should be structured. The new Access database will be saved in a folder called _fpdb, and will be given a default name like new_page_1.mdb.

This feature, like all database-related functionality in FrontPage, requires server extensions and ASP. You must give the form page a new filename extension, .asp, before publishing it.

After you publish the Web, you can use the form to add records to the new database. This database file can be loaded with Microsoft Access 2000, or you can use another feature of FrontPage 2000 to display records on your FrontPage Web.

Display Database Records on a Web

FrontPage 2000, with the assistance of server extensions, can display database records on a Web page. You can pick any Access or Excel database on your Web, or another database file that can be loaded over the World Wide Web.

You can import a database file to a Web by choosing File, Import. When you imported
pictures and other files to a Web, FrontPage 2000 simply added the files to a folder in
your Web. Importing a database adds an extra step. If the database is in a format that
FrontPage 2000 recognizes, you'll be asked to create a new database connection that's
associated with this file, as shown in Figure 23.2.

FIGURE 23.2

*Creating a connection
for a new database.*

Every database is accessed from a FrontPage Web through a connection. You refer to this
connection instead of the database filename when you access its records. When you created a new Access database from a form page, a default name was given to that connection.

Once you've imported a database and created a connection for it, you're ready to start
using that data on your Web. Choose Insert, Database, Results to display records from a
database on a Web page. A database wizard will open that enables you to select one of
the following database connections:

- A connection to a sample database.
- An existing connection that has already been added to a page on the current Web.
- A new connection.

Normally, you should have an existing connection to work with, either because you
imported the database or you created it from a form page.

Next, choose how data should be displayed on the Web page:

- Which database table to display records from.
- Which fields in the database to display.
- Which records to display (all records or a selection of records).
- How many records to display on a page.

A table in a database is a grouping of records containing the same type of information. A
movie database could have a table for movies and another table for actors and actresses,
for example.

If you know Structured Query Language (SQL), you can use it to determine which records should be displayed. With the aforementioned movie database, you might want to limit the display to movies released during the current year.

Figure 23.3 shows the dialog you use to determine the fields that will be displayed for each record.

FIGURE 23.3

Choosing which database fields to display.

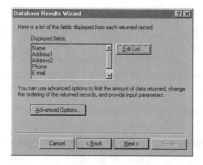

The last step in using the Database Results Wizard is to choose how the records will be displayed on a Web page. You can structure the information in several different ways, including paragraphs, lists, and tables. You also can limit each results page to a few records rather than displaying all records on a single page.

After you decide how results will be displayed, the Database Results Wizard creates a placeholder on a Web page for these results, as shown in Figure 23.4.

FIGURE 23.4

Editing a Web page containing database results.

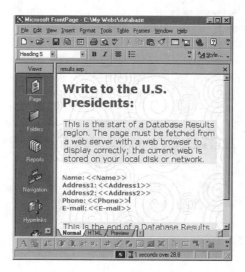

23

In Page view, database results will show up as two areas of highlighted text and a record placeholder, as shown in Figure 23.4. The text explains how to view the records from the database. Click this text to open the Database Results Wizard again and make changes. The placeholder contains a combination of text and database column values. Each column value represents a field in the database and is surrounded by "<<" and ">>" characters.

You can move the text of the placeholder around, delete database column values, and add column values by choosing Insert, Database, Column Value.

In Figure 23.5, five column values appear to the left of text: Name, Address1, Address2, Phone, and E-mail. Each value is listed on its own line, and there's a line break separating the lines. There's also a blank line at the end. The figure shows how this page looks after it's published and the database records are displayed.

FIGURE 23.5

Database results published on a Web.

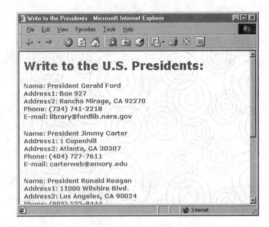

The way you format the placeholder within Page view determines how each database record is displayed on the finished product.

Workshop: Create an Access-Driven Web

An unusual aspect of FrontPage 2000's support for Microsoft Access 2000 is that you never need the latter software. You can create an Access database, query the database for specific records, and display those records entirely within FrontPage.

This hour's workshop is to create an Access-driven FrontPage Web without ever running Microsoft Access 2000. The purpose of the Web is twofold:

- To add records to a database.
- To display those records with one of the fields sorted in alphabetical order.

The database should be created specifically for this Web. Use the database to store something with at least four different fields, such as the following:

- Celebrity birthdays and birthplaces, along with their name and profession.
- Your favorite Web sites, with the title, the address, and a short description of each.
- Dallas Cowboys players, their positions, crimes they have been accused of committing.

If possible, one of the fields in the database should have a small number of possible answers. For example, you might have a category for a Web site's database such as "News," "Sports," "Personal," "Tech," or "Other."

After you've created the database, develop another page for displaying all of its records. You can choose any of the layout formats, but make sure the records are displayed alphabetically according to one of the fields.

Solution: Work with Data on a Web

Figure 23.6 shows a results page that displays celebrity birthdays.

FIGURE 23.6

Displaying an Access birthday database on the Web.

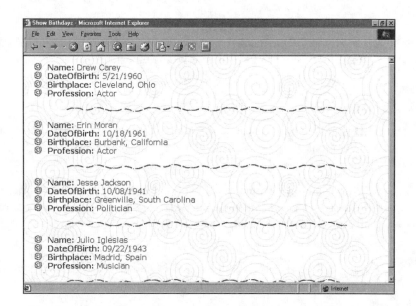

The first step in creating an Access Web from within FrontPage 2000 is to develop an input form. This form will be used to add new records to the database.

The birthdays database has four fields: Name, DateOfBirth, BirthPlace, and Profession. Each of these uses a text box on the form, except for Profession, which uses a drop-down menu. This menu limits the choice of professions, so the database will only have a Profession value equal to one of the menu options. In this example, those options are "Actor," "Politician," and "Musician."

Arranging records alphabetically is done in the Database Results Wizard as you're choosing which fields to display. The Advanced Options button opens the Advanced Options dialog, shown in Figure 23.7. Use this to pick a field that will be used to alphabetize records. The Ordering button enables you to choose the main field to alphabetize by. You also can choose the order of secondary fields to use when two records have identical fields.

FIGURE 23.7

Changing how records are displayed on a page.

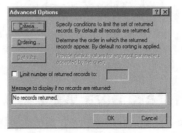

For example, consider a database where two records have a LastName field of "Flintstone." This could be alphabetized by LastName and then FirstName, so Fred Flintstone would be listed before Wilma Flintstone.

Summary

If your Web hosting service supports Active Server Pages and FrontPage Server Extensions, you can create, edit, and display the contents of an Access database from your FrontPage Webs.

Working directly with a database often makes more sense than offering its contents as text on Web pages. Manually editing text is a time-consuming task, especially if the database is updated frequently. Displaying database results on a Web page offers immediate access to that data.

During the next hour, you'll see how FrontPage works with another member of the Office 2000 family: Microsoft Excel.

Q&A

Q **Is there a way to rename a database connection? The default `new_page_1` isn't very descriptive of what the connection is used for.**

A You can't change the name, but it's relatively easy to create a new database connection to replace it.

When a new Access database is created from a form page, FrontPage 2000 uses the filename of the page to name the connection. Since the filename of a new page is called something like `new_page_1.htm` when you create it, the connection ends up with a name like `new_page_1`.

To prevent this from happening, give the page a better name before you use it to create a new database.

23

Exercises

Challenge your knowledge of FrontPage 2000 database connections with the following exercises:

- Create a database of products with the name, price, category, and a short description of each. Use this database to offer a Web with different pages that display the records in each category.

- If you have Microsoft Access 2000, use it to open one of the databases that FrontPage 2000 developed during this hour. Add records from within Access, and check to see that they're displayed on the Web with all the other records.

HOUR 24

Use Office Components and Launch Your Web

FrontPage 2000 is the first version of the software to be included in Microsoft Office 2000, the group of productivity applications that combines Word, Excel, Access, PowerPoint, and other programs into a suite. As the World Wide Web becomes more important to business productivity, Web-related features have been implemented in several different ways within Office 2000.

Most notable is the new common file format: HTML. In the past, each Office program has relied on a different format for its files. There were .mdb files for Access, .xls for Excel, .doc for Word, and none of them could be understood by the others. Now, although the original formats remain, you also can save data from each Office 2000 program as Web pages. These pages can even be read back into the programs later without losing any information.

During this last hour of the book, you'll learn how to bring more of Office 2000 to your FrontPage Web. You'll add spreadsheets that work in a Web browser the same way they would in Microsoft Excel 2000. To present the data from spreadsheets and other sources, you'll add an Office chart to a page that charts data in lines, pies, and other visual ways. When you're done, you'll take a final look at how FrontPage 2000 is used to publish on the World Wide Web.

Add a Spreadsheet to a Page

If you're offering numerical data on your FrontPage Web, one of the most effective ways to present it is as an Excel 2000 spreadsheet.

In the past, Excel spreadsheets had to be downloaded from the World Wide Web before they could be viewed. The user saved the file and then opened it in Excel if they had a copy of that software.

FrontPage 2000 makes this a speedier process by supporting Excel spreadsheets that run directly within a Web browser. You can put them on a page like any other component.

The spreadsheet and other Office components you'll learn about during this hour are implemented as ActiveX controls. *ActiveX* is a standard for creating interactive programs that run on Web pages. It was developed by Microsoft and is supported only by Internet Explorer 3.0 and later. For this reason, if your browser-compatibility settings for a Web include Netscape Navigator or WebTV, you can't add the spreadsheet, chart, or pivot table to the Web.

Choose Insert, Component, Office Spreadsheet to add an Excel spreadsheet to a Web page. The spreadsheet will appear in Page view just as it will appear on a Web page. It works like a spreadsheet, too, so you can enter values, formulas, and functions directly into it.

Figure 24.1 shows an Excel spreadsheet control on a Web page.

You can set up as much of the spreadsheet as you want within Page view, and this information will be retained when the page is loaded by a browser. When a person using Internet Explorer loads the page, the browser will check to see whether they already have Office 2000 controls on their system. If not, they will be given a chance to download and install the controls immediately. This happens automatically when you put one of these Office 2000 ActiveX controls on a Web page.

Visitors can change the values of the spreadsheet to see how it affects other calculations on the control, manipulating it as if they were using Excel 2000. These changes do not permanently affect the spreadsheet and cannot be saved with the browser.

FIGURE 24.1

Displaying a functional spreadsheet on a Web page.

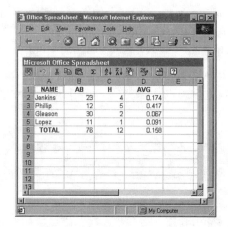

Add a Chart to a Page

Another way to enhance data presentation on your FrontPage Web is to add a graphical chart. The Office Chart component can be used to visually display the values from a data source, such as an Excel spreadsheet, Microsoft Access 2000 database, or a database that supports SQL.

The most common way to use an Office Chart component is to link it to an Excel spreadsheet on the same page. After adding the spreadsheet, choose Insert, Component, Office Chart to add a chart to the same page. This chart will be added as an ActiveX control, and you'll need Internet Explorer to view it.

An Office Chart wizard will guide you through the process of designing a chart. Figure 24.2 shows the wizard's first set of questions.

FIGURE 24.2

Creating an Office chart on a Web page.

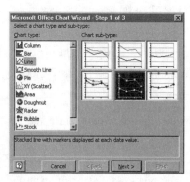

There are a dozen different ways to chart data with this control, including line graphs, bar charts, pies, doughnuts, and a few more unusual options. The Office Chart Wizard enables you to label the chart and display more than one set of values.

If the chart graphs data on an Excel spreadsheet, changes to the spreadsheet are immediately reflected in the chart. Figure 24.3 shows a spreadsheet-chart combination on a Web page.

FIGURE 24.3

Charting Excel data on the Web.

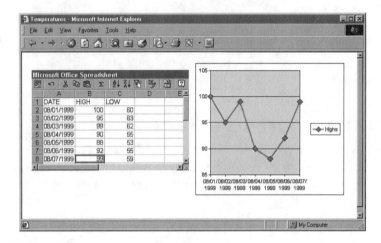

Add a Pivot Table to a Page

The third of the Office components is the most complex. Pivot tables offer a way to present data in a spreadsheet-like grid that can be easily rearranged.

For example, if you have a list of sales figures for a group of car salespersons and it's organized by year and car model, a pivot table can be rearranged several times to answer each of the following questions:

- Which salesperson sold the most Oldsmobiles during each year?
- How has each salesperson improved on a year-to-year basis?
- How many Saturns have been sold in each year?

Each of these questions requires that the same data be looked at in a different way. Pivot tables enable you to do this.

You add a pivot table to a page by choosing Insert, Component, Office PivotTable. However, you must first prepare the pivot table using an external program such as Access or Excel. You also may need to configure an OLE server or ODBC database connectivity source, so the task of establishing a pivot table is much more complicated than the other Office 2000 components.

> One of the benefits of Office 2000's increased Web support is that you can publish files created in Excel, Access, and other programs directly to a Web site. You also can save files from another Office 2000 program and import them to a FrontPage 2000 Web by running FrontPage and choosing File, Import.

Workshop: Publish and Promote a Real Web

Rather than focusing on the Office 2000 components introduced during this hour, this last workshop opens up the whole 24-hour chronology of this book for reassessment.

Your task is to publish a real FrontPage 2000 Web on the World Wide Web, something you're ready to leave online for the Web's multimillion-mouse audience to point-and-click their way through. If you bought this book with a specific project in mind, now's your chance to put the first version of it online.

Rather than publishing the Web directly to a server, create a copy of it on your system and publish it after everything's in place. This gives you a backup copy of the Web if the server crashes or goes out of business, and it also can be a faster way to work. Opening and closing Web pages over a dial-up Internet connection can be interminably slow at 56.6Kbps or 28.8Kbps modem speeds.

Before you start adding features to the Web, set the browser compatibility to match your desired audience. If you're still not sure, targeting Netscape Navigator and Internet Explorer 3.0 and later is a safe choice. You'll lose some of the newest features in FrontPage 2000, like Dynamic HTML and Cascading Style Sheets, but you'll cover more than 85 percent of the general audience currently surfing the World Wide Web.

The ideal place to publish your FrontPage Web is on a Microsoft Internet Information Server equipped with FrontPage Server Extensions. This may be more difficult to find than a host that uses Apache or another server program, but it lets you take advantage of FrontPage 2000 features such as site management, access control, and Active Server Pages.

Tell the World About Your Web

The final step in taking your FrontPage Web online is one with which FrontPage 2000 offers no help: telling the world about it.

24

There are several different software packages and Web sites that offer ways to promote your site and add it to popular directories, such as Yahoo, Snap, and Excite. After you publish your first Web, promote it by doing the following:

- Visit Yahoo at `http://www.yahoo.com` and find the directory page that your Web should be listed on. Follow Yahoo's guidelines for submitting your site to be listed in their directory.

- Visit the search engine AltaVista at `http://www.altavista.com`, and HotBot at `http://www.hotbot.com`. You can add your Web to these directories simply by submitting its address. The search engines will eventually visit your site and add all pages they can find that are linked to the home page.

- Visit the site-promotion service Submit It! at `http://www.submit-it.com` to announce your new Web simultaneously to many different Web directories and search engines. There are presently free features and pay features of Submit It!, so you can try out the free version to see if it's worth paying for later.

These are just a few of the places you can promote a new Web and get it listed in directories and search engines. They're among the most prominent places, though, so you can attract some visitors to your site quickly.

If you're having trouble finding the right page in Yahoo for your Web, search for a site that's similar to yours. If it has a listing in Yahoo, you can go directly to that page.

The prospects for getting a new Web site into Yahoo are generally dismal. There are far more submissions than the editors can evaluate, so you may have to try a few different times over several months to get a listing.

Buying ads on Yahoo changes everything, of course. The company markets several different ad campaigns for Web publishers who are trying to get into the directory, including a way to buy a space at the front of the submission line so editors see it more quickly.

Other Promotional Options

If your Web is devoted to a hobby or some other personal topic, you might want to consider joining a Web ring. Web rings are groups of sites with common subject matter that provide links to each other. If you've just published a Web comparing Scary Spice's impact on British society to that of Winston Churchill, you can probably find a Spice Girls Web ring that's looking for new members.

To find out more about Web rings, visit `http://www.webring.org`.

A new Web publisher should also consider acquiring a domain specifically for that site. At a current cost of $70 for the first two years and $35 for each successive year, the InterNIC registration authority will sell you a domain name in the `.com`, `.net`, and `.org` domains. For more information and to search for domains that are currently available, visit `http://www.internic.net`.

Make Your Web Spam-Proof

A last word of advice about your FrontPage Web: Don't use the `mailto` link. This is a way to send someone mail by clicking an email address on a Web page. For example, to add a link to the address `nowhere@noplace.com`, the following hyperlink is used: `mailto:nowhere@noplace.com`.

While these links are useful to visitors, they're being added to the mailing lists of those who send unsolicited commercial email—more commonly known as "spam"—at a prodigious rate. Spammers use programs that traverse the World Wide Web, looking for email addresses to add to their databases. One of the first things a new Web publisher learns is how quickly this can happen.

24

> The author of this book has published more than a dozen World Wide Web sites, each with a different email address that makes it easier to route incoming email. That was the *idea*, at least. In practice, it has become a remarkably efficient way to route the same "make-money-fast" schemes and pornographic advertisements into several different folders, because each email address was found by spammers.

If you can use FrontPage 2000's feedback form to receive email, providing a link to the form page instead of an email address is a good way to reduce the amount of unsolicited mail you receive.

Another, more drastic step is to edit the HTML of any page that contains your email address and replace the @ character with &64;. For example, here's the original HTML:

```
<a href="feedback.htm">Send mail to nowhere@noplace.com</a>
```

Here's the updated version:

```
<a href="feedback.htm">Send mail to nowhere&64;noplace.com</a>
```

The &64; is an HTML code for the @ character. It shows up on a page as if you used @, but most of the programs that hunt for email addresses skip right past it.

Some Web publishers replace all text versions of their email address with graphics that show the same address. This also makes them impossible for Web-surfing programs to find.

Publishing and promoting your first Web gives you a chance to develop working experience with this new medium. FrontPage 2000 simplifies many of the tasks required to develop an interesting Web, but there are no wizards in the program that substitute for the knowledge you'll gain by publishing a site on the World Wide Web. (Although Microsoft's probably working on one for release with FrontPage 2012.)

Summary

Twenty-four hours ago, give or take, you had a copy of FrontPage 2000 somewhere in the vicinity of your computer. After finishing all of the hour-long lessons in this book, you should have quite a bit of FrontPage 2000 knowledge in the vicinity of your brain.

FrontPage 2000, like most programs in the Office productivity suite, offers many more features than its users will generally need. At this point, you've mastered its essential features, including themes, templates, wizards, views, components, scripting, access control, and publishing. You've taken a barnstorming tour of the hot-button topics of World Wide Web development: HTML, Dynamic HTML, Cascading Style Sheets, Java, ActiveX, JavaScript, VBScript, and Active Server Pages. And you've also learned more about Office 2000, which is destined to quickly supplant the previous version of Office as the world's most popular productivity suite.

All of this stuff is taking up space in your brain along with things like sports trivia, the Magna Carta, restaurant tip mathematics, and the casts of television sitcoms from the '70s. Make the most of that real estate by using FrontPage 2000 to publish your own Webs.

Your pages will be at home on the World Wide Web, regardless of whether the things you're interested in are serious, significant, or silly. It's the second-largest repository of useful and useless information in the world.

As the author of this book, I hope you're as pleased with your FrontPage 2000 expertise as I am of my comprehensive knowledge of *Happy Days*.

I also hope you don't have to wait 20 years to use it.

Q&A

Q When I add a pivot table to a new page, it says "no data source". How can I fix this?

A Unlike the other Office components, the pivot table must be developed in Access or Excel before you can work with it on a FrontPage 2000 Web.

Pivot tables require a data source to be configured and the table to be fully arranged. These processes are documented in Access and Excel rather than in FrontPage, and you may need to master that software before you're ready to work with pivot table components in FrontPage 2000.

Exercises

Challenge your knowledge of FrontPage 2000 Office components with the following exercises:

- Create an Excel spreadsheet that contains a stock's high and low prices for two weeks, making up a fictitious stock if you don't have access to real data. Add an Office chart that graphs both figures for all 14 days.

- Visit this book's World Wide Web site at http://www.fp2k.com/24 to learn more about FrontPage 2000 and this book. Pat yourself on the back a few times, too—if anyone else sees you, tell them you're doing an ergonomic exercise.

24

PART VII

Appendixes

Hour

APPENDIX A

HTML 4.0 Quick Reference

All World Wide Web documents are created using Hypertext Markup Language, also called HTML. This language enables you to create Web documents by "marking up" a document with hidden tags. These HTML tags determine the presentation, structure, and interactivity of a Web document and are surrounded by the < and > characters. Some examples are the <P> tag for paragraphs, the <BR> tag for line breaks, and the <IMG> tag for images.

Although you don't see any of these tags when a Web document is loaded into a browser, you see all of the effects they create on the document.

For the most part, you'll probably create Web pages in FrontPage 2000 without ever looking at these HTML tags. Many people find it easier to work with an editor like FrontPage 2000 that works with HTML behind the scenes, hiding the complexities of the language.

To see the HTML tags being used to create a FrontPage 2000 Web document, click the HTML tab at the bottom edge of the FrontPage editor.

This appendix provides a quick way to look up the purpose and function of any HTML tag that you encounter in a document. It covers HTML 4.0, the current version of the language according to the World Wide Web Consortium.

> The World Wide Web Consortium, also called the W3C, created HTML in the early 1990s. The organization continues to shepherd the language and all future developments related to it. For a full HTML 4.0 specification, visit the following Web page: `http://www.w3.org/MarkUp/`.

The following terms are used throughout this appendix:

- A URI is a Uniform Resource Identifier, which identifies a resource on the World Wide Web. In other words, this is the address of a Web page or another type of document on the Web.

- Metadata is information that describes a document rather than being part of that document.

- A Deprecated element is something introduced in a prior version of HTML that has been replaced as of HTML 4.0.

Common Attributes

Many of the tags in HTML 4.0 have the same attributes. The following list describes the most commonplace ones:

- `accesskey="character"`—On form controls and anchors, a single character that can be entered to access the document element.

- `align="text"`—The alignment of information in a section of a document.

- `alt="text"`—Alternate text that describes images, forms, objects, and other parts of a document.

- `char="character"`—The character that acts as an axis of alignment when the contents of a table are being lined up.

- `charoff="number"`—The number of spaces to offset the axis character when you're aligning table contents.

- class="*text*"—One or more class names to assign to the document element, separated by blank spaces.
- dir="*text*"—The direction of text and tables—either "ltr" (left-to-right) or "rtl" (right-to-left).
- disabled—An attribute that disables a control on a form so that it cannot handle user input.
- id="*text*"—The name to give the document element.
- lang="*text*"—The language used in a document element's attributes and its enclosed text.
- name="*text*"—A name for the document element.
- onblur="*script*"—An event that occurs when a document element loses the user input focus.
- onchange="*script*"—An event that occurs when a document element loses the user input focus and its value was changed while it had the focus.
- onclick="*script*"—An event that occurs when the user clicks the mouse on the document element.
- ondblclick="*script*"—An event that occurs when the user double-clicks the mouse over the document element.
- onfocus="*script*"—An event that occurs when a document element receives the user input focus.
- onkeydown="*script*"—An event that occurs when a key is pressed.
- onkeypress="*script*"—An event that occurs when a key is pressed and released.
- onkeyup="*script*"—An event that occurs when a key is released.
- onload="*script*"—An event that occurs when an entire document or all frames within a frameset have been loaded.
- onmousedown="*script*"—An event that occurs when the user clicks the mouse while the cursor is over the document element.
- onmouseout="*script*"—An event that occurs when a cursor that is over a document element moves away from that element.
- onmouseover="*script*"—An event that occurs when a mouse cursor is moved over a document element.
- onmousemove="*script*"—An event that occurs when a mouse cursor is moved while over a document element.

A

- `onmouseup="script"`—An event that occurs when the user releases the mouse button while the cursor is over the document element.
- `onreset="script"`—An event that occurs when all controls on a form have been reset.
- `onselect="script"`—An event that occurs when text in a text-editing user control has been selected.
- `="script"`—An event that occurs when a form is submitted.
- `onunload="script"`—An event that occurs when a document has been unloaded from a window or frame.
- `readonly`—An attribute indicating that the value in a form control cannot be edited.
- `style="text"`—Style information for this individual document element.
- `tabindex="number"`—The place in the tab order of the document element.
- `target="text"`—The name of the frame in which a document should be opened.
- `title="text"`—Explanatory text about a document element.
- `usemap="URI"`—The URI of an imagemap to associate with the document element, which must match the `name` attribute of an existing `<MAP>` element.
- `valign="text"`—The vertical alignment of information within table cells.

Tags

Each of the following sections defines a tag that's a part of the HTML 4.0 specification for the language.

The tags are listed here using uppercase letters. Although traditionally the case of tags has been irrelevant, it seems that the W3C's future specifications may require most tags to use only lowercase letters (`<!DOCTYPE>` being the only exception listed here). What this means is that if you find yourself coding HTML, you want to be sure that you are using lowercase tags or you may find yourself having to change them a few years down the road.

<!DOCTYPE…>

- **Purpose**: This tag appears as the first line of a document and declares the HTML version that it uses.
- **Start Tag**: Required
- **End Tag**: Not allowed
- **Attributes**: None
- **Deprecated Attributes**: None
- **Other Attributes**: None

One of the following three <!DOCTYPE> tags is used:

```
<!DOCTYPE HTML PUBLIC "-//W3C//DTD HTML 4.0//EN"
    "http://www.w3.org/TR/REC-html40/strict.dtd">

<!DOCTYPE HTML PUBLIC "-//W3C//DTD HTML 4.0 Transitional//EN"
    "http://www.w3.org/TR/REC-html40/loose.dtd">

<!DOCTYPE HTML PUBLIC "-//W3C//DTD HTML 4.0 Frameset//EN"
    "http://www.w3.org/TR/REC-html40/frameset.dtd">
```

Each of these tags contains a URI. The filenames of these URIs are strict.dtd, loose.dtd, and frameset.dtd, respectively. These names describe the level of HTML 4.0 support in the document, as follows:

- **Strict**: Document doesn't use anything that has been deprecated and doesn't use frames.
- **Loose**: Document uses some deprecated elements of the language that involve visual presentation.
- **Frameset**: Document uses the same deprecated elements as the preceding level and also contains frames.

Ideally, the strict <!DOCTYPE> should be declared because it is fully compliant with HTML 4.0. The main reason to use the loose <!DOCTYPE> is because some presentation-related elements of HTML 4.0 such as style sheets are not fully adopted by the Web browser developers yet.

<A>...</A>

- **Purpose**: This tag encloses an anchor—a part of a document that is associated with another resource on the World Wide Web. It also can be used to create an association between two sections of the same document.

A

- **Start Tag**: Required
- **End Tag**: Required
- **Special Attributes**:

  coords="*text*"—The coordinates of the geometric shape of an imagemap area associated with the anchor

  name="*text*"—The name of the anchor

  href="*URI*"—A resource on the Web, specified by its URI, that the anchor should be associated with

  hreflang="*text*"—The language of the resource identified by an href attribute

  type="*name*"—The content type of the associated resource on the Web

  rel="*link_types*"—The relationship of the current document to the associated resource on the Web

  rev="*link_types*"—The relationship of the associated resource on the Web to the current document

  shape="*text*"—The geometric shape of an imagemap area associated with the anchor

  charset="text"—The character set of the associated resource on the Web

- **Deprecated Attributes**: None
- **Other Attributes**: accesskey, class, dir, id, lang, onblur, onclick, ondblclick, onfocus, onkeydown, onkeypress, onkeyup, onmousedown, onmousemove, onmouseout, onmouseover, onmouseup, style, tabindex, target, title

<ABBR>...</ABBR>

- **Purpose**: This tag encloses text that is an abbreviation.
- **Start Tag**: Required
- **End Tag**: Required
- **Special Attributes**: None
- **Deprecated Attributes**: None
- **Other Attributes**: class, dir, id, lang, onclick, ondblclick, onkeydown, onkeypress, onkeyup, onmousedown, onmousemove, onmouseout, onmouseover, onmouseup, style, title

<ACRONYM>...</ACRONYM>

- **Purpose**: This tag encloses text that is an acronym.
- **Start Tag**: Required
- **End Tag**: Required
- **Special Attributes**: None
- **Deprecated Attributes**: None
- **Other Attributes**: class, dir, id, lang, onclick, ondblclick, onkeydown, onkeypress, onkeyup, onmousedown, onmousemove, onmouseout, onmouseover, onmouseup, style, title

<ADDRESS>...</ADDRESS>

- **Purpose**: This tag encloses contact information about the author of an entire document or a specific section of a document. Most Web browsers display this information in a different manner than other text.
- **Start Tag**: Required
- **End Tag**: Required
- **Special Attributes**: None
- **Deprecated Attributes**: None
- **Other Attributes**: class, dir, id, lang, onclick, ondblclick, onkeydown, onkeypress, onkeyup, onmousedown, onmousemove, onmouseout, onmouseover, onmouseup

<APPLET>

- **Purpose**: This tag has been deprecated. Most browsers today support the <OBJECT> tag for Java applets. In the case of the Java Plug-In one would use the <EMBED> tag just as one would for any other plug-in.

<AREA>

- **Purpose**: This tag indicates an area on an imagemap that should be associated with a link.
- **Start Tag**: Required
- **End Tag**: Not allowed

A

- **Special Attributes**:

  href="*URI*"—A URI that the imagemap area should be associated with.

  shape="*text*"—The geometric shape of the area.

  coords="*text*"—The coordinates of the geometric shape.

  nohref—This attribute indicates that the area has no link associated with it.

- **Deprecated Attributes**: None
- **Other Attributes**: accesskey, alt, class, dir, id, lang, name, onblur, onclick, ondblclick, onfocus, onkeydown, onkeypress, onkeyup, onmousedown, onmousemove, onmouseout, onmouseover, onmouseup, style, tabindex, target, title

\<B>...\</B>

- **Purpose**: This tag encloses text that should be displayed in boldface. Although it has not been deprecated, the HTML 4.0 specification advises that style sheets are a better alternative.
- **Start Tag**: Required
- **End Tag**: Required
- **Special Attributes**: None
- **Deprecated Attributes**: None
- **Other Attributes**: class, dir, id, lang, onclick, ondblclick, onkeydown, onkeypress, onkeyup, onmousedown, onmousemove, onmouseout, onmouseover, onmouseup, style, title

\<BASE>

- **Purpose**: This tag is used to explicitly define the base URI for the document. This base URI will be combined with each relative URI in the document to form a full address to a resource on the Web.
- **Start Tag**: Required
- **End Tag**: Not allowed
- **Special Attributes**:

  href="*URI*"—The base URI of the document.

- **Deprecated Attributes**: None
- **Other Attributes**: target

\<BASEFONT\>...\</BASEFONT\>

- **Purpose**: This tag has been deprecated.

\<BIG\>...\</BIG\>

- **Purpose**: This tag encloses text that should be displayed in a larger-than-normal font. Although it has not been deprecated, the HTML 4.0 specification advises that style sheets are a better alternative.
- **Start Tag**: Required
- **End Tag**: Required
- **Special Attributes**: None
- **Deprecated Attributes**: None
- **Other Attributes**: `class, dir, id, lang, onclick, ondblclick, onkeydown, onkeypress, onkeyup, onmousedown, onmousemove, onmouseout, onmouseover, onmouseup, style, title`

\<BLOCKQUOTE\>...\</BLOCKQUOTE\>

- **Purpose**: This tag encloses a block of quoted text, which will be indented and displayed in its own paragraph when the document is viewed. A shorter quote can be enclosed within the `<Q>` tag.
- **Start Tag**: Required
- **End Tag**: Required
- **Special Attributes**:

    `cite="URI"`—The address of a document containing information about the source of the quotation.
- **Deprecated Attributes**: None
- **Other Attributes**: `class, dir, id, lang, onclick, ondblclick, onkeydown, onkeypress, onkeyup, onmousedown, onmousemove, onmouseout, onmouseover, onmouseup, style, title`

The `<BLOCKQUOTE>` tag commonly is used to indent a block of text even if it's not a quotation. This usage has been deprecated in HTML 4.0, in favor of using style sheets to achieve the same effect.

A

\<BODY>...\</BODY>

- **Purpose**: This tag encloses the content of the document, which should be displayed when it's loaded by a program such as a Web browser. Several popular presentation attributes have been deprecated, in favor of using the \<STYLE> tag to accomplish the same task.
- **Start Tag**: Optional
- **End Tag**: Optional
- **Special Attributes**: None
- **Deprecated Attributes**: alink, background, bgcolor, link, text, vlink
- **Other Attributes**: class, dir, id, lang, onclick, ondblclick, onkeydown, onkeyup, onkeypress, onload, onmousedown, onmousemove, onmouseout, onmouseover, onmouseup, onunload, style, title

\

- **Purpose**: This tag inserts a line break in a document, causing subsequent text and other elements to be displayed on a new line.
- **Start Tag**: Required
- **End Tag**: Not allowed
- **Special Attributes**: None
- **Deprecated Attributes**: clear
- **Other Attributes**: class, id, style, title

\<BUTTON>...\</BUTTON>

- **Purpose**: This tag adds a button control to a form.
- **Start Tag**: Required
- **End Tag**: Required
- **Special Attributes**:

  name="*text*"—The name of the button.

  value="*text*"—The initial value of the button.

  type="*text*"—The type of button to add to the form.
- **Deprecated Attributes**: None
- **Other Attributes**: accesskey, class, dir, disabled, id, lang, onblur, onclick, ondblclick, onfocus, onkeydown, onkeyup, onkeypress, onmousedown, onmousemove, onmouseout, onmouseover, onmouseup, style, tabindex, title

<CAPTION>...</CAPTION>

- **Purpose**: This tag encloses a short description of a table. The <CAPTION> tag must immediately follow a <TABLE> tag, and a table can have only one caption.
- **Start Tag**: Required
- **End Tag**: Required
- **Special Attributes**: None
- **Deprecated Attributes**: align
- **Other Attributes**: class, dir, id, lang, onclick, ondblclick, onkeydown, onkeyup, onkeypress, onload, onmousedown, onmousemove, onmouseout, onmouseover, onmouseup, onunload, style, title

<CENTER>...</CENTER>

- **Purpose**: This tag has been deprecated.

<CITE>...</CITE>

- **Purpose**: This tag encloses a citation or some other kind of reference to another source.
- **Start Tag**: Required
- **End Tag**: Required
- **Special Attributes**: None
- **Deprecated Attributes**: None
- **Other Attributes**: class, dir, id, lang, onclick, ondblclick, onkeydown, onkeypress, onkeyup, onmousedown, onmousemove, onmouseout, onmouseover, onmouseup, style, title

A

<CODE>...</CODE>

- **Purpose**: This tag encloses text that reprints source code from a computer programming language or similar information.
- **Start Tag**: Required
- **End Tag**: Required
- **Special Attributes**: None
- **Deprecated Attributes**: None
- **Other Attributes**: class, dir, id, lang, onclick, ondblclick, onkeydown, onkeypress, onkeyup, onmousedown, onmousemove, onmouseout, onmouseover, onmouseup, style, title

<COL>...</COL>

- **Purpose**: This tag encloses a column in a table so that it can be structured.
- **Start Tag**: Required
- **End Tag**: Not allowed
- **Special Attributes**:

  span="*number*"—The number of columns in the column group.

  width="*number*"—The default width for columns in the column group.

- **Deprecated Attributes**: None
- **Other Attributes**: align, char, charoff, class, dir, id, lang, onclick, ondblclick, onkeydown, onkeypress, onkeyup, onmousedown, onmousemove, onmouseout, onmouseover, onmouseup, style, title, valign

<COLGROUP>...</COLGROUP>

- **Purpose**: This tag encloses a group of columns in a table so that they can be structured at the same time.
- **Start Tag**: Required
- **End Tag**: Optional
- **Special Attributes**:

  span="*number*"—The number of columns in the column group.

  width="*number*"—The default width for columns in the column group.

- **Deprecated Attributes**: None
- **Other Attributes**: align, char, charoff, class, dir, id, lang, onclick, ondblclick, onkeydown, onkeypress, onkeyup, onmousedown, onmousemove, onmouseout, onmouseover, onmouseup, style, title, valign

<DEL>...</DEL>

- **Purpose**: This tag encloses a section of a document that has been deleted since a previous edition of the document. Text within this tag often is displayed by using strikethrough characters.
- **Start Tag**: Required
- **End Tag**: Required

- **Special Attributes**:

  `cite="URI"`—The address of a document containing information about the inserted section.

  `datetime="date_and_time"`—The time and date that the insertion was made.

- **Other Attributes**: `class, dir, id, lang, onclick, ondblclick, onkeydown, onkeypress, onkeyup, onmousedown, onmousemove, onmouseout, onmouseover, onmouseup, style, title`

<DD>...</DD>

- **Purpose**: This tag encloses a block of text that provides a definition for a term, which itself is enclosed within a <DD> tag. A list of terms and definitions is enclosed within a <DL> tag.
- **Start Tag**: Required
- **End Tag**: Optional
- **Special Attributes**: `class, dir, id, lang, onclick, ondblclick, onkeydown, onkeypress, onkeyup, onmousedown, onmousemove, onmouseout, onmouseover, onmouseup, style, title`

<DFN>...</DFN>

- **Purpose**: This tag encloses text that's either a definition or something that's being defined.
- **Start Tag**: Required
- **End Tag**: Required
- **Special Attributes**: None
- **Deprecated Attributes**: None
- **Other Attributes**: `class, dir, id, lang, onclick, ondblclick, onkeydown, onkeyup, onmousedown, onmousemove, onmouseout, onmouseover, onmouseup, style, title`

<DIR>...</DIR>

- **Purpose**: This tag has been deprecated.

A

<DIV>...</DIV>

- **Purpose**: This tag encloses a section of a document into its own block. It's used as a way to organize the content internally and can be used with attributes to affect the presentation of the section.
- **Start Tag**: Required
- **End Tag**: Required
- **Special Attributes**: None
- **Deprecated Attributes**: align
- **Other Attributes**: class, dir, id, lang, onclick, ondblclick, onkeydown, onkeypress, onkeyup, onmousedown, onmousemove, onmouseout, onmouseover, onmouseup, style, title

<DL>...</DL>

- **Purpose**: This tag encloses a list of terms and their definitions. The terms and definitions are enclosed within <DT> and <DD> tags, respectively.
- **Start Tag**: Required
- **End Tag**: Required
- **Special Attributes**: class, dir, id, lang, onclick, ondblclick, onkeydown, onkeypress, onkeyup, onmousedown, onmousemove, onmouseout, onmouseover, onmouseup, style, title

<DT>...</DT>

- **Purpose**: <DT> defines a block of text as a single term in a definition type list. A collection of terms and definitions are enclosed within a <DL> tag.
- **Start Tag**: Required
- **End Tag**: Optional
- **Special Attributes**: class, dir, id, lang, onclick, ondblclick, onkeydown, onkeypress, onkeyup, onmousedown, onmousemove, onmouseout, onmouseover, onmouseup, style, title

<EM>...</EM>

- **Purpose**: This tag encloses text that needs a special emphasis. Most Web browsers will display this text in italics. For a stronger emphasis, use the <STRONG> tag.
- **Start Tag**: Required
- **End Tag**: Required

- **Special Attributes**: None
- **Deprecated Attributes**: None
- **Other Attributes**: `class`, `dir`, `id`, `lang`, `onclick`, `ondblclick`, `onkeydown`, `onkeypress`, `onkeyup`, `onmousedown`, `onmousemove`, `onmouseout`, `onmouseover`, `onmouseup`, `style`, `title`

`<FIELDSET>...</FIELDSET>`

- **Purpose**: This tag encloses a group of related controls on a form.
- **Start Tag**: Required
- **End Tag**: Required
- **Special Attributes**: None
- **Deprecated Attributes**: `align`
- **Other Attributes**: `accesskey`, `class`, `dir`, `id`, `lang`, `onclick`, `ondblclick`, `onkeydown`, `onkeypress`, `onkeyup`, `onmousedown`, `onmousemove`, `onmouseout`, `onmouseover`, `onmouseup`, `style`, `title`

`<FONT>...</FONT>`

- **Purpose**: This tag has been deprecated.

`<FORM>...</FORM>`

- **Purpose**: This tag encloses a group of related controls that take information from the person browsing the document.
- **Start Tag**: Required
- **End Tag**: Required
- **Special Attributes**:

  `action="URI"`—The URI that will receive and process the results of the form.

  `method="text"`—The method that will be used to transmit the form results.

  `enctype="text"`—The content type used to transmit the form results.

  `accept-charset="text"`—One or more character sets, separated by commas, that must be accepted in the form results.

  `accept="text"`—One or more content types, separated by commas, that can be transmitted successfully by using the form.

A

- **Deprecated Attributes**: None
- **Other Attributes**: class, dir, id, lang, onclick, ondblclick, onkeydown, onkeypress, onkeyup, onmousedown, onmousemove, onmouseout, onmouseover, onmouseup, onreset, onsubmit, style, target, title

\<FRAME>...\</FRAME>

- **Purpose**: This tag encloses a frame and establishes its appearance.
- **Start Tag**: Required
- **End Tag**: Not allowed
- **Special Attributes**:

  name="*text*"—The name of the frame.

  longdesc="*URI*"—The URI to a document that contains a long description of the frame.

  src="*URI*"—The URI of a document that contains the contents of the frame.

  noresize—An attribute that indicates the frame cannot be resized.

  scrolling="*text*"—How scrolling is handled for the frame.

  frameborder="*number*"—Whether a border exists around the frame.

  marginwidth="*number*"—The space between the frame's contents and its left and right borders.

  marginheight="*number*"—The space between the frame's contents and its top and bottom borders.

- **Deprecated Attributes**: None
- **Other Attributes**: class, id, style, target, title

\<FRAMESET>...\</FRAMESET>

- **Purpose**: This tag encloses information that establishes the arrangement of frames in a document. It's used in place of the \<BODY> tag and should immediately follow the document's header.
- **Start Tag**: Required
- **End Tag**: Required
- **Special Attributes**:

  rows="*list*"—The height of each vertical frame in the frameset, with values separated by commas.

  cols="*list*"—The width of each horizontal frame in the frameset, with values separated by commas.

- **Deprecated Attributes**: None
- **Other Attributes**: class, id, onload, onunload, style, title

\<HEAD\>...\</HEAD\>

- **Purpose**: This tag encloses header information that describes a document, such as its title and a description of its content. The information inside this tag is not displayed when the page is shown in a browser.
- **Start Tag**: Optional
- **End Tag**: Optional
- **Special Attributes**:

  profile="*URI*"—The address of a document containing information about the metadata that can be defined in the header.
- **Deprecated Attributes**: None
- **Other Attributes**: lang, dir

\<H1\>...\</H1\>, \<H2\>...\</H2\>, \<H3\>...\</H3\>, \<H4\>...\</H4\>, \<H5\>...\</H5\>, and \<H6\>...\</H6\>

- **Purpose**: Each of these tags encloses a heading—also called a *headline*—that is presented on a document. These headings range from \<H1\> (most prominent) to \<H6\> (least prominent).
- **Start Tag**: Required
- **End Tag**: Required
- **Special Attributes**: None
- **Deprecated Attributes**: align
- **Other Attributes**: class, dir, id, lang, onclick, ondblclick, onkeydown, onkeypress, onkeyup, onmousedown, onmousemove, onmouseout, onmouseover, onmouseup, style, title

\<HR\>

- **Purpose**: This tag causes a horizontal line—also called a *rule*—to be displayed as part of a document.
- **Start Tag**: Required
- **End Tag**: Not allowed
- **Special Attributes**: None

- **Deprecated Attributes**: `align`, `noshade`, `size`, `width`
- **Other Attributes**: `class`, `dir`, `id`, `lang`, `onclick`, `ondblclick`, `onkeydown`, `onkeypress`, `onkeyup`, `onmousedown`, `onmousemove`, `onmouseout`, `onmouseover`, `onmouseup`, `style`, `title`

`<HTML>...</HTML>`

- **Purpose**: This tag encloses an HTML document in its entirety.
- **Start Tag**: Optional
- **End Tag**: Optional
- **Special Attributes**: None
- **Deprecated Attributes**: `version`
- **Other Attributes**: `lang`, `dir`

`<I>...</I>`

- **Purpose**: This tag encloses text that should be italicized. Although it hasn't been deprecated, the HTML 4.0 specification advises that style sheets are a better alternative.
- **Start Tag**: Required
- **End Tag**: Required
- **Special Attributes**: None
- **Deprecated Attributes**: None
- **Other Attributes**: `class`, `dir`, `id`, `lang`, `onclick`, `ondblclick`, `onkeydown`, `onkeypress`, `onkeyup`, `onmousedown`, `onmousemove`, `onmouseout`, `onmouseover`, `onmouseup`, `style`, `title`

`<IFRAME>...</IFRAME>`

- **Purpose**: This tag encloses a frame that is inserted into a document in the same manner as images and other objects.
- **Start Tag**: Required
- **End Tag**: Required
- **Special Attributes**:

  `frameborder="number"`—Whether a border exists around the frame.

  `longdesc="URI"`—The URI of a document containing a long description of the frame.

marginheight="*number*"—The space between the frame's contents and its top and bottom borders.

marginwidth="*number*"—The space between the frame's contents and its left and right borders.

name="*text*"—The name of the frame.

scrolling="*text*"—How scrolling is handled for the frame.

src="*URI*"—The URI of a document that contains the contents of the frame.

width="*number*"—The width of the frame.

height="*number*"—The height of the frame.

- **Deprecated Attributes**: None
- **Other Attributes**: align, class, id, name, style, target, title

<IMG>

- **Purpose**: This tag encloses an image file that's displayed as part of the document. The <OBJECT> tag also can be used to display image files.
- **Start Tag**: Required
- **End Tag**: Not allowed
- **Special Attributes**:

height="*number*"—The height of the image.

hspace="*number*"—The amount of whitespace to insert in a document between the image and the other information to the left and right of it.

ismap—An attribute that indicates the image is a server-side imagemap.

src="*URI*"—The URI of the image file.

longdesc="*URI*"—The URI of a comprehensive description of the image and any imagemaps it contains.

vspace="*number*"—The amount of whitespace to insert in a document between the image and the other information above and below it.

width="*number*"—The width of the image.

- **Deprecated Attributes**: align, border
- **Other Attributes**: alt, class, dir, id, ismap, lang, onclick, ondblclick, onkeydown, onkeypress, onkeyup, onmousedown, onmousemove, onmouseout, onmouseover, onmouseup, style, title, usemap

A

<INPUT>

- **Purpose**: This tag encloses a control that is part of a form.
- **Start Tag**: Required
- **End Tag**: Not allowed
- **Special Attributes**:

  accept—A list of content types, separated by commas, that can be transmitted successfully by the server that's processing the form.

  name="*text*"—The name of the control.

  type="*text*"—The type of control to include on the form.

  value="*text*"—The initial value of the control.

  size="*number*"—The size of the control's input area.

  maxlength="*number*"—The maximum number of characters that can be entered into a control's text input area.

  checked—This attribute indicates that a radio or check box control should be selected when the form is first displayed.

  src="*URI*"—The URI of an image to display as a Submit button.

- **Deprecated Attributes**: None
- **Other Attributes**: accesskey, align, alt, class, dir, disabled, id, lang, onblur, onchange, onclick, ondblclick, onfocus, onkeydown, onkeypress, onkeyup, onmousedown, onmouseover, onmousemove, onmouseout, onmouseup, onselect, readonly, style, tabindex, title, usemap

<INS>...</INS>

- **Purpose**: This tag encloses a section of a document that has been inserted since a previous edition of the document.
- **Start Tag**: Required
- **End Tag**: Required
- **Special Attributes**:

  cite="*URI*"—The address of a document containing information about the inserted section.

  datetime="*date_and_time*"—The time and date that the insertion was made.

- **Other Attributes**: class, dir, id, lang, onclick, ondblclick, onkeydown, onkeypress, onkeyup, onmousedown, onmousemove, onmouseout, onmouseover, onmouseup, style, title

`<ISINDEX>`

- **Purpose**: This tag has been deprecated.

`<KBD>...</KBD>`

- **Purpose**: This tag encloses text that should be entered by a user in a computer program or similar information.
- **Start Tag**: Required
- **End Tag**: Required
- **Special Attributes**: None
- **Deprecated Attributes**: None
- **Other Attributes**: class, dir, id, lang, onclick, ondblclick, onkeydown, onkeypress, onkeyup, onmousedown, onmousemove, onmouseout, onmouseover, onmouseup, style, title

`<LABEL>...</LABEL>`

- **Purpose**: This tag is used to provide a label for form controls that don't already have them.
- **Start Tag**: Required
- **End Tag**: Required
- **Special Attributes**:

  for="text"—The ID name of the control that this label is associated with.
- **Deprecated Attributes**: None
- **Other Attributes**: accesskey, class, dir, id, lang, onblur, onclick, ondblclick, onfocus, onkeydown, onkeypress, onkeyup, onmousedown, onmousemove, onmouseout, onmouseover, onmouseup, style, title

`<LEGEND>...</LEGEND>`

- **Purpose**: This tag provides a caption for a group of controls that have been associated with each other using the `<FIELDSET>` tag. This tag must be enclosed within the `<FIELDSET>` tag.
- **Start Tag**: Required
- **End Tag**: Required
- **Special Attributes**: None
- **Deprecated Attributes**: align

A

- **Other Attributes**: accesskey, class, dir, id, lang, onclick, ondblclick, onkeydown, onkeypress, onkeyup, onmousedown, onmousemove, onmouseout, onmouseover, onmouseup, style, title

\<LI>...\</LI>

- **Purpose**: This tag encloses a list of items that will be individually numbered. Each item in the list is identified by the \<LI> tag. To display a list without numbering, use the \<UL> tag.
- **Start Tag**: Required
- **End Tag**: Optional
- **Special Attributes**: None
- **Deprecated Attributes**: compact, type, value
- **Other Attributes**: class, dir, id, lang, onclick, ondblclick, onkeydown, onkeypress, onkeyup, onmousedown, onmousemove, onmouseout, onmouseover, onmouseup, style, title

\<LINK>...\</LINK>

- **Purpose**: This tag defines a link—a relationship between this document and other resources. More than one of these relationships can be defined, but \<LINK> can be used only in the header section of a document.
- **Start Tag**: Required
- **End Tag**: Not allowed
- **Special Attributes**:

  name="*text*"—The name of the anchor.

  href="*URI*"—A resource on the Web, specified by its URI, that the anchor should be associated with.

  hreflang="*text*"—The language of the resource identified by an href attribute.

  media="*text*"—The intended medium of style sheet information.

  type="*name*"—The content type of the associated resource on the Web.

  rel="*link_types*"—The relationship of the current document to the associated resource on the Web.

  rev="*link_types*"—The relationship of the associated resource on the Web to the current document.

  charset="*text*"—The character set of the associated resource on the Web.

- **Deprecated Attributes**: None
- **Other Attributes**: accesskey, class, dir, id, lang, onclick, ondblclick, onkeydown, onkeypress, onkeyup, onmousedown, onmousemove, onmouseout, onmouseover, onmouseup, style, tabindex, target, title

<MAP>...</MAP>

- **Purpose**: This tag encloses a client-side imagemap that associates areas on an object with links.
- **Start Tag**: Required
- **End Tag**: Required
- **Special Attributes**:

  name="text"—The name of the imagemap.
- **Deprecated Attributes**: None
- **Other Attributes**: class, dir, id, lang, onclick, ondblclick, onkeydown, onkeypress, onkeyup, onmousedown, onmousemove, onmouseout, onmouseover, onmouseup, style, title

<MENU>...</MENU>

- **Purpose**: This tag has been deprecated.

<META>

- **Purpose**: This tag defines a metadata property for the document, which can contain several different properties.
- **Start Tag**: Required
- **End Tag**: Not allowed
- **Special Attributes**:

  name="text"—The name of the property.

  content="text"—The value of the property.

  http-equiv="text"—The name of an HTTP Response Header that will be set to this tag's value (http-equiv is used as an alternative to the name attribute).

  scheme="text"—Additional information that describes how the content attribute has been used.
- **Deprecated Attributes**: None
- **Other Attributes**: lang, dir

A

<NOFRAMES>...</NOFRAMES>

- **Purpose**: This tag encloses content that is an alternative to frames in the same document. Browsers that don't support frames will display this alternative content instead. The <NOFRAMES> tag should be used within a <FRAMESET> tag.
- **Start Tag**: Required
- **End Tag**: Required
- **Special Attributes**: None
- **Deprecated Attributes**: None
- **Other Attributes**: class, dir, lang, id, onclick, ondblclick, onkeydown, onkeypress, onkeyup, onmousedown, onmousemove, onmouseout, onmouseover, onmouseup, style, title

<NOSCRIPT>...</NOSCRIPT>

- **Purpose**: This tag encloses content that is displayed when a script is not executed, either because the browsing software doesn't handle scripts or because it doesn't handle the script language being used.
- **Start Tag**: Required
- **End Tag**: Required
- **Special Attributes**:

  src="URI"—The URI of a document containing the script.

  type="text"—The scripting language being used.

  defer—This attribute indicates that the script doesn't add any content to the document.

- **Deprecated Attributes**: language
- **Other Attributes**: class, dir, id, lang, onclick, ondblclick, onkeydown, onkeypress, onkeyup, onmousedown, onmousemove, onmouseout, onmouseover, onmouseup, style, title

<OBJECT>...</OBJECT>

- **Purpose**: This tag encloses an object that is presented as part of the document. Objects can be files, interactive programs, and other HTML documents.
- **Start Tag**: Required
- **End Tag**: Required

- **Special Attributes**:

classid=*"URI"*—The URI of an object's implementation, which can be used in place of the data attribute or in conjunction with it, depending on the type of object.

codebase=*"URI"*—The base URI for other URIs specified as attributes of the object.

codetype=*"text"*—The content type of the data identified by the classid attribute.

data=*"URI"*—The URI of the data associated with the object.

height=*"number"*—The height of the object.

hspace=*"number"*—The amount of whitespace to insert in a document between the object and the other information to the left and right of it.

width=*"number"*—The width of the object.

type=*"text"*—The content type of the data identified by the data attribute.

archive=*"URIs"*—The URIs of any archive files that contain classid and data for faster downloading.

declare—An attribute that indicates this object is being declared but should not be presented until a subsequent <OBJECT> tag does so.

standby=*"text"*—A message that should be displayed while the object is being downloaded.

vspace=*"number"*—The amount of whitespace to insert in a document between the image and the other information above and below it.

- **Deprecated Attributes**: align, border
- **Other Attributes**: class, dir, id, lang, name, onclick, ondblclick, onkeydown, onkeypress, onkeyup, onmousedown, onmousemove, onmouseout, onmouseover, onmouseup, style, tabindex, title, usemap

<OL>...</OL>

- **Purpose**: This tag encloses a list of items that will be individually numbered. Each item in the list is identified by the <LI> tag. To display a list without numbering, the <UL> tag is used.
- **Start Tag**: Required
- **End Tag**: Required
- **Special Attributes**: None

- **Deprecated Attributes**: compact, start, type
- **Other Attributes**: class, dir, id, lang, onclick, ondblclick, onkeydown, onkeypress, onkeyup, onmousedown, onmousemove, onmouseout, onmouseover, onmouseup, style, title

<OPTION>...</OPTION>

- **Purpose**: This tag adds a choice to a menu control on a form.
- **Start Tag**: Required
- **End Tag**: Optional
- **Special Attributes**:

  selected—This attribute indicates that this option should be selected when the menu is first displayed.

  value="text"—The initial value of the option.

  label="text"—A shorter label of the option that can be used as an alternative.
- **Deprecated Attributes**: None
- **Other Attributes**: class, dir, disabled, id, lang, onclick, ondblclick, onkeydown, onkeypress, onkeyup, onmousedown, onmousemove, onmouseover, onmouseout, onmouseup, style, title

<OPTGROUP>...</OPTGROUP>

- **Purpose**: This tag encloses a group of menu options on a form.
- **Start Tag**: Required
- **End Tag**: Required
- **Special Attributes**:

  label="text"—The label for the option group.
- **Deprecated Attributes**: None
- **Other Attributes**: class, dir, disabled, id, lang, onblur, onchange, onclick, ondblclick, onkeydown, onkeypress, onkeyup, onmousedown, onmousemove, onmouseout, onmouseover, onmouseup, onfocus, style, title

<P>...</P>

- **Purpose**: This tag encloses a paragraph of text.
- **Start Tag**: Required
- **End Tag**: Optional

- **Special Attributes**: None
- **Deprecated Attributes**: `align`
- **Other Attributes**: `class`, `dir`, `id`, `lang`, `onclick`, `ondblclick`, `onkeydown`, `onkeypress`, `onkeyup`, `onmousedown`, `onmousemove`, `onmouseout`, `onmouseover`, `onmouseup`, `style`, `title`

Many HTML authors use one or more <P> tags without any text as a way to insert whitespace into a document. This is discouraged in the HTML 4.0 specification, which says that HTML browsing software should ignore repeated <P> tags without any text.

<PARAM>

- **Purpose**: This tag establishes a parameter—a value that will be provided to an object before it's presented as part of a document. More than one parameter can be used, but all of them should be enclosed within the related <OBJECT> tag.
- **Start Tag**: Required
- **End Tag**: Not allowed
- **Special Attributes**:

  `name="text"`—The name of the parameter.

  `value="text"`—The value of the parameter, which can be a string of text, an object, or a URI to a resource where one or more values are stored.

  `valuetype="text"`—The type of information stored as the parameter's value.

  `type="text"`—The content type of the URI specified in `value`.

- **Deprecated Attributes**: None
- **Other Attributes:** `id`

<PRE>...</PRE>

- **Purpose**: This tag encloses text that should not be formatted in the same manner as other HTML text. Most Web browsers will display this preformatted text in a monospace font with all whitespace intact, rather than ignoring repeated space characters as HTML normally does. Word-wrapping also may not occur, causing text to flow outside the right margin of the browser window.
- **Start Tag**: Required
- **End Tag**: Required
- **Special Attributes**: None
- **Deprecated Attributes**: `width`

A

- **Other Attributes**: `class`, `dir`, `id`, `lang`, `onclick`, `ondblclick`, `onkeydown`, `onkeypress`, `onkeyup`, `onmousedown`, `onmousemove`, `onmouseout`, `onmouseover`, `onmouseup`, `style`, `title`

`<Q>`...`</Q>`

- **Purpose**: This tag encloses a short amount of quoted text, which will be displayed with quotation marks around it when the document is viewed. Unlike a longer quotation enclosed within the `<BLOCKQUOTE>` tag, this text will not be set apart from other content by paragraph breaks.
- **Start Tag**: Required
- **End Tag**: Required
- **Special Attributes**:

  `cite="URI"`—The address of a document that contains information about the source of the quotation.
- **Deprecated Attributes**: None
- **Other Attributes**: `class`, `dir`, `id`, `lang`, `onclick`, `ondblclick`, `onkeydown`, `onkeypress`, `onkeyup`, `onmousedown`, `onmousemove`, `onmouseout`, `onmouseover`, `onmouseup`, `style`, `title`

`<S>`...`</S>`

- **Purpose**: This tag has been deprecated.

`<SAMP>`...`</SAMP>`

- **Purpose**: This tag encloses text that reprints output from a computer program, a script, or another similar process.
- **Start Tag**: Required
- **End Tag**: Required
- **Special Attributes**: None
- **Deprecated Attributes**: None
- **Other Attributes**: `class`, `dir`, `id`, `lang`, `onclick`, `ondblclick`, `onkeydown`, `onkeypress`, `onkeyup`, `onmousedown`, `onmousemove`, `onmouseout`, `onmouseover`, `onmouseup`, `style`, `title`

\<SCRIPT>...\</SCRIPT>

- **Purpose**: This tag places an executable script within a document.
- **Start Tag**: Required
- **End Tag**: Required
- **Special Attributes**:

  src="*URI*"—The URI of a document containing the script.

  type="*text*"—The scripting language being used.

  defer—This attribute indicates that the script doesn't add any content to the document.
- **Deprecated Attributes**: language
- **Other Attributes**: charset

\<SELECT>...\</SELECT>

- **Purpose**: This tag adds a menu control to a form.
- **Start Tag**: Required
- **End Tag**: Required
- **Special Attributes**:

  name="*text*"—The name of the button.

  size="*number*"—The number of items to display in a menu, presented as a scrolling list box.

  multiple—This attribute indicates that more than one item can be selected from the menu.
- **Deprecated Attributes**: None
- **Other Attributes**: class, dir, disabled, id, lang, onclick, ondblclick, onkeydown, onkeyup, onkeypress, onmousedown, onmousemove, onmouseout, onmouseover, onmouseup, style, tabindex, title

\<SMALL>...\</SMALL>

- **Purpose**: This tag encloses text that should be displayed in a smaller-than-normal font. Although it has not been deprecated, the HTML 4.0 specification advises that style sheets are a better alternative.
- **Start Tag**: Required
- **End Tag**: Required
- **Special Attributes**: None

A

- **Deprecated Attributes**: None
- **Other Attributes**: class, dir, id, lang, onclick, ondblclick, onkeydown, onkeypress, onkeyup, onmousedown, onmousemove, onmouseout, onmouseover, onmouseup, style, title

\<SPAN>...\</SPAN>

- **Purpose**: This tag encloses a small section of a document into its own block. Like \<DIV>, it's used to organize the content internally and can be used with attributes to change the presentation of the section.
- **Start Tag**: Required
- **End Tag**: Required
- **Special Attributes**: None
- **Deprecated Attributes**: None
- **Other Attributes**: align, class, dir, id, lang, onclick, ondblclick, onkeydown, onkeypress, onkeyup, onmousedown, onmousemove, onmouseout, onmouseover, onmouseup, style, title

\<STRIKE>...\</STRIKE>

- **Purpose**: This tag has been deprecated.

\<STRONG>...\</STRONG>

- **Purpose**: This tag encloses text that needs a strong emphasis. Most Web browsers display this text in bold. You can place a lesser emphasis on text with the \<EM> tag.
- **Start Tag**: Required
- **End Tag**: Required
- **Special Attributes**: None
- **Deprecated Attributes**: None
- **Other Attributes**: class, dir, id, lang, onclick, ondblclick, onkeydown, onkeypress, onkeyup, onmousedown, onmousemove, onmouseout, onmouseover, onmouseup, style, title

\<STYLE>...\</STYLE>

- **Purpose**: This tag establishes style sheet rules in the header of a document.
- **Start Tag**: Required
- **End Tag**: Required

- **Special Attributes**:

  type="*text*"—The style sheet language being used.

  media="*text*"—The intended medium on which this style sheet will be displayed.
- **Deprecated Attributes**: None
- **Other Attributes**: dir, lang, title

\<SUB\>...\</SUB\>

- **Purpose**: This tag encloses text that is a subscript.
- **Start Tag**: Required
- **End Tag**: Required
- **Special Attributes**: None
- **Deprecated Attributes**: None
- **Other Attributes**: class, dir, id, lang, onclick, ondblclick, onkeydown, onkeypress, onkeyup, onmousedown, onmousemove, onmouseout, onmouseover, onmouseup, style, title

\<SUP\>...\</SUP\>

- **Purpose**: This tag encloses text that is a superscript.
- **Start Tag**: Required
- **End Tag**: Required
- **Special Attributes**: None
- **Deprecated Attributes**: None
- **Other Attributes**: class, dir, id, lang, onclick, ondblclick, onkeydown, onkeypress, onkeyup, onmousedown, onmousemove, onmouseout, onmouseover, onmouseup, style, title

\<TABLE\>...\</TABLE\>

- **Purpose**: This tag encloses information that has been organized into a table containing rows and columns of rectangular cells.
- **Start Tag**: Required
- **End Tag**: Required

A

- **Special Attributes**:

  border="*number*"—The width of the border around the table, or "0" if the border should not be displayed.

  cellpadding="*number*"—The amount of space between the contents of a table cell and its borders.

  cellspacing="*number*"—The amount of space between cells in the table.

  frame="*text*"—The sides of a frame surrounding the table that are visible, if any.

  summary="*text*"—A summary of the purpose and structure of the table, for the benefit of nonvisual Web browsing software.

  rules="*text*"—The rules (lines) that will appear between cells in a table, if any.

  width="*number*"—The desired width of the table, expressed in either pixels or as a percentage of the space available in the browser.

- **Deprecated Attributes**: align, bgcolor
- **Other Attributes**: class, dir, frame, id, lang, onclick, ondblclick, onkeydown, onkeypress, onkeyup, onmousedown, onmousemove, onmouseout, onmouseover, onmouseup, style, title

\<TBODY>...\</TBODY>

- **Purpose**: This tag encloses one or more rows of a table's cells—the actual body of the table. If a table contains either a \<THEAD> or a \<TFOOT> row, the \<TBODY> tag must be used to hold the body of the table. A table's body must contain the same number of columns as its header and footer.
- **Start Tag**: Optional
- **End Tag**: Optional
- **Special Attributes**: None
- **Deprecated Attributes**: None
- **Other Attributes**: align, char, charoff, class, dir, id, lang, onclick, ondblclick, onkeydown, onkeypress, onkeyup, onmousedown, onmousemove, onmouseout, onmouseover, onmouseup, style, title, valign

\<TD>...\</TD>

- **Purpose**: This tag encloses a cell in a table that doesn't contain header information.
- **Start Tag**: Required
- **End Tag**: Optional

- **Special Attributes**:

  headers=`"text"`—The header cells that provide information about the current cell, with the `id` attributes of the different cells separated by spaces.

  scope=`"text"`—The set of table cells that this header cell provides information about.

  abbr=`"text"`—An abbreviated version of the cell's content.

  axis=`"categories"`—A list of categories, separated by commas, that the cell belongs to.

  rowspan=`"number"`—The number of rows occupied by the cell.

  colspan=`"number"`—The number of columns occupied by the cell.

- **Deprecated Attributes**: `bgcolor, nowrap, height, width`

- **Other Attributes**: `align, char, charoff, class, dir, id, lang, onclick, ondblclick, onkeydown, onkeypress, onkeyup, onmousedown, onmousemove, onmouseout, onmouseover, onmouseup, style, title, valign`

<TEXTAREA>...</TEXTAREA>

- **Purpose**: This tag adds a text input area control to a form.
- **Start Tag**: Required
- **End Tag**: Required
- **Special Attributes**:

  name=`"text"`—The name of the control.

  rows=`"number"`—The number of rows in the text area.

  cols=`"number"`—The number of columns in the text area.

- **Deprecated Attributes**: None
- **Other Attributes**: `class, dir, disabled, id, lang, onblur, onchange, onclick, ondblclick, onfocus, onkeydown, onkeypress, onkeyup, onmousedown, onmousemove, onmouseout, onmouseover, onmouseup, onselect, readonly, style, tabindex, title`

<TFOOT>...</TFOOT>

- **Purpose**: This tag encloses a table row that appears as a footer below all other rows of the table. Like the `<THEAD>` tag, this footer can be used to provide information about the specific columns in the table. It must contain the same number of columns as the `<TBODY>` and `<TFOOT>` table rows it is associated with. A table's footer must appear before any `<TBODY>` tags in that table.

A

- **Start Tag**: Required
- **End Tag**: Optional
- **Special Attributes**: None
- **Deprecated Attributes**: None
- **Other Attributes**: align, char, charoff, class, dir, id, lang, onclick, ondblclick, onkeydown, onkeypress, onkeyup, onmousedown, onmousemove, onmouseout, onmouseover, onmouseup, style, title, valign

`<TH>...</TH>`

- **Purpose**: This tag encloses a cell in a table that contains header information.
- **Start Tag**: Required
- **End Tag**: Optional
- **Special Attributes**:

    headers="*text*"—The header cells that provide information about the current cell, with the id attributes of the different cells separated by spaces.

    scope="*text*"—The set of table cells that this header cell provides information about.

    abbr="*text*"—An abbreviated version of the cell's content.

    axis="*categories*"—A list of categories, separated by commas, that the cell belongs to.

    rowspan="*number*"—The number of rows occupied by the cell.

    colspan="*number*"—The number of columns occupied by the cell.

- **Deprecated Attributes**: bgcolor, nowrap, height, width
- **Other Attributes**: align, char, charoff, class, dir, id, lang, onclick, ondblclick, onkeydown, onkeypress, onkeyup, onmousedown, onmousemove, onmouseout, onmouseover, onmouseup, style, title, valign

`<THEAD>...</THEAD>`

- **Purpose**: This tag encloses a table row that appears as a header above all other rows of the table. Like the <TFOOT> tag, this header can be used to provide information about the specific columns in the table. It must contain the same number of columns as the <TBODY> and <THEAD> table rows it's associated with. A table's header must appear before any <TBODY> tags in that table.
- **Start Tag**: Required

- **End Tag**: Optional
- **Special Attributes**: None
- **Deprecated Attributes**: None
- **Other Attributes**: `align, char, charoff, class, dir, id, lang, onclick, ondblclick, onkeydown, onkeypress, onkeyup, onmousedown, onmousemove, onmouseout, onmouseover, onmouseup, style, title, valign`

`<TITLE>...</TITLE>`

- **Purpose**: This tag encloses the title of the document. In most Web browsers, the title is displayed in the browser window's title bar.
- **Start Tag**: Required
- **End Tag**: Required
- **Special Attributes**: None
- **Deprecated Attributes**: None
- **Other Attributes**: `lang, dir`

`<TR>...</TR>`

- **Purpose**: This tag encloses a row of cells in a table.
- **Start Tag**: Required
- **End Tag**: Optional
- **Special Attributes**: None
- **Deprecated Attributes**: None
- **Other Attributes**: `align, char, charoff, class, dir, id, lang, onclick, ondblclick, onkeydown, onkeypress, onkeyup, onmousedown, onmousemove, onmouseout, onmouseover, onmouseup, style, title, valign`

`<TT>...</TT>`

- **Purpose**: This tag encloses text that should be displayed in a monospace or tele-type font. Although this tag hasn't been deprecated, the HTML 4.0 specification advises that style sheets are a better alternative.
- **Start Tag**: Required
- **End Tag**: Required
- **Special Attributes**: None
- **Deprecated Attributes**: None

A

- **Other Attributes**: `class, dir, id, lang, onclick, ondblclick, onkeydown, onkeypress, onkeyup, onmousedown, onmousemove, onmouseout, onmouseover, onmouseup, style, title`

<U>...</U>

- **Purpose**: This tag has been deprecated.

<UL>...</UL>

- **Purpose**: This tag encloses a list of items that won't be individually numbered. Each item in the list is identified by the `<LI>` tag. Most Web browsers display these unordered lists with a bullet character preceding each item. A numbered list requires the `<OL>` tag.
- **Start Tag**: Required
- **End Tag**: Required
- **Special Attributes**: None
- **Deprecated Attributes**: `compact, type`
- **Other Attributes**: `class, dir, id, lang, onclick, ondblclick, onkeydown, onkeypress, onkeyup, onmousedown, onmousemove, onmouseout, onmouseover, onmouseup, style, title`

<VAR>...</VAR>

- **Purpose**: This tag encloses text that represents a variable name or a command-line argument for a computer program.
- **Start Tag**: Required
- **End Tag**: Required
- **Special Attributes**: None
- **Deprecated Attributes**: None
- **Other Attributes**: `class, dir, id, lang, onclick, ondblclick, onkeydown, onkeypress, onkeyup, onmousedown, onmousemove, onmouseout, onmouseover, onmouseup, style, title`

APPENDIX B

FrontPage 2000 Templates

One of the ways that FrontPage 2000 speeds up Web design is through the use of templates. Like their namesakes in Microsoft Word and other software, templates are default versions of a document that can be customized.

An example in FrontPage 2000 is the guest book template, which makes it easy to collect feedback from your Web's visitors and present it as a page on the site. This template can be used with any Web hosted on a server equipped with FrontPage Server Extensions.

FrontPage 2000 has Web templates, for the creation of entire Webs, and page templates, which can be used to add pages to a Web.

The following sections describe templates that are available with FrontPage 2000. The graphics and FrontPage 2000 components used with each template are listed also.

Page Templates

Normal Page

Description: An empty page.

Graphics: None

FrontPage 2000 Components: None

Bibliography

Description: A list of references for the sources in an academic paper.

Graphics: None

FrontPage 2000 Components: Comment TimeStamp

Confirmation Page

Description: A page for replying to a user who has submitted feedback.

Graphics: None

FrontPage 2000 Components: ConfirmationField, Comment

Feedback Form

Description: A form for collecting feedback from a user about your Web and saving it with the FrontPage Save Results component.

Graphics: None

FrontPage 2000 Components: Comment, SaveResults, TimeStamp

FIGURE B.1

The Feedback Form page template.

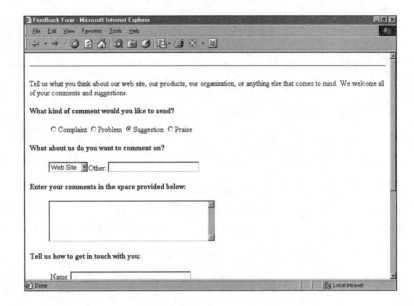

Frequently Asked Questions

Description: A page with a list of frequently asked questions and their answers.

Graphics: None

FrontPage 2000 Components: Comment, TimeStamp

Guest Book

Description: A page for collecting a user's guest book comments and saving them to a guest book page called guestlog.htm.

Graphics: None

FrontPage 2000 Components: Include, Comment, SaveResults, TimeStamp

B

FIGURE B.2

The Guest Book page template.

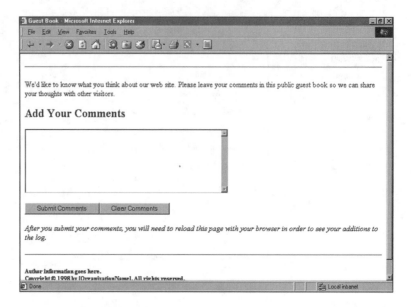

Narrow Left-Aligned Body

Description: A page with a narrow column of text on the left and a wider image on the right. Despite the name, the text uses right alignment.

Graphics: earth.jpg

FrontPage 2000 Components: None

FIGURE B.3

The Narrow Left-Aligned Body page template.

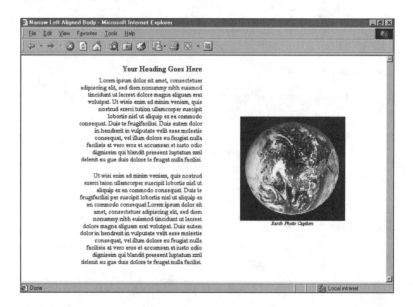

Narrow Right-Aligned Body

Description: A page with a narrow column of left-aligned text on the right and a wider image on the left.

Graphics: `firework.jpg`

FrontPage 2000 Components: None

FIGURE B.4

The Narrow Right-Aligned Body page template.

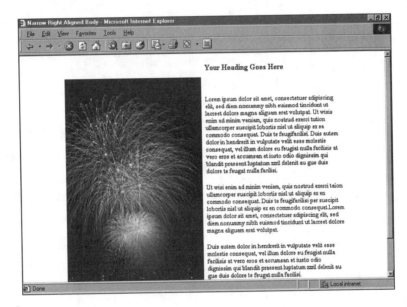

One-Column Body

Description: A page with a column of centered text running down the middle of the page.

Graphics: None

FrontPage 2000 Components: None

B

FIGURE B.5

*The One-Column Body
page template.*

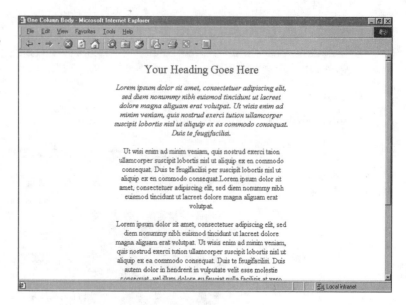

One-Column Body with Contents and Sidebar

Description: A column of text with a narrow table of contents on the left and a sidebar on the right containing text and images.

Graphics: `fish.jpg`, `Leopard.jpg`, `earth.jpg`

Components: None

FIGURE B.6

*The One-Column Body
with Contents and
Sidebar page template.*

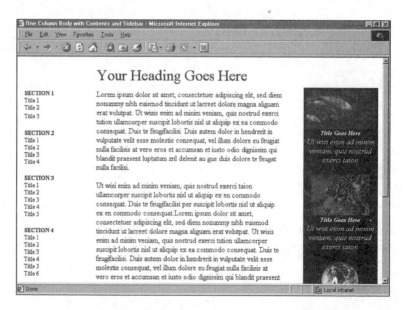

One-Column Body with Contents on Left

Description: A column of text with a narrow table of contents on the left.

Graphics: `fish.jpg`

Components: None

FIGURE B.7

The One-Column Body with Contents on Left page template.

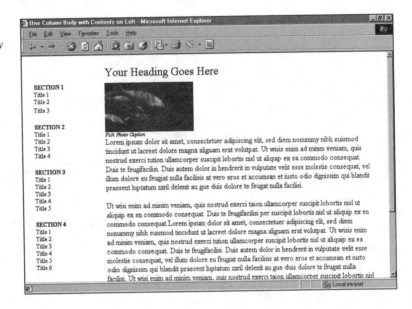

One-Column Body with Contents on Right

Description: A column of text with a narrow table of contents on the right.

Graphics: `cake.jpg`

Components: None

B

FIGURE B.8

The One-Column Body with Contents on Right page template.

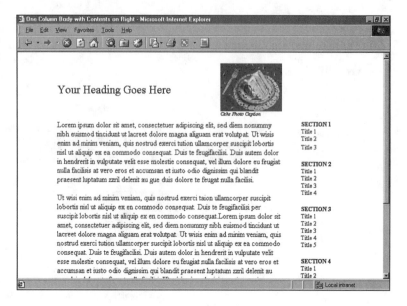

One-Column Body with Staggered Sidebar

Description: A column of text with alternating columns of text and images to the left.

Graphics: cake.jpg

Components: None

FIGURE B.9

The One-Column Body with Staggered Sidebar page template.

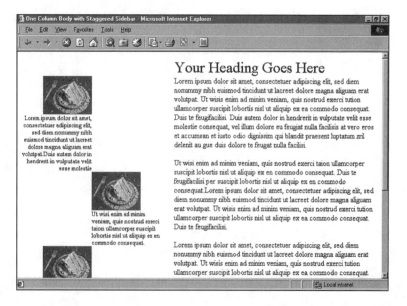

One-Column Body with Two Sidebars

Description: A column of text with a thin sidebar on the left for links and an image sidebar on the right.

Graphics: `Sunflowr.jpg`

Components: None

FIGURE B.10

The One-Column Body with Two Sidebars page template.

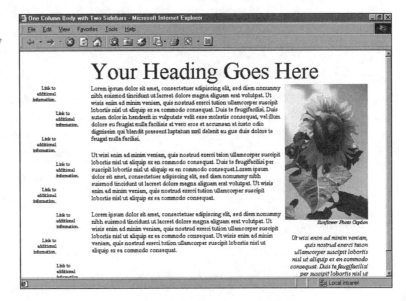

One-Column Body with Two-Column Sidebar

Description: A column of text with two thin sidebars on the right.

Graphics: Sunflowr.jpg

Components: None

B

FIGURE B.11

The One-Column Body with Two-Column Sidebar page template.

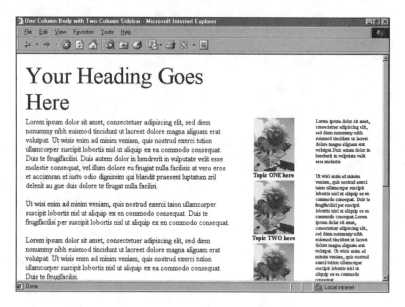

Search Page

Description: A page that can be used to search the text of the Web.

Graphics: None

Components: Comment, Search, TimeStamp

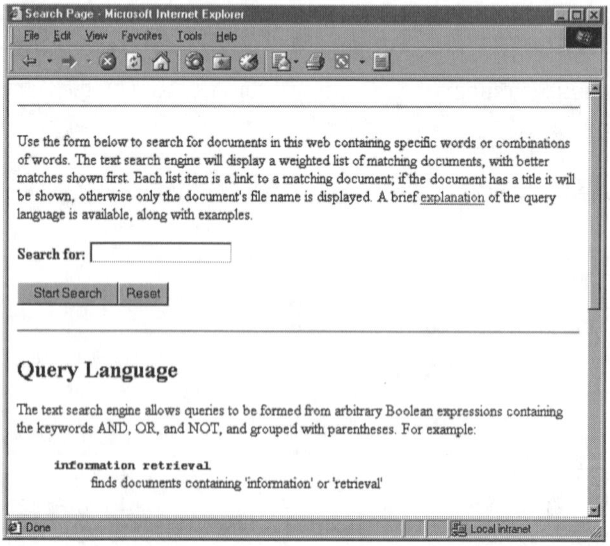

FIGURE B.12

The Search Page template.

Table of Contents

Description: A page containing the Table of Contents component, which lists all pages on a Web that are accessible from `index.htm`.

Graphics: None

Components: Outline, TimeStamp

FIGURE B.13.

*The Table of Contents
page template.*

Three-Column Body

Description: A page with three columns of text.

Graphics: None

Components: None

B

FIGURE B.14

The Three-Column Body page template.

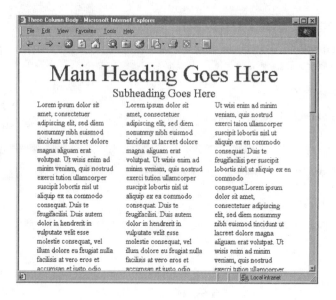

Two-Column Body

Description: A page with two columns of text.

Graphics: None

Components: None

FIGURE B.15

The Two-Column Body page template.

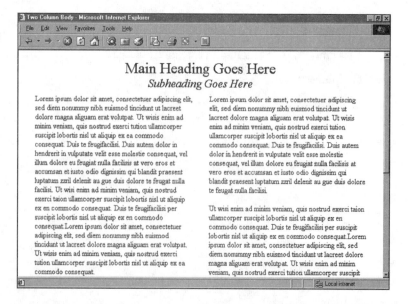

Two-Column Body with Contents and Sidebar

Description: Two columns of text with a narrow table of contents on the left and a sidebar on the right.

Graphics: None

Components: None

FIGURE B.16

The Two-Column Body with Contents and Sidebar page template.

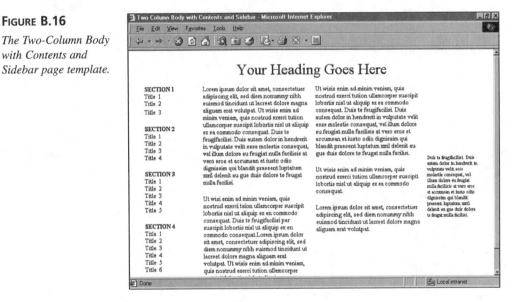

Two-Column Body with Contents on the Left

Description: Two columns of text with a narrow table of contents on the left.

Graphics: `Fish.jpg`

Components: None

B

FIGURE B.17

*The Two-Column Body
with Contents on Left
page template.*

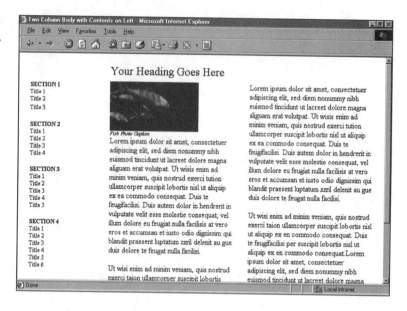

Two-Column Staggered Body

Description: Alternating columns of text and images.

Graphics: `earth.jpg`, `Leopard.jpg`, `Crane.jpg`, `Fish.jpg`

Components: None

FIGURE B.18

*The Two-Column
Staggered Body page
template.*

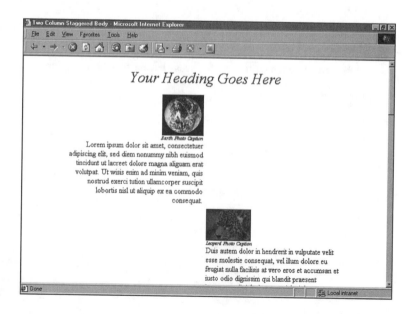

Two-Column Staggered Body with Contents and Sidebar

Description: Alternating columns of text and images with a table of contents on the left and a sidebar on the right.

Graphics: None

Components: None

FIGURE B.19

The Two-Column Staggered Body with Contents and Sidebar page template.

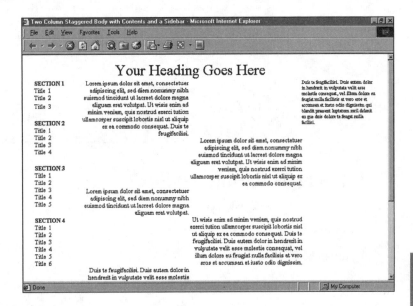

User Registration

Description: A page enabling users to register themselves as a member of a sub-Web on a server (not permitted on all FrontPage 2000-enabled servers, for security reasons).

Graphics: None

Components: Comment, Registration, TimeStamp

FIGURE B.20

The User Registration page template.

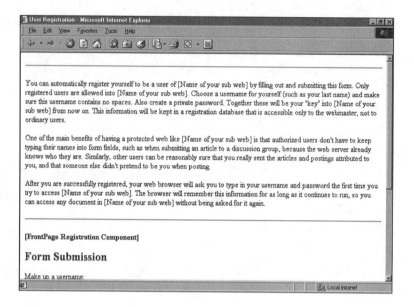

Wide Body with Headings

Description: A single, wide column of text with numerous subheadings.

Graphics: None

Components: None

FIGURE B.21

The Wide Body with Headings page template.

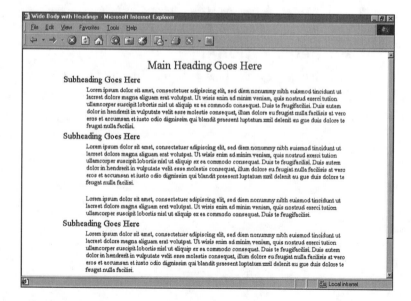

APPENDIX C

FrontPage 2000 Themes

When you're designing a Web for the first time in FrontPage 2000, one of the most daunting tasks is developing the graphical appearance of the site. A Web often includes the following visual features:

- A graphical background, such as a stripe down one side or an image file that is repeated several different times to fill the browser window
- An image file displaying a logo
- Graphical headlines
- Graphical buttons for site navigation

If you don't have the ability, time, or desire to create graphics of your own, you might want to use one of Microsoft's Web themes. Themes are a quick way to define a consistent graphical appearance for your Web. FrontPage 2000 includes more than a dozen different themes that would be appropriate for personal, commercial, or academic Webs.

Themes can be applied to a single page within a Web or to the entire Web itself. You can select them by clicking Format, Theme after loading the Web into FrontPage 2000. After you select a theme, you can customize the colors, configuration, and graphics that it uses.

Each of the following sections describes one of the themes that is a standard part of FrontPage 2000. You also can install additional themes by choosing Format, Theme and selecting (Install Additional Themes) instead of picking a theme.

Artsy

FIGURE C.1

The Artsy theme on a Web page.

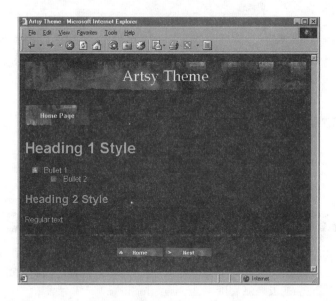

Description: Autumn colors and torn paper icons over a dark background of a Greek statue.

Predominant Colors: Black, copper, and yellow

Fonts: Arial, Helvetica

Blank

FIGURE C.2

The Blank theme on a Web page.

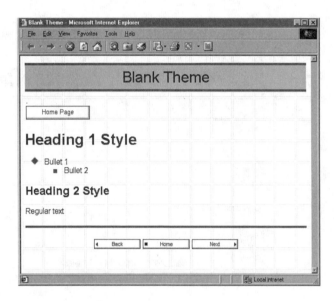

Description: A gray top-of-page banner over white background tiles and simple visual elements.

Predominant Colors: White, blue, and light gray

Fonts: Arial, Helvetica

C

Blends

FIGURE C.3

The Blends theme on a Web page.

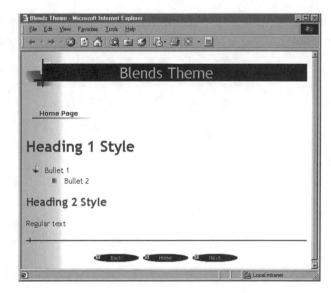

Description: Bright colors, black icons, and black page banners over a side-striped background.

Predominant Colors: Red, yellow, blue, and black

Fonts: Trebuchet MS, Arial, Helvetica

Blueprint

FIGURE C.4

*The Blueprint theme
on a Web page.*

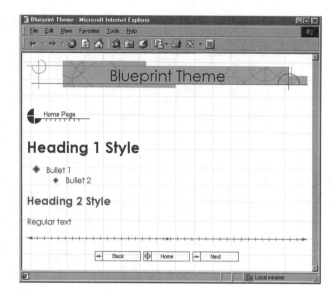

Description: A white graph paper background over draftsman's markings.

Predominant Colors: Light blue, dark blue, and white

Fonts: Century Gothic, Arial, Helvetica

C

Bold Stripes

FIGURE C.5

*The Bold Stripes
theme on a Web page.*

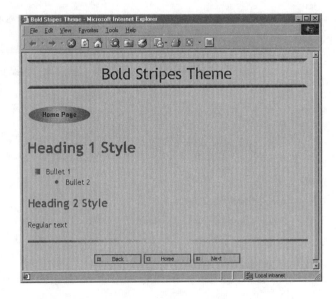

Description: Blue headings and gray icons over faint gray-striped wallpaper,

Predominant Colors: Blue, black, and gray

Fonts: Trebuchet MS, Arial, Helvetica

Capsules

FIGURE C.6

The Capsules theme on a Web page.

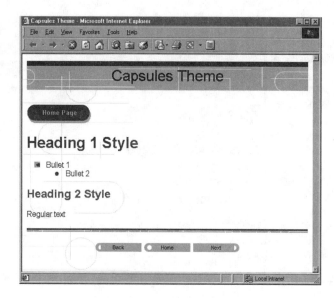

Description: Simple, rounded-edge graphics over a background of random-looking lines and half-circles.

Predominant Colors: Blue, light green, and white

Fonts: Arial, Helvetica

C

Citrus Punch

FIGURE C.7

*The Citrus Punch
theme on a Web page.*

Description: Informal tropical graphics over a flowery pattern of red, green, and yellow.

Predominant Colors: Bright orange, yellow, bright green, and red

Fonts: Verdana, Arial, Helvetica

Expedition

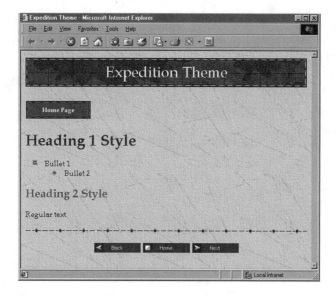

Description: Adventurous, "Indiana Jones"-style images and a weathered canvas background.

Predominant Colors: Tan, brown, and black

Fonts: Book Antiqua, Times New Roman, Times

C

Industrial

FIGURE C.9

The Industrial theme on a Web page.

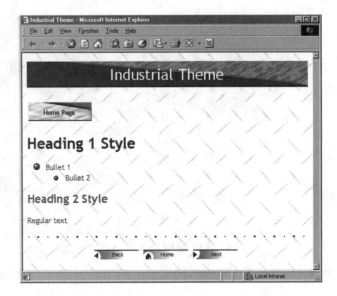

Description: A corrugated white metal background underneath rectangular metallic buttons.

Predominant Colors: Blue, light blue, white, and gray

Fonts: Trebuchet MS, Arial, Helvetica

Rice Paper

FIGURE C.10

The Rice Paper theme on a Web page.

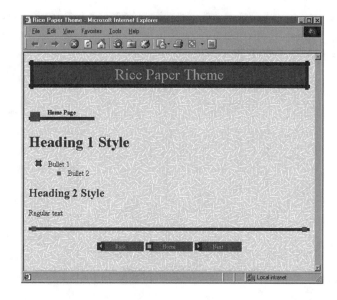

Description: Textured green banners and dark headings and text for easy viewing on an intricate patterned background.

Predominant Colors: Dark green, yellow, and gray green

Fonts: Times New Roman, Times

C

Romanesque

FIGURE C.11

*The Romanesque
theme on a Web page.*

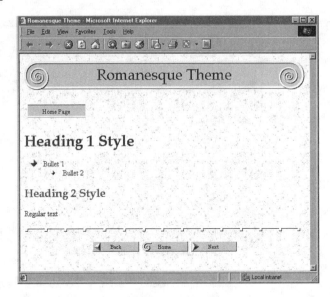

Description: Yellow Roman columns and buttons over a spotted white background image.

Predominant Colors: Mustard yellow, white, and red

Fonts: Book Antiqua, Times New Roman, Times

Straight Edge

FIGURE C.12

*The Straight Edge
theme on a Web page.*

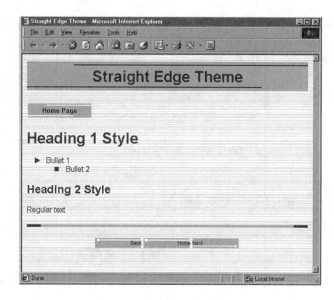

Description: Simple square graphics featuring lines that move across the page banner.

Predominant Colors: Khaki, white, and lime green

Fonts: Arial, Helvetica

C

Sumi Painting

Description: Ragged-edge watercolor graphics on a textured drawing paper surface.

Predominant Colors: Light blue, dark blue, and white

Fonts: Verdana, Arial, Helvetica

APPENDIX D

Upgrading from Prior Versions of FrontPage

One of the new features of FrontPage 2000 and the other programs in the Office 2000 suite is improved installation. The software setup process has been simplified, making it easier to use successfully. The software also has a new diagnostic feature, making it easier to fix any installation errors that may occur. Ideally, FrontPage users should be able to install the version 2000 upgrade easily by using the Microsoft Installation Wizard.

This appendix offers some guidance for any problems that you may encounter along the way.

Installing FrontPage 2000

Microsoft FrontPage 2000 is available as a standalone product and as part of the Office 2000 suite of programs. The following minimum system requirements have been recommended by Microsoft:

- A Pentium with 32MB of memory
- A CD-ROM drive
- A VGA monitor (although a Super VGA, 256-color monitor is preferred)
- A Microsoft-compatible mouse
- Windows 95 or NT Workstation 4.0
- A 9,600-baud modem (although 28,800-baud is preferred)

Installing the whole Office suite, which includes FrontPage 2000, requires approximately 280MB of hard drive space. You can reduce this amount during installation by choosing not to install some Office programs.

Server Extensions

Among the optional features you can use with FrontPage 2000 are FrontPage Server Extensions and Office Server Extensions. These programs extend a Web server's capabilities to support interactive features like a guestbook, a feedback form, and a discussion forum. Office Server Extensions are an enhanced version of FrontPage Server Extensions that enable additional Web functionality in Office 2000 programs.

Office Server Extensions require the Windows NT operating system and one of two servers: Microsoft Internet Information Server 4.0 (Windows NT Server 4.0) or Personal Web Server 4.0 (Windows NT Workstation 4.0).

FrontPage Server Extensions have the same requirements, but they're also available for other servers, such as Apache, which is widely used on Linux systems. You need either Office Server Extensions or FrontPage Server Extensions to use some Web publishing features in FrontPage 2000:

- Remote management of a Web
- Form submission using a FrontPage 2000 component instead of a CGI program
- Working directly with a Microsoft Access 2000 database on a Web
- Use of other FrontPage 2000 components

FrontPage Server Extensions are supported by the Personal Web Server that can be installed with Windows 98. These extensions are also supported on some Web hosting services. Check with your service provider to make sure they're supported before you use these features in your Webs.

Self-Repairing Application

One of the new features of FrontPage 2000 is its capability to repair itself. When the program is launched, it will make sure that all essential files and program libraries are present on your system. If any of these files or libraries are not found, a dialog box will appear that enables you to reinstall the missing elements.

Users who have installed FrontPage 2000 from a network may not have to do anything to cause the software to repair itself. Network administrators have the option of placing these files on the network for use during self-repair.

If FrontPage 2000 was installed from your CD-ROM, you'll need to keep those CDs handy in case the self-repair feature is ever needed.

This self-repair function is a part of all Microsoft Office 2000 products.

Conflicts with Previous Editions

By default, FrontPage 2000 will be installed in place of any version of FrontPage that's already on your system. The software is backward-compatible, so you'll be able to load Webs created with FrontPage 98 and earlier versions of the software.

However, you should back up all existing Webs before you install the new version to make sure that they're not overwritten during the upgrade.

> At the time of this writing, the installation of Office 2000 conflicts with pre-release versions of Microsoft Visual Studio 6.0. You must either upgrade Visual Studio 6.0 to the full release or uninstall it before you can use the current Office 2000 on your system.

If you want to keep a previous edition of FrontPage 2000 on your system, you must choose the Customize option during installation. The dialog box that includes this option is shown in Figure D.1.

D

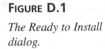

FIGURE D.1

The Ready to Install dialog.

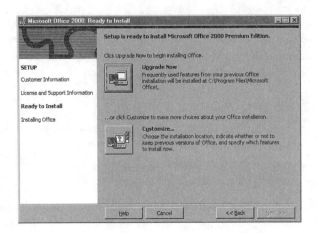

If you choose a custom installation, you'll be able to make the following configuration choices:

- The drive and folder where the software should be installed
- Whether to save previous versions of the software or to delete them during installation

You'll also be able to choose where specific elements of the software are stored. By default, most programs and files related to FrontPage 2000 are stored on your hard drive. One exception is a group of additional FrontPage 2000 themes.

During a customized installation, you can choose which elements of the software to save to your hard drive, which elements to run from the CD-ROM, and which elements to install only when they're first requested by a user.

The additional FrontPage 2000 themes fall into the third category. They won't be installed unless you select the Install Additional Themes dialog when you're defining a theme within the FrontPage editor.

If you have enough hard drive space on your system, you'll find it more convenient to keep the default options and install most of the program onto your hard drive.

Figure D.2 shows an installation dialog where the location of FrontPage elements can be selected.

FIGURE D.2

The Select Features dialog box.

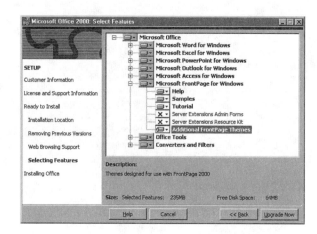

APPENDIX E

FrontPage Internet Resources

According to the World Wide Web search engine AltaVista, there are more than 120,000 Web pages that mention Microsoft FrontPage in some manner. Unless you have a few decades to kill, or an available pool of cheap labor, you might not want to sift through all of these pages individually to find useful FrontPage sites.

This appendix covers the best Internet resources currently available for Microsoft FrontPage. You can find tips, bug-troubleshooting help, discussion forums, and many other useful bits of information that aren't in the official Microsoft FrontPage 2000 documentation. You'll also come across some good examples of Webs designed with FrontPage.

Although many of these resources are devoted to earlier editions of FrontPage, they may have been expanded to cover FrontPage 2000 as well by the time you read this.

Web Sites, Discussion Groups, and Mailing Lists

The most important resource, as far as this book is concerned, is this book's official World Wide Web site:

`http://www.fp2k.com/24`

Visit this Web site for the latest details on corrections, clarifications, and other information that supplements this book. You also can use it to send email to author Rogers Cadenhead.

Web Sites

Microsoft FrontPage: `http://www.microsoft.com/frontpage/`

Microsoft's official home page for FrontPage 2000 and past versions of the software. Go here first for product specifications, technical support, and online ordering. You can search through Microsoft's database for information on bug fixes related to FrontPage, find out about free offers that you're eligible for, and subscribe to *Microsoft FrontPage Bulletin*, a monthly email newsletter.

Chris's FrontPage Information Web: `http://jazzpiano.com/frontpage/`

If you'd like the perspective of an experienced FrontPage Web designer, try Chris Calabrese's FrontPage Web site. A FrontPage user since January 1997, Calabrese has compiled quick tips, problem solutions, and a guide to Internet resources for FrontPage users. The site covered FrontPage 97 and FrontPage 98 at the time of this writing.

The FrontPage Network: `http://www.frontpagenetwork.com/`

Another clearinghouse of FrontPage information and links, the FrontPage Network includes frequently asked question (FAQ) files for several useful topics, such as themes, Personal Web Server, email, hover buttons, and frames. There also are numerous how-to articles, user tips, and discussion forums. This is also one of the first sites outside of Microsoft that covers FrontPage 2000.

Dynamic Net FrontPage Support: `http://dynamicnet.net/support/frontpage.htm`

Although it's not as extensive as some of the other FrontPage Web sites, Dynamic Net's FrontPage Support site offers links to useful documents published by Microsoft, tips on newsgroups, Web sites, and books related to the software, and other information. It's one of the only sites that focuses on Active Server Pages in addition to FrontPage.

FrontPage World: `http://www.frontpageworld.com`

A guide to FrontPage that's published by Paul Colligan, one of the editors of this book. There's a guide to books, sites, and training programs available for FrontPage 2000, as well as an exclusive newsletter.

Web Hosting Providers that Support FrontPage: `http://microsoft.saltmine.com/frontpage/wpp/list/`

A database of Web hosting providers who support FrontPage. This can be viewed by state or in alphabetical order, and there's an associated database for international providers. Several of the providers offer free hosting, which is useful when you're experimenting with the software.

The Complete Webmaster: `http://abiglime.com/webmaster/articles/frontpage.htm`

The Complete Webmaster, an online zine for Web developers, has published more than 30 helpful articles about FrontPage since September 1997. There also are sections of the site devoted to other Web technology you might be interested in, such as CGI, Java, and JavaScript.

Acme Information Services: `http://www.acmeinfo.com/`

Acme, an Internet service provider in Minneapolis, Minn., is the first company that offered FrontPage 2000 hosting. As a result, they're experienced with the issues that can arise in hosting and publishing FrontPage Webs.

Mailing Lists and Discussion Forums

Microsoft FrontPage Bulletin: `http://www.microsoft.com/frontpage/bulletins/bulletin.htm`

Microsoft's official email FrontPage newsletter, which is published monthly. The *Bulletin* includes release news, user tips, expert advice, and special offers. To find out how to subscribe, visit the Web page `http://www.microsoft.com/frontpage/bulletins/bulletin.htm`. If this address has been changed, you should be able to find it on Microsoft's official FrontPage site at `http://www.microsoft.com/frontpage/`.

FrontPage Awareness Forum:
`http://frontpage.netnation.com/HyperNews/get/frontpage.html`

An unofficial Web-based discussion board for FrontPage, using HyperNews software.

Microsoft FrontPage Client Newsgroup: `news://microsoft.public.frontpage.client`

If you can handle the large number of messages posted each day, this Usenet newsgroup is a great way to get personal support from other FrontPage users. If you don't have access to a news server that carries Microsoft newsgroups like this one, you can read it on the Deja News Web site at `http://www.dejanews.com`.

FrontPage Mailing List at St. Johns

St. Johns University hosts an active FrontPage mailing list that includes up to 40 messages a day from users of the software. To receive subscription information via email, send a message to `listserv@maelstrom.stjohns.edu` with the text "info frontpage" as the body of your message.

FrontPage Users Digest Mailing List at Webcom

Webcom, a large Web hosting provider, hosts a FrontPage mailing list that can be delivered in digest form—all messages posted during a day are grouped into a single message. To receive subscription information via email, send a message to `front page-users-digest-request@webcom.com` with "info frontpage-user-digest" as the body of the message.

GLOSSARY

Glossary

accessibility   Refers to the various issues involved with ensuring that differently abled people can use Web pages and navigate Web sites.

action   In DHTML and scripting, an action is what happens when an event occurs. *See also* **event** and **object**.

active graphics   In FrontPage themes, refers to navigation buttons that change in appearance when the user passes the mouse pointer over them, and that provide navigational cues (for example, a button is highlighted to indicate the current page).

Active Server Pages (ASP)   A technology developed by Microsoft that allows users whose servers have ASP capabilities to easily script Web pages.

active Web pages   Web pages enhanced with programs, scripts, and other Web technologies that respond to user input or contain animated special effects.

ActiveX   A Microsoft technology that enables Web developers to take bits and pieces of programming code and put them together to create programs that run on Web pages. ActiveX only works in Internet Explorer.

ActiveX control   An ActiveX program that loads in a Web browser.

alternative text   Text that appears when a visitor's Web browser cannot display a picture or embedded object.

animated GIF   A group of GIF images that are assembled into simple animations that run in a Web browser.

article   A message posted to a discussion Web or newsgroup.

aspect ratio   The width-to-height ratio of a picture. Most image programs have an aspect ratio feature to ensure that pictures are resized proportionally.

audio   Sound on your computer. Common audio file formats include AU, WAV, and MIDI.

AVI   Audio Video Interleaved, Microsoft's popular video format.

background image   An image that repeats across a Web page to form a patterned background.

background sound   An audio file that plays when a Web page loads in a Web browser.

bandwidth   The amount of data transferred over the Internet or via a particular connection. Bandwidth is measured in Kilobites per second. *See also* **Kbps**.

banner   In FrontPage themes, the text graphic that appears near the top of a Web page that contains the page's topic.

banner ad   An advertisement that appears on a Web site (usually at the top of a page).

bookmark   In FrontPage, a target on a Web page that links to a particular section on that Web page. In Netscape Navigator, a favorite Web page that you can visit by pulling it down from a list instead of having to type the URL. *See also* **internal links** and **target**.

browse   To surf the Web or to look for a file on your computer through a dialog box, such as the Open dialog box.

browser   An application, such as Internet Explorer or Netscape Navigator, for viewing Web pages.

browser compatibility   Issues involved with making sure pages appear correctly in different Web browsers and different versions of Web browsers.

browser-safe colors   216 colors that are displayed correctly in a Web browser, regardless of the computer or operating system the visitor is using.

bullet list An indented list of items preceded by a decorative character that calls attention to each item.

bulletin board A Web site that allows users to have ongoing discussions. Bulletin boards generally contain a table of contents page with links to individual messages, pages with the text for each message, and a page with a Web form so users can post and reply to messages. *See also* **discussion Web**.

Cascading Style Sheets (CSS) A Web technology that allows you to create a document with built-in custom formatting styles that you can apply to pages throughout a Web site. Style sheets work similarly to the styles in desktop publishing and word processing documents.

CGI script A script that runs on a server and enables you to program a Web page. The most common example of a CGI script is a form processor that gathers data from a Web form. FrontPage components allow users to do things that used to require CGI scripting. *See also* **scripting language**.

child level In objects and Web pages, child level elements are lower in the hierarchy. For example, when you create FrontPage navigation bars in the Navigation view, child level pages are represented as pages that fall under a main section page.

client A computer that connects to a server to access a network, the Internet, or other data. Also refers to browsers, email programs, and other applications that allow users to get information and services from a server.

client-side Refers to technologies like DHTML, cascading style sheets, Java applets, and ActiveX controls, which rely on a Web browser or other client application. For example, only version 4.0 browsers and higher support DHTML.

closed network A group of computers within an organization that are connected to each other (usually through a server) so people within the organization can communicate and exchange files. Closed networks can only be accessed by authorized users.

collapsible outline A list of items that allows Web page visitors to click an item and display additional list items.

color depth The number of colors that a computer screen can display or that an image can include. Options include millions of colors (16.7 million colors, true color, 24-bit color), thousands of colors (67,000 colors, high color, 16-bit color), and 256 colors (8-bit color). Higher color depths generally enable better-quality image displays.

color scheme The colors of a Web page's background, text, and links.

Common Gateway Interface (CGI)   A set of commands and scripting languages that can run on most standard servers. Perl is a popular CGI scripting language. *See also* **CGI script**.

components   In FrontPage, menu items that add features to a Web page that would otherwise require programming or scripting.

continuous tone image   An image with complex shading and gradation of colors, like a photograph or an oil painting. On the Web, these images work best when formatted as JPEGs.

CSS   *See* **cascading style sheets**.

data   Web pages, email messages, pictures, documents, and anything else that is stored on your computer or transferred over networks or over the Internet.

data access pages   In FrontPage, a set of Web pages that allows visitors to search (and sometimes add entries to) a database stored on the server.

default   The automatic setting that determines the behavior of an application or an element that is created or manipulated within an application. Most defaults can be changed by clicking a toolbar button, selecting a menu item, or changing settings in a dialog box. For example, FrontPage automatically aligns text and images to the left, but you can realign them to the center.

definition description   The indented text that follows a definition term in a definition list. *See also* **definition list**.

definition list   A list consisting of main entries followed by indented items with additional information. This type of list is generally used in tables of contents and other documents that contain titles or definitions followed by an explanation or description.

definition term   The main entry in a definition list, which is followed by a definition description in a definition list. *See also* **definition list**.

delay   In animation, the amount of time that elapses between frames, and in video and audio, the amount of time that elapses between loops. *See also* **loop**.

DHTML   *See* **Dynamic HTML**.

dialog box   A box with a message or set of options that appears on the computer screen after you perform an action, click a toolbar button, or select a menu item.

directory path   The location of a file in relation to a computer or Web.

directory server   A type of server that allows users to conference online with NetMeeting.

discussion Web   A type of FrontPage Web where visitors can read and post messages to each other. *See also* **bulletin board.**

display settings   The resolution and color depth of a computer screen's display. Common settings are 640×480 at 256 colors (8-bit) or 800×600 at millions of colors (24-bit).

docking a toolbar   Anchoring a floating toolbar to the top, right, bottom, or left of the application window.

domain name   The address of a server or group of servers, as in fp2k.com. *See also* **virtual domain**.

double-click   To click the mouse button twice in quick succession.

download   To get data from a server.

dynamic database   An online database that visitors can interact with via the Web and that is updated automatically when the data changes.

Dynamic HTML (DHTML)   A Web technology that enables Web developers to position, layer, and animate Web page elements, set up collapsible lists, and load special fonts to a Web browser.

dynamic Web pages   *See* **active Web pages**.

email link   A link that enables the visitor to send email to a specified address.

embedded files   A file and plug-in application (complete with toolbar buttons) that appears as part of your Web page layout, such as a QuickTime movie with player controls. FrontPage also uses the term *embed* when you save Web pages that contain images that you've edited with the Picture toolbar. In this context, *embed* means adding the pictures to your Web page. *See also* **inline files**.

event   In DHTML and scripting, an event is something that happens to a Web page or object that triggers an action. *See also* **action** and **object**.

Extensible Markup Language (XML)   An up-and-coming Web technology that enables Web developers to create custom HTML tags that add greater Web page capabilities and better integrate Web pages with databases. Version 5.0 Web browsers support XML.

external files   Files that are launched separately from a Web page when a visitor clicks a link, rather than appearing as embedded or inline files that are part of the Web page layout. *See also* **inline files** and **embedded files**.

external links   Hyperlinks to pages on other Web sites. *See also* **hyperlinks**.

filename extension   A period and a string of characters added to a filename that tell computers and Web browsers the file type. For example, `image.jpeg` designates a JPEG file.

flame   An angry message sent by email or posted to a discussion Web or newsgroup.

floating toolbar   A toolbar that floats in the middle of an application window when displayed. You can anchor a floating toolbar by dragging it to the top, bottom, left, or right of the application window. *See also* **docking a toolbar**.

form   On the Web, a page with form fields that allows users to enter information, select options, and post data to the server.

form field   A text box, scrolling list, button, or other page element that appears on a Web form so visitors can enter information, select options, and send data.

form handler   A CGI script or FrontPage component installed on a server that processes form data, such as by adding the information to a database or sending it to an email address.

frames   Divide a Web page into separate areas with individual Web documents.

frameset document   A Web page that tells which pages to display in which frames.

FrontPage navigation bar   A type of navigation bar that you can generate automatically with FrontPage. *See also* **navigation bar**.

FrontPage Server Extensions   Special software that extends a server's capabilities so FrontPage users can do things that would normally require programming. Many FrontPage features only work on a server with FrontPage server extensions.

FrontPage Web   A Web site created in FrontPage.

GIF   Graphic Interchange Format, an image file format for the Web that works well for line art and flat-color pictures. The GIF format also allows you to create animations from GIF files and create transparent GIFs. *See also* **animated GIF** and **transparent GIF**.

GIF animation   *See* **animated GIF**.

graphical bullets   Bullets that are created as images, rather than text.

graphical text   An image that contains text.

horizontal line   A Web page element that inserts a line on the Web page. Horizontal lines are commonly used to create separators for different types of information or sections on a Web page. Some people also use the terms *horizontal rule* or *page divider*.

horizontal spacing   The amount of space between the left and right sides of an image or other page.

hot spot   An area on an image map that functions as a link.

hover button   In FrontPage, an image or text link that changes in appearance when a visitor passes their mouse pointer over it or clicks it.

HTML   Hypertext Markup Language, a coding language used for creating Web pages.

HTTP   Hypertext Transfer Protocol, the set of server, communications, and browser technologies that enables Web pages to be used on the Internet.

hyperlink rollover   A piece of text or an image that changes its appearance when a visitor passes the cursor over it.

hyperlinks   Text or pictures on a Web page that you can click on to jump to another Web page or download a file.

Hypertext Markup Language (HTML)   *See* **HTML**.

Hypertext Transfer Protocol   *See* **HTTP**.

icon   A graphic that represents a concept or action. For example, in most computer applications a folder icon represents a directory that contains files, or a button that you can click to open a file.

image map   A picture with clickable hot spots that function as links. *See also* **hot spots**.

inheritance   A programming and Web concept in which child level elements (objects that are lower in the hierarchy) inherit characteristics from parent elements. For example, level 2 headings are generally smaller than level 1 headings, but still appear in the same font as the level 1 headings. *See also* **child level** and **parent level**.

inline files   Files that appear on a Web page, such as images or embedded movies or soundtracks. *See also* **external files**.

internal links   Links to targets within the same Web page. *See also* **bookmark** and **target**.

Internet   A vast global network that allows people to view Web pages, send and receive email messages, participate in newsgroups, join chat rooms, and more.

Internet service provider (ISP)   A company or organization that allows you to connect to the Internet through their server. In general, these ISPs charge a flat monthly rate and also host Web sites.

intranet   A closed office network that works similarly to the Internet and uses Internet programs like Web browsers and email programs to share information among coworkers.

ISP   *See* **Internet service provider**.

Java   Sun Microsystems' popular programming language for creating applications that run in a Web browser.

Java applets   Programs written in Java.

JavaScript   Netscape's popular client-side scripting language for programming Web pages. *See also* **scripting language** and **client-side**.

JPEG   Joint Picture Experts Group. A Web image file format that works well for continuous tone images. *See also* **continuous tone image**.

JScript   Microsoft's answer to JavaScript. JScript works with Internet Explorer, or in any browser when the Web server supports Active Server Pages.

Kbps   Kilobits per second, the unit of measurement for modem and connection speeds on the Internet, as in 56.6Kbps. The faster the modem, the more quickly you can download data.

key combination   A shortcut that allows the user to press a combination of keys instead of selecting commands from a menu.

keyword   A descriptive word entered when using a search engine form to search for information on the Web or on an individual Web site.

layer   To arrange text and images so they overlap, or to position them one on top of one another.

line art   Images with simple lines and solid colors. On the Web, these images work best when formatted as GIFs.

links   *See* **hyperlinks**.

local files   Files on the same computer, or on a computer on a local network to which you're directly connected.

local links   Links to pages on the same Web site. *See also* **external links**, **internal links**, and **hyperlinks**.

local network   A group of computers that are directly connected to each other, usually through a local server. Most offices and other organizations have local networks. *See also* **intranet** and **closed network**.

local server   A server that hosts a local network.

loop   In multimedia, a loop occurs each time the file plays.

low-res image   A low-quality image with a small file size that appears as a placeholder on a Web page until the larger, higher-quality image finishes loading.

main page   The Web page that visitors automatically go to when they enter a URL that doesn't point to a specific document(as in http://www.fp2k.com/24/ rather than http://www.fp2k.com/24/feedback.htm). Each Web folder, Web, and sub-Web should contain one (and only one) main page that is named either index.htm, index.html, default.htm, or default.html.

marquee   An animated text message that scrolls on a Web page.

meta-information   Information about a Web page. Meta-information can't be displayed in Web browsers, but it gives search engine spiders and other applications important information, including a summary and keywords for the Web page. *See also* **spider**.

modem   A device used to connect a computer to a telephone line.

moderator   The person who runs a discussion Web or newsgroup.

monitor settings   *See* **display settings**.

mouse over   When a visitor passes the mouse pointer over a text or image link. *See also* **hyperlink rollover**.

navigation bar   A row of graphics or text links that appears consistently throughout a Web site (or sections within a Web site) to help visitors navigate the site.

navigation map   *See* **jump map**.

nested sub-Web   A FrontPage Web within a Web that can have individual settings apart from the root Web.

numbered list   An indented list of items, each preceded by a number.

object   In DHTML and scripting, a picture, block of text, or other Web page element that performs an action when an event occurs. *Object* is also used as a general term for a page element or a snippet of programming code. *See also* **action**, **event**, and **page elements**.

Office viewers   Browser plug-ins that allow visitors to view Microsoft Word, Excel, and PowerPoint files even if they don't have those applications.

operating system   The software that runs your computer and tells it how to work with other applications.

overlay   A page layout with overlapping or layered text and image elements. *See also* **layer**.

page elements   A general term for Web files and things that you put on a Web page, including text, images, embedded files, scripts, and FrontPage components.

page title   Text that appears in the browser's title bar when a page appears in a Web browser.

parent level   In Web pages and programming, the top elements in a hierarchy. In the FrontPage Navigation view, a parent level page is generally the main page for a section, with child level pages organized beneath it. *See also* **child level** and **same level**.

Perl   A popular CGI scripting language. *See also* **CGI script** and **common gateway interface**.

permissions   In server administration, sets of passwords and access levels that allow coworkers to administer, edit, or view Web pages.

photorealistic image   *See* **continuous tone image**.

pixel   Short for "picture element." Computer screens display words, pictures, and other elements as little dots that blend together. Each dot is a pixel.

plug-in   An application that extends a Web browser's capabilities so it can launch files that browsers don't normally support. For example, the Shockwave plug-in allows you to view Shockwave movies on a Web page.

PNG   Portable Network Graphic, an up-and-coming Web image format supported by 5.0 Web browsers, FrontPage, and newer versions of imaging programs.

Portable Document Format (PDF)   Adobe's technology for creating online Acrobat documents that retain their fonts and layouts and that can be viewed with the Acrobat Reader plug-in.

positioning   Placing an image or block of text in an exact location for a precise page layout.

processor   Another name for the central processing unit (CPU), the device that determines how quickly your computer runs.

programming language   A language like C++, Java, or Visual Basic that allows programmers to write powerful software applications.

properties   Details about a Web page, image, or other type of file or Web page element.

publish   To upload files from a FrontPage Web to a server. *See also* **upload**.

QuickTime   Apple's popular video format.

ratings   On the Web, meta-information intended for programs that block out inappropriate Web pages. Web site ratings are somewhat like movie ratings.

remote files   Files on a computer that you can connect to by dialing up an Internet account. *See also* **local files**.

remote server   A server that you can connect to by dialing up your Internet account. *See also* **local server**.

repeating page elements   Pictures, links, and text that appear on pages throughout a Web site, such as a navigation bar.

reports   Lists of Web site details generated automatically by FrontPage in the Reports view.

resample   In FrontPage, the process of using the Picture toolbar to change the dimensions of the image itself, rather than simply telling the Web browser to display the image at a different size through the Image Properties dialog box.

resolution   The number of dots (pixels) per inch used to render an image, or the display resolution for a computer screen. On the Web, images are formatted at 72 or 96 dots per inch (DPI). Standard computer display resolutions include 640×480, 800×600, and 1280×1024 (Super VGA). *See also* **display settings** and **pixel**.

right-click   To click an object on the computer screen with the right mouse button to display a shortcut menu.

rollover   *See* **hyperlink rollover** and **mouse over**.

root Web   The main Web that contains all of the files and folders for a FrontPage Web.

round-trip HTML   Microsoft's term for FrontPage and Microsoft Office's capability to convert files to Web pages and back to the original format for editing without losing any information.

same level   In Web pages and programming, elements that occupy the same level in a hierarchy. In the FrontPage Navigation view, parent level pages appear on the same level, with child level pages organized beneath them. *See also* **child level** and **parent level**.

screen real estate   The amount of available space on a computer screen for displaying application windows.

scripting language   A simplified programming language that allows even non-programmers to create Web pages. Scripting languages rely on another application—such as a Web browser or a server application—in order to run. Popular scripting languages include JavaScript and Perl.

search engine   A technology that enables people to search databases on the Web. This term is also used for search sites like Yahoo!, WebCrawler, and HotBot.

search form   A text field with a Submit button. Visitors can type keywords and click the button to display a list of links that meet the search criteria. Some search forms also include pull-down lists or items with check boxes so users can select additional items to narrow down the search.

search page   A Web page with a search form.

server   A computer that stores data and serves it up to users who request it, or that allows users to connect to the Internet.

server-side   Technologies that rely on a server's capabilities. For example, many FrontPage features require a server with FrontPage extensions.

shared borders   A FrontPage feature that makes it easy to create repeating page elements on the top, right, bottom, or left page border, and to apply them to other pages.

Shockwave movie   A multimedia file created with one of Macromedia's applications, including Director and Flash.

shortcut menu   A menu that appears when you click a page element with the right mouse button.

site search engine   A search engine that only searches the contents of a particular Web site, rather than the entire Web. The FrontPage Search component allows users to create a searchable Web site.

slow pages   Pages that take a long time to load in the browser due to large (or many) images, large quantities of text, elaborate animations, and other factors. A Web page should take no longer than 20-30 seconds to load. The FrontPage status bar displays the estimated download time for the current Web page.

source code   The HTML code behind the Web pages. In FrontPage you can click the HTML tab in the Page view to see the source code. *See also* **HTML**.

spam   Advertisements and promotional announcements sent by email or posted to a discussion Web or newsgroup.

spider   Programs used by search engine companies like Lycos and Altavista to automatically find and catalog Web pages. Spiders are also called *robots*.

static database   Information from a database that is formatted as a set of Web pages, and that doesn't allow visitors to retrieve information or otherwise interact with the database itself.

static Web pages   Web pages that contain no animated elements, programmed components, collapsible lists, hover buttons, or other elements that the user interacts with. *See also* **active Web pages**.

style sheets   *See* **cascading style sheets**.

table   A Web page element consisting of rows, columns, and cells that helps Web designers arrange images, text, and other page elements.

target   An area of a Web page that is defined so you can create a link to it from within the same Web page. In FrontPage, targets are called bookmarks. *See also* **bookmark** and **internal links**.

tasks   In FrontPage, items that appear in the Tasks view as reminders of work that needs to be done on a Web site.

themes   In FrontPage, professional, prefab Web page designs that you can apply to a Web site.

thread   Articles posted to a discussion Web or newsgroup in response to a particular message.

toolbar   A row of buttons in an application window that users can click to perform tasks.

transparent GIF   A GIF image with the background color removed so it appears to float against the Web page's background.

uniform resource locator (URL)   An Internet address, as in `http://www.fp2k.com/`.

upload   To send files to a server or publish files to a FrontPage Web site. *See also* **download** and **publish**.

VBScript   Microsoft's scripting language for Internet Explorer or active server pages.

vertical spacing   The amount of space between the top and bottom of a Web page element and the surrounding text.

video   Movies. Popular video formats include AVI and QuickTime.

virtual domain   A domain that is hosted on another server. Many people sign up for a domain name, as in `mydomain.com`, but host it on their ISP's or Web hosting company's server instead of their own.

Web   *See* **World Wide Web** or **FrontPage Web**.

Web hosting company   A company that provides Web hosting services but not dial-up Internet access.

Web-safe colors   *See* **browser-safe colors**.

Web server   A program that enables a server to host, manage, and serve up Web pages.

Web site address   *See* **uniform resource locator**.

whitespace   The amount of empty space on a Web page that contains no text, images, or other elements. A reasonable amount of whitespace is essential for good design, readability, and an uncluttered look.

wizard   An application built into a program that takes users through the steps of a complicated process, such as setting up a FrontPage Web.

workgroup   A group of people who work together, or groups of people who share the same FrontPage Web access privileges.

World Wide Web   The part of the Internet devoted to Web pages.

WYSIWYG   What you see is what you get, an expression describing publishing software that displays a page exactly as it will appear when it is published.

XML   *See* **Extensible Markup Language**.

ZIP   A popular file compression format for Windows.

INDEX

Symbols

3-D button, 136

A

Accessibility add-in, 170
accessing root folders, 157
active graphics (themes), 39
Active Server Pages. *See* ASP
ActiveX
  component files, 79
  controls, 191
Add button, 218
Add Connection button, 269
add-ins, 168, 170
Add-ins command (Tools menu), 168

adding
  animation to Web pages, 146
  backgrounds to Web pages, 67
  banners, 123
  borders to Web pages, 64
  charts, 279-280
  check boxes to forms, 217
  drop-down menus to forms, 217
  forms to Web pages, 56
  frames to Webs, 103, 108
  graphics, 114, 218-219
  hit counters with HTML, 230
  labels to forms, 216
  links to graphics, 127, 129
  Navigation bars, 81, 83, 123
  new paragraph style, 243
  pivot tables, 280-281
  pushbuttons, 218-219
  questions to forms, 200

  Radio buttons to forms, 217
  search engines, 249
  spreadsheets, 278
  tables to Web pages, 92-93
  text
    to graphics, 137-138
    to Web pages, 68-71
  text boxes to forms, 215
adjusting frames, 104-105
advertisments, 282
aligning
  cells, 97
  graphics, 115-117
animating
  GIF files, 146
  Webs, 145-146
  with dynamic HTML, 148-149
applying
  styles to pages, 241
  themes, 38-39
articles, discussion Webs, 263
Artsy theme, 342
asking questions (forms), 201, 203